The Craft
of Family Therapy

D1603413

The Craft of Family Therapy

Challenging Certainties

Salvador Minuchin
Michael D. Reiter
Charmaine Borda

With Contributions From:
Sarah A. Walker
Roseann Pascale
Helen T. M. Reynolds

Routledge
Taylor & Francis Group

LONDON AND NEW YORK

First published 2014 by Routledge
2 Park Square, Milton Park, Abingdon, Oxon OX14 4RN

52 Vanderbilt Avenue, New York, NY 10017

Routledge is an imprint of the Taylor & Francis Group, an informa business

© 2014 Taylor & Francis

The right of Salvador Minuchin, Michael D. Reiter, and Charmaine Borda to be identified as authors of this work has been asserted by them in accordance with sections 77 and 78 of the Copyright, Designs and Patents Act 1988.

All rights reserved. No part of this book may be reprinted or reproduced or utilised in any form or by any electronic, mechanical, or other means, now known or hereafter invented, including photocopying and recording, or in any information storage or retrieval system, without permission in writing from the publishers.

Trademark notice: Product or corporate names may be trademarks or registered trademarks, and are used only for identification and explanation without intent to infringe.

Library of Congress Cataloging-in-Publication Data
Minuchin, Salvador.
The craft of family therapy : challenging certainties / by Salvador Minuchin, Michael D. Reiter,
Charmaine Borda ; with contributions from Sarah A. Walker, Roseann Pascale, Helen T.M. Reynolds.
    pages cm
  Includes bibliographical references and index.
 1. Family psychotherapy.   I. Reiter, Michael D.   II. Borda, Charmaine.   III. Walker, Sarah A.
IV. Pascale, Roseann.   V. Reynolds, Helen T. M.   VI. Title.
RC488.5.M543 2013
616.89'156—dc23   2013013912

ISBN: 978-0-415-70811-1 (hbk)
ISBN: 978-0-415-70812-8 (pbk)

Typeset in Minion
by Apex CoVantage, LLC

For Pat, who has co-authored our lives for more than sixty years.

—SM

To my wonderful wife Yukari, who has supported me as a person and allowed me to engage in my various pursuits.

—MDR

For my daughters, Britnie and Ariana; you inspire me.

—CB

CONTENTS

PROLOGUE

There are many ways of learning how to become a family therapist. These methods have changed over the last 50 years or so. When family therapy first began, with the seminal article of Don Jackson on family homeostasis (1957), there were no family therapy theories. There were no introductory textbooks on different family therapy approaches. The field was not yet established, and the ideas and understandings of how families functioned and what to do with them were hidden within the families that were being seen. Practitioners learned by viewing and doing. The originators of the field—people like Nathan Ackerman, Murray Bowen, Jay Haley, Don Jackson, Salvador Minuchin, Virginia Satir, Carl Whitaker, Lyman Wynne, and others—developed their understanding through meeting with families and then evaluating what happened in the session.

Over time, these examples of experiential learning were developed into theories of how to therapeutically engage families, and institutes were created where therapists could learn how to work in this new way. To get training as a family therapist, a clinician, who was probably originally an individual therapist, might attend one of the institutes of family therapy, such as the Mental Research Institute in Palo Alto, CA (with Don Jackson, Jay Haley, Virginia Satir, and others); the Philadelphia Child Guidance Center (headed by Salvador Minuchin); the Georgetown Family Institute (headed by Murray Bowen); the Ackerman Institute in New York; or the Family Therapy Institute of Washington, D.C. (headed by Jay Haley and Cloe Madanes). The therapy room was the classroom, where the learning took place by doing. These institutes mainly provided a particular view of why families have difficulties and what therapists could do to help them. The people who came to learn were offered training that was grounded primarily in one approach. They were not bombarded with the multitude of different theories that the present generation of students is struggling to assimilate.

Currently, new practitioners in family therapy are trained in university settings, rather than in institutes. Learning comes from textbooks for classes that try to provide a wide foundation for the field, so that people have the knowledge designated as necessary by state licensing boards. The brunt of learning comes in the classroom rather than the therapy room. Students are expected to digest a variety of approaches, and then are asked to use one or more of these theories as a guideline for their practice when they begin to see families.

The current process represents a shift from an <u>inductive</u> mode of understanding to a <u>deductive</u> mode. It seems to us that the loss of an inductive process for becoming a family therapist has severe consequences for the quality of a student's work in the therapy room. For that reason, we have decided to write this book. We are promoting an inductive method of learning how to become a family therapist, and exploring, through illustration, how learning comes from doing.

Some history, first, in order to illustrate this point of view in action:

In the late 1960s, when I (Minuchin) was the Director of the Philadelphia Child Guidance Clinic, the families that came to the clinic for treatment were mostly African American or Latino—many of them on welfare. The staff of the clinic was 100% Caucasian. It was clear that we needed to recruit minority people as staff, and we searched the local community for people we could train, as "paraprofessionals," to become family therapists. At the beginning of the 1970s, we applied for and received a training grant from the National Institute of Mental Health (NIMH) to train up to 18 people for 2 years.

For the trainers—Jay Haley, Braulio Montalvo, Marianne Walters, myself, and others—how to train was a quandary. Haley was enthusiastic about the idea of training people who had not been "contaminated" by academic knowledge, and we developed a training program that was totally inductive. Trainees were going to learn by looking at and studying their experiences as they became involved in the practice of family therapy. Live supervision would be essential, since we needed to protect the trainees, the families, and the clinic.

Haley developed a manual of how to survive the first interview, which provided step-by-step directions on how to conduct the session. After every session, the trainers met with the trainees and watched a video of the session, then asked the "students" what they learned from the work and what questions their work elicited. The concept and hope underlying this training procedure was that we could tap into the life experience of our trainees. We assumed that their previous problem-solving responses to conflict might be similar to some of the ways our clients responded, and that we could help these "therapists" to tame and improve their spontaneous responses, transforming them into therapeutic interventions. We hoped, also, that we could learn techniques that would improve our work with a low socioeconomic population that was not familiar to our staff. These were not the techniques being taught in universities but ways of being, as people, with families we did not know well, and that would be useful and effective.

The grant was extended twice and during this period we trained 24 paraprofessionals, some of whom continued to study and became social workers, all of whom became family therapy practitioners.

After that experience, I continued training professional family therapists for several decades before retiring, but when Charmaine Borda and Michael Reiter, family therapy faculty at Nova Southeastern University, asked if I would conduct an informal training practicum for graduate students, it was a request I could not refuse. Here was an opportunity to work with bright young people who were just beginning their experience as practitioners.

The training in universities, now, is almost the opposite of the training I conducted at the Child Guidance Clinic. At the universities, training in family therapy is generally a deductive process. Students first learn the theories that are the foundations of the diverse schools of family therapy and then apply theory to practice. Through this procedure, trainees are generally learning to be restrained, protective, and respectful of the client, to avoid entering into conflict with patients, and to search for the techniques that "truly fit" the problem that the clients present. In effect, they are training for cautiousness, guarding against the imposition of their own framework on problems that the family presents. If my view about this training is correct, it is a training that discourages the students from looking at themselves as resources in the therapeutic practice.

In accepting the invitation of my young colleagues, I have joined them in exploring a different, more inductive process of training. We started out without a clear curriculum, and, instead, simply asking the students to bring videotapes from the therapy sessions they were conducting in practicum situations. We observed the style and nature of their work and talked with them about their experiences. Over time, we have been able to move toward the development of a method for training in the craft of family therapy.

Our first observations of the students at work provided important building blocks for this development. As they began to interview families, their styles of interviewing presented some common characteristics. They were, of course, anxious, since they had scant experience with encounters involving more than one person, and they usually were polite and proceeded with caution. They asked questions that were frequently a paraphrasing of the client's last statement (i.e., "So you said that it troubled you when you saw what your daughter was doing?"), as well as questions that encouraged clients to continue explaining, and questions directed at tracking the narrative but which did not open up new explorations. Paradoxically, they also became quickly engaged in trying to explain, support, protect, or improve the family drama.

The combination put these new practitioners in a quandary. They were becoming naïve improvers, engaged in monitoring narrow aspects of the family presentation before they had a clear knowledge of how the family members related, their history, or their efforts at problem solving. They felt the need to do something to demonstrate their competence and became engaged in responding to family problems before knowing the family. Most did not know how to be silent or how to use silence as a tool. And, noticeably, they focused mostly on the pathology the family offered as the reason for requesting help, ignoring the exploration of strength, resilience, and resources by which family members might become helpers of each other.

Our students came with different life experiences, but we noticed a major commonality in their presentation of their cases: They didn't include themselves in the process. They would describe the family dynamics, sometimes with surprising clarity, but always as if they were objective, neutral observers. When we asked for feedback from the students observing the tapes, they responded with alternative descriptions of the family's transactions, but the participation of the therapist in producing this behavior was not mentioned.

These lacunae, empty spaces in observing and describing the therapeutic process, were surprising to me. I remembered that at the beginning of the family therapist movement, all training programs struggled with the issue of the participation of the therapist in the therapeutic process, and with the therapist's awareness of that reality. At that time, most trainees in family therapy came with some experience in psychodynamic individual therapy, and many had undergone their own psychotherapy or psychoanalysis. The family therapy trainers needed to address the necessity of providing an alternative to the long, intensive involvement in self-observation that psychodynamic therapy provided.

Many institutes began to include a focus on the self of the therapist in the first year of training. Virginia Satir scheduled retreats with her students and their families, in which the students explored their participation at different stages of development in their families of origin, using the techniques of psychodrama. Carl Whitaker promoted the idea that therapists should access and utilize themselves in the therapy room, and that to do this they would need to come to terms with their own thoughts (Whitaker, 1989). Murray Bowen focused on the self of the therapist, especially in relation to his or her family of origin. He stated, "I believe and teach that the family therapist usually has the very same problems in his own family that are present in families he sees professionally, and that he has a responsibility to define himself in his own family if he is to function adequately in his professional work" (Bowen, 1972, p. 468). All of these master therapists believed that training to become a family therapist started with an exploration of one's own self, which would then aid the trainee inside the therapy room.

The university training programs of today, it seems, have shifted from a focus on the self of the therapist to a focus on what has become known as core competencies.[1] These competencies are concerned primarily with how to conceptualize cases and how to structure and engage in therapy sessions. There are several competencies that refer to the therapist's awareness of the impact the family is having on him or her, but, overwhelmingly, the trainee is expected to be thinking about *what to do* rather than *who they are*. With the introduction of these core competencies, graduate family therapy programs are now expected to train their students to fulfill these guidelines; there is no longer an emphasis on helping students with other aspects of development, such as the person of the therapist.

Through my professional career, as well as in this current training program, I have considered that the therapist's awareness of an intervention is an essential part of the formation of an effective therapist. In our program, the students started their presentations describing relevant aspects of their own life and the ways in which these experiences molded their therapeutic style. Only then did they describe the characteristics of the family they were presenting. After that, they examined the techniques and strategies they had used. In our discussions throughout the training, I continuously invoked the metaphor of a therapist who has formed, on the left shoulder, a homunculus, who is engaged in observing the therapist's mental processes and is involved in silent dialogues with the therapist as s/he works.

This book is the product of the authors' time with the family therapist trainees. We wanted to develop a primer that would help move trainees from theory into a world of craft. In doing so, we have organized what follows as two books in one, written by two different sets of authors. In the first half, Minuchin explores several of his own past sessions,[2] providing you with an overview of the concepts that he believes are important for therapists to think about and implement in the first sessions with a family. In the second half, the authors, with the crucial help of their students, describe the sometimes arduous process for novice therapists trying to put these concepts into action.

Welcome to your journey through the craft of family therapy.

---

1 The American Association of Marriage and Family developed a list of 128 core competencies that a family therapy trainee should be able to demonstrate at the licensure stage.

2 Identifying information has been changed in all of the cases to ensure the anonymity of the client families.

ACKNOWLEDGMENTS

We would like to thank all of the students who participated in the Friday Supervision sessions. Some students came for only one semester while others were with us for several years. They all helped us to put these ideas into perspective and were the impetus for us to write this book. The students are, in alphabetical order: Jinan Amra, Kelsy Anderson, Yajaira Arias, Stephanie Ashwell, Doreen Blake, Eva Brown, Geoffrey Carlo, Jason Carter, Jacqueline Clarke, Jeff Cotton, Elizabeth David, Julianna M. Deans, Yolle-Guida Dervil, Sandra DiMarco, Paulette Edwards, Kendall G. Elias, Kristina Fecik, Simone Finnis, Cindy George, Diana Giraldez, Maria Teresa Gonzalez, James Guerin, Katherine S. Hatzitheodorou, Addis A. Hunter, Andrea Jambeck, Sherline Jean-Louis, Todd Workman Jesness, Valeria Galante Lado, Norlene (Rose) LaFavor, Alona Leviner-Sommer, Lystra Lewis, Deana Litowitz, Anitra Moss, Michelle Moyer-Tsai,Sonia Mucarsel (Neale), Tuyet A. Nguyen, Laura Richter, AnneMarie M. Rodewald, Michelle M. Rodriguez, Carolyn M. Rose, Kelly Scavone, Daniela Sichel, Brett Simpson, Michelle Small, Meagan Smart, Ali Taeb, Juan Turon, Sarah Walker, and Seidy V. White.

We also want to thank Pat Minuchin for her work in editing the manuscript, and Elizabeth David for her invaluable assistance in preparing the book. Finally, we'd like to thank Marta Moldvai at Routledge and Kimberly Cleary at Apex, for their support and skill in guiding us through the process that has brought this book to completion.

Part I
Concepts and Practice of the Craft

1

THE CRAFT OF FAMILY THERAPY

When a family comes into your office, what do you do? What is the correct way to start the session? Do you ask about the problem? Do you offer your services as a healer? Do you smile and ask about the trip to the office? Are you silent until one family member begins to talk? Yes, yes, yes, and yes. The problem with therapy is that it is an encounter between strangers preparing themselves for a significant journey together. Therefore, the early joining in the process will be idiosyncratic, depending on the particular family and the particular therapist. It's a journey that starts in uncertainty.

Most new therapists will probably fall back on theory as a way to reduce their anxiety so that they can function. But which theory do you choose to operate from? How do you choose a theory that will enable you to be effective? In fact, there is no clear answer, and the question is perhaps too simple. Whatever model you choose to work from, even if it is from an integrative position, there is more to therapy than simply the concepts and techniques of that approach. Two therapists may use the same technique, even with the same family, and for one therapist that technique seems to help the family, while the other therapist finds that it flops.

Many young therapists would find this puzzling. That's because they look at therapy as a course of action in which the therapist observes a family and implements techniques to help them with their problems. They do not understand the complexity of the process. The craft of therapy includes not only an understanding of the characteristics of the family and a grasp of techniques that can facilitate change, but also an awareness of how they, the therapists, are functioning within the therapeutic system.

We will be exploring the craft of therapy throughout the book, but we begin by offering an imaginary "therapist pouch" to prepare the reader for the journey. It is somewhat similar to a journeyman's bag in which the worker carries the tools that will be needed for the most frequent jobs.

To fill the family therapist's pouch, we have included items that help in the task of rearranging relationships. They are grouped under the following headings: Basic

Principles; Techniques; Working with Subsystems; and The Self of the Therapist. Each group of tools is presented separately in the following section, but they are also intertwined, available as both separate and combined resources.

The pouch offers a useful framework for the beginning of this journey. It also serves as a resource during the therapeutic process. When a therapist adopts a distant position from the family, temporarily shielded from the demand for action, he or she can observe and think, drawing on the pouch to plan the most appropriate and effective route for intervention.

THE FAMILY THERAPIST POUCH
Basic Principles
1. Joining is the Essential Element
This is the first item in the pouch. Joining is not a skill or a technique. It's a mindset constructed out of respect, empathy, curiosity, and a commitment to healing. It signals the establishment of a work-oriented system. Joining happens from the first contact with the family to the final goodbye at termination. Through this connection, the therapist is able to engage the family to support as well as challenge.

2. All Families That Come to Therapy are "Wrong" in Their Assumptions
This statement may seem startling, at first. What seasoned therapists know, however, is that clients come to therapy because they have a limited view of their situation. Families are "wrong" because they're certain they know the reality of their situation, and that there are no alternatives to their story. Their ingrained perception is that the problem is an individual experience, rather than maintained by the whole group. As a systemic therapist, you know this is incorrect. Symptoms occur within a context of relational interactions. You know, also, that family members are using fewer resources than they have, and that they have been trapped into traveling the road already taken.

3. The Family's Certainty is the Enemy of Change
The more clients maintain their certainty about the problem, the less open they are to viewing the situation differently, and thus they will be unlikely to alter their way of being with one another. The therapist may be uncertain as to what the problem is, but s/he knows it can be viewed from a wider lens than the zoomed-in focus that the family members are using.

Techniques
4. Challenging the Family's Certainty
An important function of the therapist is to challenge the family's certainty about the problem. That entails introducing doubt, encouraging curiosity, presenting alternatives, and offering hope. Each family is idiosyncratic. The members have chosen their own alternatives and ways of relating with each other throughout their lives, so their resistance to the therapist's suggestions is natural, and often strong. Nonetheless, there are many ways to challenge their certainty.

For instance, the therapist may challenge a repetitive pathological interaction that always ends in stalemate. The challenge is usually difficult for the family to accept, but the therapist can facilitate acceptance by offering a combined message of support and challenge. S/he might say, "There is a mystery here. You four are individually very nice people [support], yet you continue to engage each other in ways that make each of your lives miserable [challenge], and this is a mystery."

Or the therapist might challenge the strong dependence of a family on his or her expertise by lessening the therapist's hierarchical status, thereby making room for members of the family to be more active in helping each other. To take that stand, a therapist must appear both uncertain and spontaneous. That is a difficult undertaking; it is achieved only slowly, as the therapist becomes a self-observing instrument of change.

5. Exploring Alternatives

As the therapist continues to challenge the family's certainty, the polemic between the family's truths and the therapist's suggestions should bring a revelation of new roads to explore. The therapist emphasizes the alternatives, encouraging explorations where family members can act as healers of each other. One of the most useful and effective tools for such explorations is "enactment," a technique developed many years ago. It will be illustrated at different points throughout the book, but because it is such a useful and important part of the "therapist's pouch," it is discussed briefly here as well.

Enactment is a process during which the therapist acts like a traffic agent, directing members of the family to enter into dialogues in his or her presence. The therapist is an audience, observing in silence their ways of relating. The patterns that are observed will be brought up later in the session as observations that family members will recognize, even though they contain novelties not recognized before.

The technique seems simple; essentially, the therapist is asking particular members of a family to talk with each other in the presence of other family members, but the implications are far-ranging. When two family members talk to each other in this context, the conversation is no longer spontaneous. It slows down and becomes an encounter that is witnessed by the rest of the family and by the therapist. The sense of agency in the participants increases and becomes an awareness that "I am talking to you while we are being observed." As a result, each one becomes more aware of "where I belong in the family group."

Both the original descriptions (Minuchin & Fishman, 1981) and those of more recent writers (Nichols & Fellenberg, 2000) have summarized useful principles for working with enactments. While the process is going on, therapists are encouraged to hesitate before interrupting; to refrain from correcting the clients or the tone of their discussion; and—of primary importance—to pay attention to the process rather than the content of their interactions. For new therapists, the narrative of the family is often the foreground, while the context of relationships within which those narratives are housed is seen as background. Enactments are not designed to bring forth the facts of what the clients are saying but, rather, the family rules that set the stage for their interactions. This process shifts the picture; content becomes background while family dynamics jump into the foreground.

Examples of enactment appear often in the sessions and discussions of this book. It will become clear that in order to become effective, therapists must not only set up these interactions but must silently review their own role as the enactment proceeds. They must find ways to bring interactions to new life so that the participants hear each other more clearly, thereby enabling family members to explore change and become healing agents for themselves and each other.

6. Using the Content of Family Communication to Access the Process of Family Dynamics

This tool is an important part of the previous point concerning enactments, but it stands alone as well, because it's available not only during enactments but throughout the therapeutic sessions. Most family members come to therapy talking about the specifics of their complaints: who did what, what the other person said, where they think the symptoms come from, etc. They have communicated these ideas countless times before, agreeing and disagreeing with each other as they do so. If the therapist stays with the family in this narrative, they will remain at the surface of their experience. If, however, the therapist hears the content as a signal of family dynamics, including the emotional content of the transaction, it's possible to move the family into uncharted territory, encouraging a conversation about relational dynamics they have not had before and opening up new pathways for thinking, perceiving, and behaving.

7. Using Humor and Metaphoric Language in Therapy

Humor, metaphoric language, and poetic imagery are excellent means for joining with a family, as well as a way to challenge certainty. Because clients come in with a familiar range of perspectives and emotions, the therapist's use of humor and unexpected imagery open up the possibility for seeing themselves and their situation in a different way.

Many beginning therapists hesitate when it comes to this possibility, fearing that their use of humor or creative language will not be well received by the family. They assume that the therapy session must be serious. We agree and disagree. Clients come in because they are in distress, and therapy is a very serious endeavor. Yet that doesn't prevent therapists and clients from being able to notice the absurd, or from finding humor even within a dire situation. When the therapist says to a precocious and intrusive child, "When did you become your mother's mother?" the family not only is amused but understands. There is something healing about unexpected language and ideas.

8. Introducing Specific Topics at Different Levels

At particular points in the sessions, the therapist may find it useful to provide new knowledge, discuss future directions, or touch on ethical responsibilities. Introduced separately or together, such topics help family members to view and behave differently with one another.

Knowledge: Because of their profession and experience, family therapists have specific knowledge about how families function that can be described to most clients in ways that are useful. Conveying concrete information about family organization, coalitions, patterns of conflict, or the function of boundaries transforms what the family has always seen as intra-psychic into a more systemic understanding. New knowledge of this kind supports a focus on dialogues and transactions rather than monologues and individual actions.

Future Directions: By attitude and specific interventions, the therapist can convey the message that the family has untapped possibilities and that changes in the way they function together can bring harmony and a sense of well-being. It is a message of hope and expectation.

Ethical Responsibilities: There are moments in therapy when the therapist can comment on the ethical principle that people are responsible for the well-being of those whom they love and are close to. It is an idea accepted by most families who come for help, despite the conflict, frustration, and despair they may come in with. This sense of belonging and responsibility within the family is also the principle that guides a therapist's effort to increase the competency of family members as healers of each other.

Working With Subsystems
9. The Individual as a Subsystem: Unwrapping the Identities of Family Members

Individuals are complex subsystems of the larger family system, and it is part of the therapist's task to expand the scope of each person's identity. Each member of a family is usually seen as a particular kind of personality, filling certain roles and functions in the larger whole. Exploring the multiple identities of family members allows them to view themselves from a wider perspective and opens up alternative ways of relating with one another.

When family members become more than they thought they were, as well as more than how other family members have rigidly viewed them, alternative ways of seeing and being become available. It's the therapist's job to bring forth how each family member can be seen as interactionally connected to others in new roles.

10. Utilizing Subsystems for the Expansion of Understanding and the Possibility of Change

Families have a variety of subsystems, though they often do not understand the reality and complexity of how they function. When therapists highlight these aspects, members can be moved beyond the rigid patterns they have been repeating. To create this shift, the therapist must deconstruct the complexity of the total family, working separately for a time with the spouses, with parents and child, with siblings, and so forth.

In the sessions described in this book, there are many examples of working with subsystems. When subsystems are examined separately, it becomes clear that each one is creating a contextual demand for certain kinds of interaction. At that point, therapist and family have the freedom to highlight implicit rules and explore multiple alternatives.

11. Unbalancing Subsystems: Promoting and Challenging Different Units

The process of unbalancing or supporting subsystems is an important tool. It facilitates change by creating stress for some units, at particular points, while supporting others, then shifting over time.

New therapists often find it difficult to take sides, even briefly. They adhere to the notion carried by the zodiac sign of Libra, believing they must always keep the family in balance. If they spend five minutes listening to the husband's complaint, they believe they must give equal time to the wife, and if they challenge the wife's position in the family, they must challenge the husband's position at the same time. They are not comfortable with the idea that differential stress is an important tool for change, or that balance will come over a longer period.

The same discomfort often comes in relation to ending a session. It's difficult for new therapists to accept the idea that each session does not have to end with all parties satisfied and hopeful about the future. When a session is coming to a close and they know family members are angry or frustrated, it's hard for them to remember that there can be a therapeutic purpose in having people leave in that state. A last push for harmony comes from anxiety, rather than thoughtfulness. The more anxious the therapist becomes, the narrower the lens s/he is using to see. You cannot fix everything in one session.

Balancing and unbalancing subsystems are complex skills, involving the therapist's empathy and concern for fairness. The nature of the task brings us to the need for self-awareness, discussed in the tools described below.

The Self of the Therapist

The effective therapist enters a session with an invisible companion, carried in on his or her left shoulder. One must think of it as a "homunculus": a diminutive mythological being that looks and thinks like the therapist and can observe and reflect on the process of intervention. This invisible companion is essential, providing the therapist with the opportunity to make informed decisions about the use of the self and about exploring the roads not yet taken.

12. Choosing the Distance from Which to Function

Throughout the session, the therapist stays aware of his or her "distance" from the family, considering when and how to change as the session develops. S/he can be close, medium, or distant from the family, and the different positions serve different purposes (Minuchin & Fishman, 1981). Therapists gain and lose possibilities when operating at each of these positions. The more proximal the position, the less the therapist can sit back and think; the more distant, the less engaged with the family. Both positions have advantages.

Inexperienced therapists tend to adopt a proximal position; they have difficulty sitting back to create distance. They feel that they, as therapists, have to do something, and they're usually very present in the interactions that occur during the session. Tools such as enactments, which allow space to sit back, breathe, and think, seem unavailable to them. With time, they learn to plan their interventions and are able to shift distance in keeping with their aims.

13. Owning Expertise When Working With Families

Therapists are experts, and they must own their expertise when they work with a family. Understandably, beginning therapists have difficulty occupying that position. They tread carefully, concerned about imposing their views on their clients. The family is coming to therapy, however, because their way of thinking and behaving is not helping them move past a current painful situation.

Along with others, such as Anderson (2012), we believe that the therapist's expertise lies partly in creating a space for dialogic conversations. But there is another aspect to be acknowledged, and it is important. Family therapists are also experts in seeing dysfunctional patterns. It's a crucial part of their task to bring these to the forefront of the family's awareness, and to guide the subsequent process of exploring alternatives.

14. The Greatest Tool the Therapist Can Use Is the Self
New therapists tend to think of themselves as the intermediary between a technique and a family, but the therapist is much more integral than that. In the process of therapy, s/he is the central tool. Challenging families to react to you is a developed skill. We hope that the concrete meaning of that statement will become increasingly obvious to the reader as the book progresses.

THE PURPOSE OF TOOLS

Tools are just that—a means to accomplish an objective. When the carpenter begins with a piece of wood, he has an end goal in mind: to change that wood into something else. The saw, chisel, hammer, and nails are a means of transforming what the carpenter first sees into what he wants it to become. The effective family therapist also uses tools as means to an end, not as ends in themselves. The craft of family therapy lies in how these tools are used to produce a difference in the family—a useful change. An enactment on its own does not move the family. But a therapist who understands that enactment is a way to view the family's interaction is able, then, to help shift the process.

Knowing how to use tools is one of the biggest obstacles for beginning therapists. They often have an understanding of techniques but they do not know how to use them in order to get to their goals. And that is the craft of family therapy.

A final note to the reader:
The therapist's pouch offers a useful framework for the beginning of the journey. It may also serve as a resource during the therapeutic process, when, as a practitioner, one can observe and think, drawing on the pouch to plan an appropriate and effective route for intervention.

I know, however, that the pouch is tightly packed, and the contents are not easily grasped before setting out. So, read this chapter only once. Come back to it after you have the read the following chapters. We hope you will find, when you come back to this chapter, that the contents and the specifics have become user-friendly.

Segue
As we move into the remaining chapters of Part I, we introduce you to four families seen by Minuchin many years ago. Written essentially by the first author, this segue and the following four chapters primarily carry the first-person voice ("I") and perspective.

By now you know that the family you are seeing for the first time presents you with a mystery and asks you to solve it. At first glance, the story they tell you seems complete, but you realize that, as it is presented, the mystery is unsolvable. The first goal of therapy, therefore, is to help them look at the context of the story since, as you do it, you open the road to alternative ways of looking at the mystery.

But therapists, as they approach this task, come with a bias, so it may be interesting to look first at the way in which different therapists have started this process.

Murray Bowen, for instance, would have said, "Don't tell me what you feel, tell me what you think"; while Susan Johnson might say, "Tell me how you *really* feel." Carl Whitaker would have said, "If you are confused, nurture that. It's only at this point that people grow up"; while Michael White would have suggested an alternative story, and I (Minuchin) say to family members, "Don't be so certain."

This diversity should alert students to the fact that they are in a field in which the beginning of therapy includes goals that will direct the practice. In the following chapters, the reader will join me as I work with four families, and will see how I use the therapist's pouch, and how techniques become connected with concepts as I operationalize the "craft of therapy."

To counter the various families' certainties and open up alternatives, I focus on three major challenges: "Externalizing the Symptom" (Chapter 2), "Unwrapping Identities" (Chapter 3), and "Deconstructing Family Organization: Exploring Subsystems" (Chapter 4). These three challenges incorporate the "Therapist's Style," which is discussed in Chapter 5.

As an educational device, I have presented the sessions as if I focused on only one goal with each family. This, of course, is never the truth, but I wanted to highlight the point that at the beginning of an encounter with a family, the therapist needs to focus on these aspects of clinical practice. As you read these chapters, it's useful to remember that therapy is both a dialogue and a polemic, and a therapist aims to become a master of both.

2

SYMPTOMS

Challenge to the Concept that the Symptom is Located in One Family Member

When a family walks into the therapy room, they come prepared with their perspective of what has been happening in the family. This usually comes in the form of an Identified Patient/symptom bearer. The family's perspective is a very individualistic one: if this one person in the family could just get his/her act together and stop doing the problematic behavior(s), things in the family would be just fine. However, the family therapist's perspective is quite different. It is an understanding that behaviors are contextual and that whatever symptoms an individual presents are tied into the familial relationship s/he is housed in.

The dialectic between an individualistic and a systemic view of symptoms leads the therapist into a dilemma: "How do I let the family know the way they are viewing the problem is wrong, while at the same time connecting with them?" To further complicate the matter, whatever symptom the family presents is a call for the therapist to act in certain ways. For instance, when they present a son who is depressed, the family is saying, "Step in and make him less depressed." A complaint about a non-affectionate partner is also a pull for the therapist to get the partner to be more affectionate. A single mother bringing in her children because she is overwhelmed with caretaking may expect the therapist to help her discipline her children. If the therapist agrees to the family's demands around the symptoms, s/he becomes another part of the family engaging in actions that will maintain the symptom.

How does the family therapist explore the symptom in a systemic manner? The therapist is like a detective uncovering a mystery. Knowing that the symptom is but one piece of a larger puzzle that, when put into the context of relationships, uncovers the mosaic of the family, the therapist begins with the symptoms but searches underneath for the relational rules in place that maintain the symptom.

Minuchin (1974) believes that symptoms represent the family's "expression of a contextual problem" (p. 152). In viewing symptoms in this manner, the therapist then has several choice points for entering the family. He can choose to focus on the presenting problem, since the family is invested in viewing the presenting complaint as the primary problem, or he might choose to reframe the symptomatic behavior as an interpersonal experience. In this case, a presenting problem of a child being aggressive is transformed into an exploration of how the rules of the family allow this behavior.

This chapter presents how a therapist can enter into a family through the symptom, and help the family to expand its viewpoint from an individualistic model of problems to a more systemic understanding. This case, taken from a session with an anorectic daughter that Minuchin conducted over 40 years ago, demonstrates how therapists can discuss the symptom in ways that do not restrict the therapist's ability to move.

In selecting a case of a family with a daughter who has been anorectic for two years, has been hospitalized a number of times, and who has been seen by a pediatrician and a psychiatrist who have agreed with the diagnosis, Minuchin is in the delicate position of needing to challenge not only the family but also the medical profession.

Minuchin did something unusual when he met with the family in the 1970s. He decided to meet them at 12 pm for a 2-hour session that included having lunch while conducting the session. He explained to the family that since the patient had problems with eating, they would have lunch together to see how the problem presented itself. He also asked the mother to bring the usual food for lunch to the session.

THE CASE[1]

Loretta Menotti, 16, is the oldest daughter of a working-class Italian American family. Her parents had come to the United States from Sicily shortly after their marriage. Neither of them completed grammar school, but they are both intelligent and competent people. The father is an unskilled civil servant; the mother is a housewife. Both speak with a marked Italian accent, and their English is sometimes more rapid than fluent. When Loretta was 14, she was admitted to a large city hospital, complaining of severe pain in her abdomen. She remained in the hospital for 2 months, not eating at times because of the intense pain. After extensive medical workups, organic causes for the pain were ruled out; the diagnosis: "psychological problems." She refused to see a psychiatrist. Two years later, Loretta had continued to lose weight and was becoming obsessed with this problem. The diagnosis this time was "simple schizophrenia with superficial depressive features." Thorazine was prescribed. Three months later, Loretta was again hospitalized, with the diagnosis of anorexia nervosa. On admission, she weighed around 80 pounds. She remained in the hospital for 6 weeks. Her eating improved, and she gained weight. The continuation of therapy on an outpatient basis was recommended, but the family did not follow through. Four months later, Loretta was again admitted to the hospital—to the intensive care unit. There her condition was stabilized, but she remained in the hospital for another 2 months, with little improvement. Her family signed her out against medical advice. She weighed 75 pounds. Her eating problems continued. She was amenorreic and depressed. She had not attended school for some months.

---

1 This case was originally presented in Minuchin, Rosman & Baker (1978), Psychosomatic Families.

The symptom is clear. The ownership of the symptom is also clear: Loretta has been sick for 2 years and she has been examined repeatedly by competent pediatricians, psychiatrists, and psychologists, and while her diagnoses varied, nobody questioned who the sick member in this family was. Loretta agrees with her doctors; she is sick and the family members (mother, father, siblings) have been involved for the last 2 years in the drama of accommodating, responding, enduring, and trying to control her symptoms. As a systemic practitioner, I (Minuchin) rejected this certainty. Loretta, I said, is the carrier of symptoms, but all the family members are active participants in maintaining this tragic dance.

This first interview is typical of the active dialog that ensues between a family, in its certainty, and the family therapist. It starts by acknowledging Loretta's pain, and exploring her symptoms and the participation of family members in promoting and maintaining her deviant behavior.

The interview is presented verbatim, followed at intervals by my discussion, in italics, concerning the thoughts and actions of the previous section.

Minuchin:	First, I want to understand what has been happening. I understand that Loretta has been losing weight for the last three years. Is that correct?
Loretta:	Right.
Father:	Two years.
Minuchin:	When did it start, Loretta?
Father:	Two years.
Mother:	It started at the beginning of Lent. I take her to St. Francis Hospital because Loretta, she don't feel too good. She got pain all over. So they want to take picture inside Loretta's stomach, but I say "No." I say, "I take my daughter home."
Minuchin:	Do you remember that, Loretta? [Loretta nods]
Mother:	So I take Loretta home because I don't want nobody to touch my daughter. So I take her home, and next day Loretta throws up. She cries. She has a pain. So I call the car service, put Loretta in the car, and take her to Dr. Smith. He calls Tenafly Hospital, and from there we go straight to Tenafly Hospital. Loretta stay in bed 2 weeks there in the hospital.
Minuchin:	[To Loretta] I would like to know from your point of view, what was it that you were having?

I am listening to what the family is saying, but I am triggered by the parents' persistence in replying to questions I posed to Loretta. I know from previous experience that Loretta's symptoms may be expected to improve as she begins to gain the autonomy proper to a 16-year-old. I also know that Loretta's dependency and her mother's concern are reciprocal elements of the same pattern: whenever I touch one, I will touch the other. But I remain silent. I am a stranger, and the family has been suffering for a long time. They need—and want—to explain.

Loretta:	The first night that I went to St. Francis Hospital was because I was having strong pains in my abdomen and my back and they found it was a kidney infection and they gave me intravenous since the pain was so great.

Minuchin:	Okay, so you went then for something very, very specific. And when you went to the Tenafly Hospital, was it a continuation of the same?
Loretta:	I don't know. I mean, they never actually said anything there.
Minuchin:	Since Mother is the major voice of the family, she will tell, but you will need to check it, because it's your life that she is describing. Okay?

The mother is clearly the most powerful member of the family—at least in relation to anything involving Loretta's illness. Everything demands that I respect that: Mother's real power, the rules of courtesy, and the necessity of maintaining enough observance of the family's accustomed patterns to join them in a therapeutic system. At the same time, I begin to signal the message that will dominate the session: Loretta should own her own experience.

Mother:	So I take her to Tenafly to my doctor. For 2 weeks they check Loretta. Loretta, she doesn't eat enough, and the doctor told me, "Take your daughter home and bring her to a psychiatrist."
Minuchin:	Hold it a moment, because I want to check something. Loretta, when you were in the hospital, you did not eat anything?
Loretta:	For a while, they put a sign up on my bed that said I wasn't supposed to eat anything because they didn't know what was causing the pain. And then I didn't have any appetite. So I had the IV's from the first time until I went home.
Minuchin:	Do you know that this happens to many people? If they are 2 or 3 days without eating, they lose the appetite. It was at this point that you stopped eating, and this was when? Two years ago?

Loretta has responded to my attention, and my polite indication that Mother is not the ultimate authority, with increased information—a good sign. My statement begins to normalize her experience, which will be one way of diminishing her status as the sick member of the family.

Loretta:	Right.
Mother:	So, I stay 2 weeks with Loretta in the hospital.
Minuchin:	You stayed in the hospital? With her?

My tone of voice conveys genuine admiration for this woman, who simply rode roughshod over the bureaucracy of an entire city hospital.

Father:	Yes, she spent many nights with her.
Minuchin:	That's wonderful. That's an Italian heart for you!
Mother:	One day, my husband told me to come home to see the kids and, "If you still want to go tomorrow, I'll take you in there." So, I said I would see what I can do. So we go home. When we go home, I got a funny feeling. Loretta, she doesn't feel good, so I say to my husband, "You better take me back to the hospital. I have a funny feeling about Loretta." He say, "Oh no, you stay here." I say, "You take me or I go." So my husband take me

there. When I go back, I find Loretta all black and blue. She has pains. She's screaming, "I have a pain all over here, I have a pain over there." She is screaming. I say, "We will call the doctor." So they say nothing is wrong with Loretta. And I say, "What do you mean nothing is wrong with Loretta? She's all black and blue." "That's all right, don't get nervous." So they give her needle, and Loretta, she sleep all night.

Minuchin: [To Mother] That means, you had the feeling—Loretta could die.

I have a problem. It is clear that Mrs. Menotti's over-involvement with Loretta is destructive. But it is an accepted pattern of the family, buttressed by all the power of the "Mother" in the Sicilian culture. I am going to have to find a way of challenging the over-involvement without challenging the "Mother." As a therapist becomes part of the therapeutic system, he responds to the family story but develops a silent monologue about what is the appropriate response to the dance he is observing. This process is invisible to the family but needs to be explicit to the therapist as he observes himself responding to them.

Minuchin: Do you have the same sense about Maria?
Mother: Yes, with everybody. All my kids.
Minuchin: I don't think Maria sends vibes. What do you think, Maria? If you have a pain, do you think Mama knows?
Maria: Yes.
Minuchin: She does! What about Father? That's a special gift. Does Daddy have that?
Maria: Yes.
Minuchin: Is that so, Carlo? Can you experience the pain of your kids as your wife does?
Father: Well, I can see by just taking a look at them. If they don't look good, then I assume there *is* something wrong, you know.
Minuchin: But Margherita says she can hear vibrations from the hospital.
Father: I brought her back from the hospital, right? The minute that we were home, she says, "I want to go back." When she got back, Loretta was in bad shape.

While we are talking about Loretta, we had begun a process of exploring family relationships. I am also beginning to challenge Mother's over-protection and over-involvement, but this intervention is not yet visible. I will expand that slowly so that when the family members recognize the challenge they will accept it as something that is already familiar.

The father claims no magical knowledge of his children's well-being, but he makes it clear that he has no intention of challenging his wife's claims. Now I know—if I didn't before— that I cannot challenge Mother or motherhood in this family. But perhaps I can challenge its definition.

Minuchin: That feeling *is* very, very important when the kids are young. That's essential. Let me ask you a little bit, Loretta. You are 16 now?
Loretta: Yes.
Minuchin: Now that you are growing up, does it sometimes bother you that Mother is still so sensitive to you?
Loretta: Sometimes.

Minuchin:	What about you, Maria? Do you feel sometimes that Mother doesn't know that you are 13, that she still thinks you are 12 or 11?
Maria:	[Sighing] I don't know. No-o-o.
Minuchin:	Sophia, what's your feeling? Sometimes she forgets that you are 15? She treats you as if you are younger?
Sophia:	Yes.
Minuchin:	This always happens. When you are very sensitive to the pains of younger kids, there is then a problem of how to become the mother of older children. A good mother of younger children sometimes becomes a difficult mother for older children. So you are still a very good mother for Maria, Giuseppi, and Enrico, but I think there is some problem with Sophia and Loretta. I think that you are too much for them.
Mother:	No. [Father laughs] How?
Loretta:	You always have arguments with me and Sophia. Always.

And here, a short time after the presentation of Loretta's symptomotology, we are talking about family development, adolescent autonomy, maternal styles of mothering, and conflicts between husband and wife, and the family members accept this exploration as part of the process of helping Loretta with her symptoms.

The family appears to be picking up the challenge. It is time for me to sit back and see how far they can carry it.

Minuchin:	Carlo, help the two girls to talk, because Mama is too strong and they are in the hot spot. Help them to say how they would like Mama to be sometimes.
Father:	Why don't you express yourselves about what the doctor is saying? At 15, you should know how to say a few words by yourself, huh?
Sophia:	I don't have too many fights with Mom.
Father:	We are talking about how you wish Mom treats you from now on, since you have become 15.
Sophia:	I don't know. She doesn't treat me bad.

Sophia is already retreating; clearly no one in this family is comfortable challenging the Mother.

Father:	Do you think Mom needs to be changed to somehow make you feel better?
Loretta:	I think that's not the point, Dad. It's not the point of changing.
Father:	What is the point?
Loretta:	Dad, you really can't change. Once you are the person you are, you have to try and then compromise a little.
Father:	But you wish that Mom could change toward you somehow.
Loretta:	I am not saying change totally. I'd rather have her worry less.
Minuchin:	What you are saying, Loretta, is that it's not a total change, but you would like your mother to be less worried about you and about the other kids.
Loretta:	M-hum.

Discussion does not go easily between Loretta and her father. Indeed, it becomes evident later in the session that the father also has areas of great Old-World rigidity and

protectiveness about his daughters' growing up, as well as considerable difficulty in stand-
ing up to his wife. The girls cannot trust their father to be an effective ally. My intervention
restates Loretta's challenge, softening it to a point that may be acceptable, and lending sup-
port to an agreement between Loretta and Father.

Minuchin:	Do you think that Mama has *too* big a heart and that sometimes that makes her worry more than is necessary?
Father:	Well, what I've seen, Mama does herself much of the things that the girls could do by themselves. She makes it too easy for them. Now they find it a little hard to begin to manage by themselves and try out this situation.
Minuchin:	That's a very interesting and very sensitive view. Can you say it again? Because I think Margherita is deaf in this ear [Touches Margherita's ear].

I selected Father as my co-therapist, increasing his authority as an observer of his wife and
her relationship with her daughters. My carefully chosen adjectives make the father my
peer: someone who understands the intricacies of psychological processes. At the same time,
a slightly seductive, humorous gesture softens my challenge to his wife. I want these people
to be able to talk together.

Father:	I am sure Margherita understood already what I'm talking about.
Minuchin:	Do you understand what he says? What do you think about that?
Mother:	Why do I have to think? I am a mother. The things they can't do, I do.
Minuchin:	Now, what about what Carlo says? That you do more than what they need?
Father:	You've been doing, and you don't mind doing anything for them, right?
Mother:	I don't. I help my kids all the time in all ways. If they want help, my kids, I give it to them. That's what I do for my kids, then, all the time.
Minuchin:	I think that you still did not hear clearly what your husband has said, and what Loretta said. So say it again, Loretta, so that Margherita can hear it.

Margherita has a stonewall defense: all she is doing is being a good mother. But now
both Carlo and Loretta are prepared to challenge the overprotective pattern, especially
since my bantering is establishing a lighter, more secure feeling. I am enjoying this very
mild flirtation, as is the whole family. Surely in this nice family, meeting a nice therapist,
it is safe to do a little exploring. But the focus of the session has changed. We are not
dealing with Loretta's symptoms but with the patterns of relationships among family
members.

The familiar certainty becomes questionable, and alternative ways of looking at relation-
ships are open.

Loretta:	That you worry too much. And you've got to try to worry less, because I am 16 and Sophia is 15 and Maria is 13 and you worry too much, as if we were 10 and not 16, or 15. And let us try to do some things ourselves. Because if we want to try something, you say, "No, let me do it, it's better if I do it."
Mother:	Wait a minute, Loretta, I give you the chance—
Loretta:	In certain things that are easy to do. But in other things, you don't dare give us a chance.
Minuchin:	Loretta, I want to congratulate you! I think you are very good. Sophia, do you help her sometimes?

Once family members learn that talking with each other is acceptable in the session I become an observer, but I enter to highlight competent behavior on the part of the identified patient (IP).

In my work with anorectics, I have observed that a capacity for direct challenge in an area not related to food is a prerequisite for symptom improvement. Accordingly, I strongly reward Loretta's competent statement while beginning to explore the possibility of amassing support for her by strengthening her position as leader of the siblings.

Sophia:	In what?
Minuchin:	Do you help Loretta? Because she took the leadership position to defend all three of you. Do you sometimes join her?
Sophia:	No.
Minuchin:	So, Loretta, you are the only fighter?
Loretta:	Yes.
Minuchin:	Carlo, you have a lovely wife. Your children have a lovely mother. But I think that she can become a problem for the children that are growing up.
Father:	Yes, I thought that, too. In the situation of these two girls, now that they wish to do things but they are not really prepared to do, just because.
Minuchin:	They didn't have any experience. Yes.
Loretta:	Yes. But there has to be some point where you have to begin.
Father:	And that causes more worry for my wife, you know, when the two girls are willing to do something that we might consider unusual.

Fifteen minutes into the session I am at the starting point of a therapeutic reframing. The family came with one Identified Patient and one symptom: Loretta's not eating. From among the natural transactions among family members, I began to highlight certain themes and jump lightly over others. I addressed myself to Mother, respecting family hierarchies, but focused on Loretta's and Father's contributions, showing interest in the manner and content of their ideas. As the theme of the mother's sensitivity, her special "gift," appeared I used it to focus on parental control and support Loretta's age-appropriate rebellion in areas that are not about eating. At the same time, I supported Loretta's position as the leader of the adolescent children, challenging her isolation as the sick member of the family.

During the remainder of the session, other typical themes appeared: the anorectic's preoccupation with her appearance and her fear of becoming overweight; the parents' desperate sense that they are prisoners in a crazy drama centered on food and eating; the daughter's sensation that she is an embattled and lonesome fighter. But the therapy keeps its focus on the battle for control and age-appropriate autonomy, expanding to include the spouse's conflict, the father's isolation from his daughters, and his inability to challenge his wife's behavior as a parent. Wherever possible, I make links between Father and Loretta; one way of introducing distance for Mother and children is to support greater proximity between Father and Loretta.

The following excerpts from the rest of the session focus on challenging those family characteristics that maintain Loretta's troubled behavior: the family's enmeshment, overprotection, and avoidance of direct confrontation (except in the area of Loretta's eating), and the position of Loretta in the covert conflict between husband and wife. The challenge and the family's established patterns of response appear against the background of a shared lunchtime. By prearrangement, food for everybody is brought into the session, and therapy continues in a context that exemplifies the family's struggle and that allows for reframing.

Deconstruction of the System: Externalization

I borrow from Michael White (2007) the term "externalization," but I give it a different meaning. White, a social constructivist, moves the symptom out from the symptom bearer and helps the family to see how the external culture imposes its demands on them. He creates a therapeutic framework in which family members, together, defend themselves from external intrusion. I prefer to explain this process as one in which the therapist pushes the symptom out of the symptom bearer and helps the family members to see the family's participation in the construction and maintenance of the symptoms in the symptom bearer.

One hour into the session, I look at my watch.

Minuchin: It is 12:15. I want to have something to eat now because I think Loretta's problem is related to what we are talking about. Loretta, I think you are a good fighter. I am impressed by you.

Father: She is, yes.

Minuchin: I am concerned about what she feels, because if she feels that she cannot fight and win, then she will probably starve herself.

Mother: She is big enough to do anything she wants to do. Sophia, the same thing.

The food is brought in. Loretta runs out of the room, crying that she will not eat. I go after her, and we return together, 5 minutes later. During those 5 minutes in the hallway, I was able to build on Loretta's positive experience of the first part of the session. Loretta and I agreed that the task for the next part would be to negotiate with her parents. Loretta was not going to eat, but she was to negotiate with her parents and win. I promised to help, and she returned to the therapy room with that understanding.

Having lunch with anorectic families allows the direct observation of transactions around eating. It also makes it possible, in some cases, to move the spotlight from the patient's eating to the interpersonal transactions among family members in relation to eating: issues of control, disobedience, blackmail, and demands for loyalty. With the explicit enactment of conflicts, it is possible to develop crises that jolt the Identified Patient and the family out of their pathological patterns (Minuchin & Fishman, 1981).

Meanwhile the mother, has distributed sandwiches and drinks, and has placed a sandwich in front of Loretta's chair. As I sat, I said to the family that I had an agreement with Loretta that she was not going to eat in the session, but that the rest of the family, and myself, should have lunch.

Minuchin: Loretta, how old does your mother think you are?

Loretta: I don't know. Apparently not 16.

Minuchin: I absolutely agree with you. Until you are 16, you will not eat.

Mother: She wins me all the time, my daughter! If I say, "No," Loretta stops eating. If we don't do it Loretta's way, we have to put our hands in the air, we have to stop everybody. I have to stop Sophia. I have to stop my husband. I have to stop the phone ring. I can't talk to nobody because Loretta, she nervous. She do anything to send me, my husband, her sister, her brothers, any way she wants. We say, "Yes, Loretta." We have to do anything she wants, and everything will be okay. If we do something else, forget about it; Loretta, she say "No."

While Mother talks, the rest of us begin to eat, and as if by design, we avoid looking in Loretta's direction.

Minuchin: Can you answer your mother, Loretta? Carlo, let Mama sit near Loretta. Loretta, talk with Mother, because she says that you are controlling the house.

I seat Mother near Loretta and encourage direct confrontation in an area that is not related to food. There is also an implicit alliance between Loretta and me that facilitates her challenging her mother.

While Loretta's experience is one of being helplessly controlled, her control of her family around food is second only to Mother's control around protection. But since psychosomatic families are conflict avoiders, all controlling maneuvers are framed under the heading of concern and protection.

My challenge to this family pattern is to encourage explicit conflict around areas of normal autonomy.

Loretta: I am not controlling nobody, Mama.
Mother: You're controlling your father; you're controlling me, Sophia, Enrico, Maria, Giuseppi. Why, Loretta?
Loretta: I'm not controlling nobody. It's just that somebody has to do something.
Mother: That's me and your father's job. You have to do something by yourself. You are not to interfere with Sophia, Maria. . .
Loretta: I want to stand by myself and you are stopping me!
Mother: No, Loretta.
Loretta: Yes, Mama! You may not realize this sometimes, but you're doing it anyway.
Mother: But sometimes, Loretta, you put us in the world in a way we can't do nothing. We have to agree with you. But sometimes we can't. And if we don't get what you want, you start crying.
Loretta: No, Mama.
Mother: Screaming. Throwing chairs around. Pulling anything the way you want.
Minuchin: She has temper tantrums? Like little children?

Now conflict is in the open. I have supported Loretta's behavior as an age-appropriate resistance to her parents' over-control. Therefore, I can support her parents' challenge of her childish behavior and still be perceived as supporting her competence. By supporting Loretta and her parents against each other, I encourage the open expression of conflicts and their reciprocal demands for more-appropriate behavior.

Father: Well, she perfectly all right when she's cool. When she blow the cool. . .
Minuchin: You agree with your wife that Loretta is the one that drives the house?
Loretta: That's not the truth! You're making me sound like a bad person!
Mother: [Gently] No, you're not a bad person.

Loretta has signaled discomfort with the level of conflict and Mother, as always, has responded protectively. My job is to block the family's pattern of transforming issues of behavior control into emotional blackmail. Therefore, I keep the conflict going.

Minuchin: She is saying that you have temper tantrums. She is saying that you are childish.
Loretta: I may yell. I may scream. But I am not childish. I don't ever throw things around.
Mother: Loretta, I don't say that.
Loretta: If anything, you throw shoes at me or whatever it is that's in your way. You're trying to make me sound like a bad person!
Mother: No, Loretta. You are not a bad person.

Again there has been a warning light and its response, but this time Loretta herself continues her point.

Loretta: I am the bad person in the family. I'm the black sheep of the family simply because I stand up and say what I feel. The other children are always good. They're always your little sweethearts because they don't open their mouths.
Mother: No, Loretta, nobody is sweetheart—
Loretta: They agree about everything with you and Daddy. Whatever you say is all right with them.
Mother: When you want something that I can't buy you, you cry for 3 days, you get nervous. You stop eating. Right away—no food. Not get up from the bed. You don't want to see nobody. You don't want to talk to nobody. And Mama cries.

Encouraging direct conflict between mother and daughter is finishing in the usual framing: "Loretta is sick, and Mama cries."

Minuchin: Is your mother saying that you are blackmailing them? That your not eating is a way of controlling them?
Loretta: That's not true!
Mother: Why you do the same thing to the hospital? You blackmail the doctor.
Loretta: I don't blackmail nobody.
Mother: That's what they told me. You don't eat. They bring food in and you give it to somebody else.
Loretta: It always turns out that I'm the liar.

The therapist reframes the symptom: Not eating is not related to food but to interpersonal control. Mother and daughter continue focusing on the use of the symptom as part of the relationship. Now both the mother and I have firmly labeled not eating as a manipulative act. But as often happens, the facts of the matter are quickly transformed into the emotional interchanges of mother and daughter: "You didn't eat in the hospital" flip-flops with "you don't trust me."

Mother:	Now, you have to tell Dr. Minuchin you stay almost 2 months with no food in the stomach. Only that kind of food they give you through the tube. You cry. Mama cries outside in the hallway when they put the tube in the nose. Mama cries.
Loretta:	I'm not going to feel sorry for you, Ma. I'm sorry because you're wrong. I am not a liar.
Mother:	You made a cake for me to eat; I don't want to eat it. You right away say, "You don't want to eat it because I made it." The doctor at the hospital told me, "Your daughter is in danger and could die." I see she don't eat nothing. Now, this morning, she get up and she come over here. Not even a glass of water. There's nothing in there. I have to worry about her.

We are firmly back in the endless fight about eating. I'll try to reintroduce an interpersonal perspective.

Minuchin:	I think that Loretta feels a loser in your family. You say that Loretta is the winner. I think she is a loser.
Mother:	I can't do anything with Loretta. Loretta says, "You don't love me because you don't want to get this," and I have to do what Loretta say.
Minuchin:	I don't think that you let her feel that she is 16.
Mother:	No, she is the winner. Loretta, Mommy don't tell you that you are 16?
Loretta:	Yeah, you tell me, but you don't make me feel it. You don't treat me like 16. You treat me like I was 2 years old.

Loretta is using my developmental construction as a crutch, to help her stand against her mother.

Minuchin:	Margherita, you do so many things for your daughter that she becomes an extremely childish, incompetent person.

This challenges the mother as a participant in Loretta's symptom and the symptom loses significance as it is reframed as childish behavior. We have now a new family dance: Father becomes a co-therapist and supports his daughter in her challenging of her mother.

Father:	Right. I have to agree with you.
Minuchin:	And at some point your daughter needs to grow up. And your wife needs to start to grow up first, so that your daughter can grow up. It's very difficult, Loretta, to fight your mother, because she is a very lovely mother. Carlo, how can you help your daughter to become 16? Because she will begin to eat only when she's 16, not before.
Father:	I wish she make clear to me what she wants to do. I wish she'd be reasonable and understand that sometimes things are not possible.

Minuchin: You know, Loretta is very childish. But I think the family, and particularly you, Margherita, support her childishness.

Mother: How? How Loretta?

Minuchin: When you tell her how to move the chair, you are treating her as if she's 6. That's how. It's very simple how. When you say to her that she can go out with a boyfriend without asking her father, because you will protect her from her father's anger, that's how. You keep her as a little child.

This type of intervention is rather typical in my work, reflecting as it does my conviction about the complementarity of human behavior. I label a family member ("Loretta, you are childish"), and at the same time assign responsibility for that label to another ("Margherita, you keep her childish"). It is a framing that suggests a route to solution: "Loretta is childish; therefore, Margherita must grow up."

Father: When the tempers rise between the two of them, it's not possible to understand Loretta. Most of the time, even a little thing creates a situation that becomes impossible because of tempers.

Minuchin: I think you need to talk to your wife about keeping her a little girl.

Father: I'll be yelling many times that she is doing just too much and won't let these girls do things that they could do. Even when they were younger. And I don't think much has been changed in that area.

Minuchin: Can Margherita hear you, or is she deaf?

Mother: No, I hear my husband. I hear what he says.

Minuchin: But I want to tell you something. Loretta, she grew up a long time ago. When she wants to be, she's a young teenager. I think you are very much tied to your mother, unable to make decisions, to take initiative. You are fighting a battle for growing up in the worst possible ways, by killing yourself so that you will demonstrate to Mama that she is wrong. I think you can be a winner, but I don't know yet that you want to. You will eat when you are 16. But I don't think you feel, act, or think like 16. And I think this is because the family, especially Mama, is always doing things for you. Mother is moving your hands; she is moving your arms. [I take Loretta's hands and arms and move them. You don't do anything for yourself. So, I think you should not eat now. But you will eat at the moment when you are 16.

One of the advantages of family therapy entails using the family members as cotherapists, becoming healers of each other. Minuchin gives a task to Carlo to intervene in the complementarity between Loretta and Mother.

My behavior, treating Loretta like a puppet, has focused her attention on me; it increases her distance from her mother. At the same time, by appropriating Loretta's control of the symptom ("You will eat only when you are 16"), I have robbed its metaphorical meaning as a banner of autonomy. Not eating is now framed as a symbol of Loretta's dependence; and since I have joined with Loretta in her struggle for autonomy, we are now cooperating to create a family context that will allow her to eat and grow. I begin a strategy to increase distance in the family.

Minuchin: Loretta, do you eat with your family?
Mother: Loretta, she don't . . .
Loretta: What do you mean, I don't eat?
Mother: You want the truth, I give you the truth.
Loretta: Just because I don't eat with you, it means I don't eat? No, don't worry. I'm better off eating without you.

Loretta's voice is rising, and her despair is reappearing. Again, I experience the pull to support her.

Minuchin: Loretta, what is your weight at this point? Write it down on this napkin so that nobody sees it. Keep it secret. I also want you to write what is your height. [I give her a napkin, on which she writes that her weight is 82 pounds.]

This secret gives Loretta control over her body. Until now, eating has been an interpersonal issue, so that not eating was a triumph of her will over her mother's. Making her weight a secret between Loretta and me moves it back to the realm of physiological matters, away from psychological control.

Minuchin: Okay, now. I want you to help me, Carlo. I don't want any arguments at home about food. What would be the best way? [To Loretta] Would you like to eat alone for one week?
Loretta: It doesn't matter.
Minuchin: I want you to make a decision. Would you like to eat with some family members, or alone, or would you like to sit with them at the table, but eat alone? Select one alternative. Which one would you prefer? Which one would make it more comfortable for you?

It is important to have Loretta set the parameter because she experiences herself as only a responder to her parents' wishes. However, her passivity forces me to make the decision for her.

Loretta: It really doesn't matter as long as nobody bothers me about what to eat or how much.
Minuchin: Loretta, you need to understand their point of view as well. If you eat with them, then they will look at what you eat and what you don't eat, because you will make their situation uncomfortable. Just for one week, I want you to eat in your room. Could you do that? Because I don't want your family to know what you eat.
Loretta: On Sunday, I want to eat with them.

This is another response typical of anorectics—Loretta doesn't know she wants something different until a decision has been made. This time, I support her assertion as a statement of autonomy.

Minuchin: Fine, on Sunday you will eat with them. Now, for the next week there will be no fights with Loretta about eating. Carlo, you will be the foreman of that.

I think that your wife is very concerned and she is not objective because she's a mother hen. She vibrates with the kids. Now, do you think you can do a thing like that?

Father: Yes.

Loretta: I don't want to be weighed. It's better for me not to know.

Minuchin: Loretta, I will weigh you because I need to know if you can maintain your weight. But this will be between you and me.

Loretta: Okay.

Both my priorities and Loretta's wishes are maintained by compromise. This can, perhaps, be a useful model for the family.

Minuchin: You see, there are negotiables and non-negotiables. In order to work with you, it is necessary to know that you will not die.

Loretta: Well, I can be weighed, but I don't want to know it. I don't want to hear about it. I don't want to know my weight.

Minuchin: If that's how you want to arrange it, okay, but if you lose weight, I will tell you.

Loretta: Okay.

Minuchin: Okay, so that is something you, Carlo, and Margherita, can be relaxed about. We will check her weight. Meanwhile, she needs to learn to handle you two and you need to learn to handle her.

Loretta: The only reason why I get mad and the only reason why I scream and yell is because I don't know what to say anymore. I've had it. It's been years since this business and I can't take it anymore. I'm tired of it. Absolutely tired of existing and the whole situation. And that's why when I say something, I don't even know what I'm saying, and when I think about it, I'm sorry I said it.

At the end of the session, I bring back the focus on eating reframed as an issue of autonomy.

Minuchin: Loretta, I think that you should not start eating with the family until you are 16. How old are you now?

Loretta: Sixteen.

Minuchin: When was your birthday?

Loretta: Last week.

Minuchin: But you are not 16 yet. And since Loretta will not start eating until she is 16, I want Loretta to eat alone. At the point at which she begins to eat, she will be exactly 16. I think, Loretta, that you should not put too much weight on because your face looks rather nice long. But you need to gain probably 10 pounds. But this is for you to decide. Because at16, you will need to do things on your own. At home, I want you, Carlo, to talk with your wife, and then talk with Loretta, about what rights does a 16-year-old have and what obligations. Can you help your wife to think like that? That a 16-year-old has obligations?

Father: I will try.

Minuchin: Can she hear?

Mother: I hear good.

Father: Do you think you need that doctor to tell you?

Mother: I don't think so.

Minuchin: Okay. Carlo, you will need to talk with Margherita. I think she has run the house for too long alone, you know. You will need to talk with your father about jobs, Loretta. Maybe he can help you with this and other things. To let Loretta know you . . .

Father: What I want for Loretta—excuse me for interrupting you—is to think different about me. She has to think about me not as an obstacle course.

Loretta: Well, I can't think it, Dad, unless you show it.

Father: I have to show you before you will believe me, huh?

Minuchin: [To Loretta] For this week, before you return again, I want you, Loretta, to talk to your father twice over half an hour. And for the first time you tell him something about you, okay? So that he will know you. [To Carlo] The second time, I want you to tell her something about yourself, Carlo. I think she needs to know you and that will be a help. Carlo will take over more of helping Loretta. Will that be a help, Margherita? Margherita, she will start eating at the point at which she is 16, and she will not die of that. If she loses weight, then we will think differently. If she maintains the weight she has now, it is safe for the moment. So, you don't worry about that.

What happened in these 2 hours? I think the reality of the Menotti family changed. Or to be less grandiose, I led its members to observe themselves from a different perspective, one that allows new possibilities. They came with one deviant member; the magnetic pull of Loretta's behavior was obfuscating their experience and directing their perspective. During the session, Margherita's values of motherhood were questioned and challenged, Carlo's under-involvement and his longing fear of tenderness were uncovered, the children's overdependence and their need for autonomy were explored and supported, and Loretta's strength as the sibling leader was rewarded. Most important, underlying each individual's move is a glimpse of the interconnectedness of their movements. The family left in a mood of hope, with a new and more productive definition of their problems.

I had lived with this family for 2 hours, and in the "condensed time" of a therapeutic session transactions have an experiential intensity that permits a holistic vision. I knew this family's strength, their flexibility, and their capacity to increase their experiential repertoire. I felt that Loretta had already begun to change, and I had seen Carlo and Margherita expand their repertoires in their transactions with me. My prognosis for the Menotti family was positive.

They continued in treatment for 4 months. Therapy focused on issues of individuation and age-appropriate autonomy. Loretta gained 21 pounds over the first three months; her weight stabilized at around 105 pounds.

A follow-up one and a half years later found Loretta working as a waitress, a job that she had held for the last six months. She had re-enrolled in school and was planning to finish high school. She had many friends, and maintained a stormy relationship with her parents.

What Can We Learn?

Who were the Menottis, when they came for therapy, and how and why did they change?

When the family first described their problems, how did the three main participants in the family drama experience themselves; how did they see the others; and how did they conceptualize their relationships?

Loretta and Margherita

Loretta and Margherita, her mother, were prisoners of their proximity: in their enmeshment, there was little space to experience a sense of personhood, a sense of agency, or a freedom in decision-making. Each one felt as if they were responders to the other's control; prisoners of the other's demands and of their affect regulation. Their observation and experience of the other family members became less significant and the background to the emotional turmoil in which they were immersed.

Carlo

Carlo, at middle distance, was able to observe both of them in their destructive clinch, and was critical of the limitations but unable to relate with either one in a constructive way. He saw himself as an acute observer of himself in his relationship with his wife and children, but not as an effective decision-maker.

How can we explain the changes among members of the family during therapy?

During the two and a half hour session, a number of encounters among the members of the therapeutic system provided an opportunity for family members to see themselves in different contexts: as members of different subsystems in which they relate in novel roles, exploring new ways of relating, and seeing and conceptualizing themselves as complex individuals able to select ways of relating.

Loretta

Loretta was joined by the therapist who insisted, from the beginning, that she alone describe her experiences; from that platform, she was able to negotiate successfully with the therapist, indicating when and where she would eat. And she accepted limitations, as she accepted the therapist's request to weigh her, though she requested not to be informed of her weight.

She joined Sophia in challenging Margherita and felt acknowledged as leader in the request for more autonomy.

She joined with Carlo in a subsystem that excluded Margherita, and in that subsystem she became an observer of her mother and of the relationship between Margherita and Carlo.

Margherita

Margherita was given a platform to describe her experience, her heroic efforts on behalf of Loretta, and of her sense of responsibility and commitment toward her children.

The therapist confirmed her competence as a mother of young children, and from an expert position he explained the need to change parenting strategies with adolescents.

The therapist joined Carlo in a challenge to Margherita's concept of motherhood, and she accepted Carlo's competence to join Loretta in a relationship that excluded her.

She had a number of dialogues with Loretta in which the affect was of low emotional intensity.

Carlo

Carlo found a sense of agency in his family. His coalitions with the therapist facilitated his challenging his powerful wife. He was able to develop a relationship of proximity with Loretta.

Sophia and Maria

Sophia and Maria were witnesses of the family dance.

Therapist

The therapist felt as a director of a play in which he was one of the main actors, and in both positions he felt competent.

- He "knew" the Menottis. He had met them in many countries and felt the familiarity with which they were relating to each other and with him.
- He joined with Margherita, flirted with her, and challenged her.
- He affiliated with Carlo, who became his co-therapist.
- He coached Loretta toward adolescence.

All the participants experienced a shift in their reality; in the context of multiple encounters their sense of being an individual and of belonging to a number of groups became multi-layered.

In their own idiosyncratic way, all the sessions of Minuchin presented in the next chapters will present a similar process.

3

UNWRAPPING FAMILY MEMBER IDENTITIES

One of the certainties that a family brings to therapy is the knowledge that the identity of their members is unique and unchangeable, and this certainty is maintained by years of daily transactions among its members. Therefore, the idea of multiple identities goes against their living experience and will be challenged.

One of the therapist's goals is to invite family members to see alternative ways of being and belonging within the family. The question becomes how to do it: how to challenge the concept of the self as a unit.

I owe the concept of "Layers of Identity" to Borges, the Argentinean poet, who, in one of his short stories, "Borges and I," describes the paradoxical relationship he, Borges the man, has with Borges the writer, who rushed to publish his most cherished experiences, leaving him (Borges the man) exposed to his (Borges the writer) readership.

Another example of layering is close to my heart. My granddaughter Colleen, who is a student of fine art, draws a figure on a piece of paper. She then draws on a transparent piece of paper another figure that she puts on top of the first and continues this process of layering until she's satisfied with the end that she achieves: where the drawing we see is the sum of all the drawings, even though each part has a single identity.

My thinking about self and identity resembles a drawing of my granddaughter or a story of Borges. A self is created in a context populated by significant "others" at different historical periods in the life of a person, but it has a single identity who partakes through life and is influenced—and exerts influence—on other selves. And while we talk about our identity as if it is a unit, in effect we can unwrap the latent identities that have formed through our lives. A therapist functions as a midwife, making available alternative ways of being that increase the flexibility of people's relating with their significant "others."

LAYERS OF IDENTITY

The therapist assumes that the family members have resources available. Therefore, after joining with family members, one of the functions of therapy is to convince family members that they are <u>not</u> who they think they are. This is a paradoxical situation that has only one answer: they are more than what they think they are. One part of challenging certainties is to introduce doubts and confusion, and then indicate possible alternatives. But to show family members they are more than what they are is resisted by our belief that our identity is our only one and that it is unique.

When the therapist suggests the "simple" systemic idea of complementarity–family members construct each other, "you can change him or her," family members answer "he/she is who they are," and they can only change themselves.

One of the ways of challenging the <u>reality</u> that the individual is unique is by demonstrating to family members the <u>reality</u> that individual is also multiple.

In this chapter, we will present a family with which the therapist's technique was multiplying the ways in which family members defined themselves, and re-establishing new relationships between these new identities.

The Smiths are a family of three: the mother and father are in their late 50s and the son is 15 years old. The family has also two married daughters. The son is depressed and spends most of his time at home in bed sleeping. He has been expelled from school and is presently at a day program for disturbed children. The family is working class: father works as a foreman in a factory and mother is a homemaker.

In this chapter, the comments in the right column signal the moments of labeling, or change of labeling, family members' views of themselves. For didactic purposes, only we have numbered the moments in which there are shifts in the identities of family members.

(Tom = S, Mother = M, Father = F)

The Interview

Minuchin: I will be available to you for this next hour to find out, first, who you are, what are your problems, and can we change them? Can you—some of you—begin to tell me, what are the issues that you have at this point?

Mother: Well, the major problem right now, which is why we came here, is Tommy's reluctance to get out of his bed in the morning to be where he's supposed to be. Right now he should be here at 9:30 in the mornings for his clinic and it isn't just getting him out of bed for clinic, it's for anything that he has to. . . . When he was going to regular school he wouldn't go up.

Mother defines Tom (S1) as the IP who is irresponsible and defiant.

Minuchin: [To Tom] You know there are people who are morning people and people who are late people. You would say that you are more of a night person?

Challenge the pathological description, attempting to normalize the IP.

Son: Not really. It's like just the morning I don't feel like doing anything. I feel active all day but. . . .

Minuchin: It's just the morning. If you would have a good alarm clock then that would solve it?

Son:	The alarm clock I got now. . . . [Tom looks at his mother]
Minuchin:	Who's the alarm clock?
Son:	Well, I got one in my room.
Minuchin:	Do you have an alarm clock or is Mother the alarm clock?
Son:	I got one.
Father:	He's got one.
Minuchin:	Are you certain she's not an alarm clock?
Son:	Yeah.
Minuchin:	Who wakes you up?
Son:	She does most of the time.
Minuchin:	So she is your alarm clock.
Son:	Fine. I guess.
Minuchin:	[To Mother] Okay, so you have a function. You are an alarm clock.
Mother:	Well, at the present time we have two alarm clocks in his bedroom . . . and me.
Minuchin:	And you still need to come in?
Mother:	Yeah. It helps him.
Minuchin:	[To Tom] I wish I could get your knack for sleeping. What's the latest that you have been able to keep sleeping? [Tom looks at Mother] Don't ask her. She's . . . we all have functions. She's an alarm clock. She's also memory bank?
Son:	About one, two o'clock.
Minuchin:	One, two o'clock. That means you can sleep. . . .
Son:	That doesn't happen. . . .
Minuchin:	That means you can sleep 12 hours straight. I would. . . . [To Father] I bet you wish to have that capacity.
Father:	Yes, I do.
Minuchin:	What time do you wake up?
Father:	Me? Four or 5. [Looks at wife as if asking for her input]

Symptom belongs to Mother and Son.

Mother (M1) is an alarm clock.

Mother (M2) is a memory bank for Tom.

Minuchin:	Not only Tom looked at her for information, you also looked at her for information. She's an amazing person. So you wake up at five o'clock in the morning. When do you go to work?	*Mother (M3) is a memory bank for Father.*
Father:	I leave about quarter to six, six o'clock.	
Minuchin:	And what's your shift?	
Father:	Uh, sometimes six, sometimes 7 to 4:30, 3:30, 5:30. It can be any time really.	
Minuchin:	You work 10 hours then?	
Father:	Sometimes ten, sometimes eleven, sometimes eight. Most of the time it's nine.	
Minuchin:	Does that give you overtime?	
Father:	Yeah.	
Minuchin:	When you can work 10 hours, you do because you are able to get a couple of hours of overtime. What kind of work do you do?	
Father:	I'm a foreman. Fabricate pipe. Fabricate steel pipe. Cut and thread it.	
Minuchin:	It must take many years to become a foreman.	*Father (F1) responsible and competent.*
Father:	Many years.	
Minuchin:	How many years?	
Father:	Thirty.	
Minuchin:	Thirty years. How old are you now?	
Father:	Fifty.	
Minuchin:	You started at 20 and you work all the time in one job? And so you moved from just a worker you moved to the boss? So you certainly have seniority at this point.	*Father (F2) is executive.*
Father:	Mmmm-hmmm.	
Minuchin:	How many workers?	
Father:	Seventeen.	
Minuchin:	Seventeen. And how many foremen?	
Father:	Two.	
Minuchin:	Two. And the other guy is also a guy who came through the ranks and worked with....	

Father:	Yeah, not quite as long as me.
Minuchin:	So you are secure in your job.
Father:	Oh, yeah.
Minuchin:	Okay. So we have a person like you that knows about time and knows about schedules and knows about responsibility and you had worked all your life.
Father:	Mmmm-hmmmm.
Minuchin:	Okay. How is it you got a kid that doesn't know about time and doesn't know about schedules, doesn't know about motivation? How did you manage?
Father:	I don't know. That's what we can't figure out.
Minuchin:	Seems strange. Right?
Father:	Yeah. If he followed the right thing he'd be efficient, I don't know.
Minuchin:	Maybe. Maybe you gave him the wrong model. Maybe he doesn't want to be like you. [To Tom] What do you think? You don't want to be like father?
Son:	Yeah, I do.
Minuchin:	You do?
Son:	Yeah, I would love to.
Minuchin:	Thirty years in the same job, working from 6 to 4. Would you like that?
Son:	Yeah.
Minuchin:	You know most people like you, you know they look at the old man and say no, that's not the life for me. You really would like to be like him?
Son:	Yeah.
Minuchin:	That's interesting. Is that what you want to do?
Son:	Yeah, I want to work at the same place he does.
Minuchin:	You would like to work at the same place he does? And be with him?

Father (F3) as an incompetent father.

Son (S2) as loyal, Father (F4) as a role model.

Son:	Yeah.	
Minuchin:	Before, you looked at Mother and you activated her. But even when you don't look at her, she's active. Mother is asking you a question and you said yes and she said yes, as well. You know, she's wired to you people! [To Mother] Are you so wired that if he answers, you shake?	*Mother (M4) constrained by connections to Tom.*
Mother:	I guess so.	
Minuchin:	[To Father] Isn't that wonderful about how families get wired?	*Family as an enmeshed system. (Challenge is hidden.)*
Father:	That's true.	
Minuchin:	[To Mother] Beautiful. You feel vibes. Did you always feel like that? Wired to people?	
Mother:	Yeah, I guess so, because I have always been responsible for people.	*Mother (M5) as caretaker.*
Minuchin:	So you two have always been responsible people. You are responsible to your job and you are responsible to your family. Is that the way in which you divide the work? Your responsibility was to provide for the family and your responsibility was to take care of the kids? And this has worked?	*Father/Mother dyad divide responsibilities for caretaking.*
Mother:	Up to this point, fine.	
Minuchin:	How many years have you been married?	
Mother:	We've been married 30 years. And we have two other children besides Tommy, too. Married daughters.	
Minuchin:	But you are the only boy in the family and you're the youngest. How old is your older sister?	
Son:	One is about 28 . . .	
Mother:	Twenty-eight and 34. Yeah.	
Minuchin:	[To Tom] You activate both of them. Very good. You looked at Dad and you activated him, and Mom activated herself by herself. Do you know how you do it? Very invisible but very strong wires. So 28 and 34. So your younger sister is really much older than you are. So you are the baby. How long will you be the baby? 'Til you're 50? Or 'til you are 20? I don't know. Some families keep babies for a long time.	*Enmeshed family system.*

Son:	Um. . . .	
Minuchin:	Ask your mother how long will you be the baby?	*Enactment begins process of challenging over-protection. Tom (S3) as baby.*
Son:	Mom?	
Mother:	'Til you grow up.	
Minuchin:	Well, that can be a lifetime. You can be 70 years old and still be the baby. You know. Can you . . . can you check what does she mean by that? How long does that take? Check up with her to know. How long will you be the baby?	
Mother:	I don't know how long you'll be the baby. 'Til you accept your responsibilities. Which I am willing to give you. But you have to accept them. When you accept responsibility for yourself then I will consider you grown.	
Minuchin:	Would you agree with that? Answer to your mom because she is putting all the responsibility on you. It's up to you to grow up. Can you talk with her about that?	*Therapist joins with Tom, suggesting he should challenge Mother's view of his incompetence.*
Son:	Yeah, why am I responsible?	
Mother:	Because it's your life. It's your responsibility.	
Minuchin:	I know people that are wired like your mom is, so closely wired to you that you don't have too much space. Your being wired keeps you young. Will your mother let you grow up? I just don't know. Do you think she will?	*Mother (M6) as over-protective, handicapping development of Tom's autonomy.*
Son:	Yeah.	
Minuchin:	You're answering too fast. I am not so certain. I just saw your mother wired to you so closely I am not certain she will let you grow up. What will happen if you grow up?	
Son:	I don't know.	
Minuchin:	What will happen to her?	
Son:	I don't know.	
Minuchin:	Talk with your father about this. What could happen to your mother if you grow up?	*Enactment dialogue between Father and Son about Mother.*

Son:	What would happen?
Father:	She'd probably relax and enjoy life. That's one thing that would happen.
Minuchin:	Ask your mom now. That's your dad's opinion. Ask your mom.
Son:	Mom? What would happen if I grow up?
Mother:	What would happen if you would grow up? I wouldn't have a baby anymore. Right? Which I am going to clarify, I don't want a baby anymore.
Minuchin:	Don't take her answer so fast, okay? Challenge that. (To father) See, I think that is a very serious thing what your Mrs. said just now, that she will not have a baby, because people that are wired like she is wired get depressed when the baby grows up. What do you think about that? She may have a problem.
Father:	Hmmm . . . I don't think so. Not really. I just think she's waiting for Tommy to grow up. Like I am. Maybe we can do things we want to do. We can go places and get it done. We want to go places and do things. We can't do it until our son grows up. Meanwhile, we've been married 30 years, we want to get out and see things a little bit, you know. And we can't because Tom holds us back.
Minuchin:	He keeps you?
Father:	Yeah.
Minuchin:	That means he is very controlling, that he keeps you hostage.
Father:	Well, you know, sometimes Tom can get into mischief, you know. So we would rather stay home and avoid all the . . .
Son:	When was the last time I did?
Father:	Well . . . I don't know.
Son:	So then why are you saying that?
Father:	Well, the fear is still there.

Increasing Tom's voice (S4) as a challenger. Mother (M7) possible depression.

Tom (S5) controlling parents. Parents as victims.

Dialogue between Son and Father. Son challenging Father.

Son:	Well, I haven't been doing anything so you have no reason to say that.
Minuchin:	That was very nice. What you just did is 15 years old. You're 15 years old?

Therapist supporting Tom's competence (S6).

Son:	Yeah.
Minuchin:	That was very nice. You see, that gives me a very important clue. It is not only you that need to grow up, because what you just said is that at times you grow up and they don't recognize it. Talk with your dad about that. That was beautiful. Go ahead, talk with him about that, because he says you are a baby. And so he needs to be . . . your jailer or your prisoner. Talk with him.

Label to Tom (S7)– jailor or prisoner. Label to Father (F5)–jailor or prisoner.

Son:	Why do you still fear it? I haven't done anything.
Father:	I just have a fear.
Son:	You've left me alone, and I haven't done anything.
Father:	I know. But we're still not too happy to go out and leave you at home.
Son:	But I am not doing nothing.
Father:	I know. Let's keep up the good work, right?
Son:	All right.
Minuchin:	[To Tom] What he's saying to me is that he is keeping you a baby because. . . . And it's not just that you're a baby, it's that your father says that he's afraid you will never grow up. What do you need to do to get him to trust you?

Therapist joins Tom in challenging Father's version of his competence. Father (F6) undermining Son).

Father:	As far as keeping you a baby goes, I don't think breaking the ice box and stealing my beer. . . .
Son:	When was the last time I did that?
Father:	Stealing my whiskey. . . .
Son:	When was the last time I did that?
Father:	I don't know. But that's not being a baby. That's being very grown up, I think. That's my opinion.

38 · Concepts and Practice of the Craft

Minuchin: But, Tom is saying to you that he has changed and that you don't recognize his change. Am I correct that's what you're saying?

Son: Yeah.

Minuchin: Okay. Talk with him. You will need to convince them. If not they will just not recognize. You need to convince them then.

Therapist joining with Tom—supporting his competence.

Son: Like I said, I changed.

Father: Well, we recognize the change. We told you that before, didn't we?

Son: Well, I haven't done anything to prove otherwise. But you're saying you still have fears.

Dialogue between Father and Son. Father insisting on Son's incompetence. Tom challenges as a normal adolescent.

Father: Well, I do. And so I still have that fear in my heart that you will do something too, well, baby-like, let's put it that way. That's why there are locks on the ice box and the cellar.

Son: Well, take them off. I am not going to do anything.

Father: Maybe I'll do that. If I took it off the cellar, you would mess the cellar up with that paint.

Son: I was just messing around. I didn't mess the cellar.

Father: Yes, you did. You were acting like a little kid down there with that paint. Didn't you?

Son: I just was messing around.

Father: Well, the screwdriver was full of paint. . . .

Son: That was in the sink.

Father: The copper tube was full of paint.

Son: That was . . . they both were in the sink.

Father: That was just messing right?

Son: Right. Because they were both in the sink when I put them there.

Father: Well, that was a very irresponsible act that you pulled there. Let me tell you.

Minuchin:	Did you do it as a mischief? Or did you do it because you're a klutz?	*(S8) The label "klutz" is an improvement over the label "baby."*
Son:	Not because I'm a klutz. I had gold paint and I painted my bike with it and there was a little bit left and I was at the sink and I spilled it and I turned the water on and all this paint flooded on top of it and got on the sink.	
Minuchin:	So it was not on purpose—some mischief— it was just because you were incompetent.	
Son:	I'm not incompetent.	
Minuchin:	That's incompetent. But that's different from being a baby. (To father) That's an incompetent youngster, you know, maybe he did not learn from you to be competent. You are a very competent man. If you had been working all this time and you're a foreman, you are probably a person that takes care of your tools and all those things. Is that true?	*Father (F7) as "competent as an individual" but "incompetent as Father."*
Father:	Yeah.	
Minuchin:	And he does not . . . he has not learned that yet.	
Father:	No. He has no respect for tools whatsoever.	
Minuchin:	And you would like to teach him that.	
Father:	Yeah.	
Minuchin:	And is he a very incompetent student that you cannot teach him?	
Father:	No. He can be. . . . He's smart. He just doesn't want to listen and that's a problem.	
Minuchin:	I am not certain. I am listening to Tom and my feeling is that there are two parts of Tom and that you are looking at the worst part of him, and certainly the worst part of him is pretty bad, but there are some aspects of him that I am listening now. You painted your bike?	*Therapist supports Tom as responsible and labels Father as biased.*
Son:	Yes.	
Minuchin:	So you were responsible there with your bike and you painted it. Try to convince your Dad that this is one of those things that it's a mistake and you learned from it. I don't know. Convince him that you are not a klutz.	

Son:	It's just a mistake, you know? Next time, I know. Next time if I spill paint, I will know to try and wash it off the floor. Cuz I thought that it would just wash down the drain.	*Tom (S9), with support of therapist, becomes responsible and competent.*
Father:	And suddenly everything is fine, right?	
Son:	All right, next time I do something I'll tell you about it.	
Minuchin:	See you have a youngster who is a little bit of a klutz. He doesn't like that, but I think he's a klutz. But I was impressed because he said he would like to be like you. Can you teach him to be like you?	*Therapist introduces the idea that Father can be healer (F8).*
Father:	Well I've been trying to teach him to be like me by getting out of bed in the morning, but he won't get out of bed, I guess. It isn't being like me. It's far from being like me.	
Minuchin:	I don't understand why you can't kick him out of bed.	
Father:	Well, I'm at work. I can't come home from work and then go back to work. That's been one of the problems.	
Minuchin:	I'll tell you why I am talking with you instead of talking with your wife. I think she's too closely wired, so I don't think she will help him to become like you. She did a marvelous job with her daughters, and I think she is doing the best that she can with Tom, but she cannot do with Tom what she did with your daughters. She just doesn't know. Here you have a kid who wants to be like you, but he's a klutz and you're very competent. And she cannot help him.	*Therapist connects Father to Tom and disconnects Tom from Mother.*
Father:	How can I help him?	
Minuchin:	So, talk with him about how you could help him to stop being a klutz.	
Father:	How can I help you?	*Father (F9) reconnects as a teacher.*
Son:	Start by helping to teach me.	
Father:	How do I teach you how to get out of bed in the morning?	
Son:	I try to get up in the morning.	

Minuchin:	Continue talking with him but ask him to be straight, ask him to be 15, ask him to be a man. Talk with him.	
Father:	I want you to be a man. And get up. All you gotta do is sit up in the bed. And sit up and you're up. That's all you gotta do. But you won't get out of bed. So how can you be a 15-year-old boy and not get up? I hear Ma three or four times calling you.	
Minuchin:	[To Mother] If you would just sit here. I think you are too closely wired to Tom. (To Tom) Talk together about what will happen. The way in which he can help you to start tomorrow to be responsible. Talk with your father and he will help you.	*Therapist rearranged the seating position putting Tom near Father and Mother near Therapist.*
Father:	How are you going to get up in the morning? What can you do?	
Minuchin:	[To Mother] You just relax. My goodness are you closely wired!	*Mother looks tense. She stretches her neck to look at Tom.*
Son:	You can try to make me go to bed earlier. Or I could try to go to bed earlier.	
Father:	Then, why don't you go to bed earlier?	
Son:	That's what I'm going to do. I'm going to try.	
Minuchin:	Let's eliminate the word "try," because tomorrow he will change, so you are his model, okay? So begin to teach him. You have a life of experience. Help this guy to get some of this experience.	
Father:	Well, we have to take something off you. Maybe your new recording machine we'll take off you.	
Son:	I'll just start getting up in the morning.	
Father:	Hear what I say?	
Son:	Yeah.	
Minuchin:	Talk about that. This is good language between a 15-year-old and his father. Begin to talk language that you will be responsible and he needs to be responsible to you. Begin to develop a program. I want this young lady that you have to begin to relax, and she has a hell of a time to relax. If Tom gets wired to you, you will help your Mrs. You want to help your Mrs., right?	*Father (F10) as a healer of Son is a healer of his Wife.*

Father:	Oh, yeah.
Minuchin:	[To Mother] I am on your side. Okay?
Mother:	I understand.
Father:	We talk about this 15 times now, same subject. You keep on saying tomorrow you're going to get up, but the same thing over, and over, and over again.
Minuchin:	Then something is wrong with what you do, sir. Something is wrong with what you do. I don't know what, but if you say that this happens and you don't like it, and he doesn't like it and you don't change it: something is wrong with what you do. Something needs to change in the house.
Father:	I don't know what could change. We're starting to punish him. What else could we do to you?
Minuchin:	Don't hook your wife. Not "we," it's you.
Father:	Maybe I can pull down your pants and give you a licking. Maybe that will straighten you out. You think so?
Son:	I don't know.
Father:	No? That might just happen next. Would you like that?
Son:	No.
Father:	So . . . tomorrow you're going to get up, right?
Son:	Yeah.
Father:	'Cuz that's what you said last week.
Minuchin:	If he said that last week and it didn't happen, you had done something wrong. You know it's clear to me. For him to change, you need to change and Mother needs to change. And that's clear. [To Mother] You need to relax, you need to be out.
Mother:	I've been trying.
Minuchin:	[To Mother] You need to not be so available. [To Father] You have a wire cutter? That's what we need to do. To cut the wire. She's wired too close. [To Mother] You need to let him grow up. If you are the memory, if you are the alarm clock, he doesn't need to grow up, so for you it's easy. Your husband will cut the wire.

Father insisting on keeping Son as the only "owner" of his behavior. Therapist labels Father as a failure (F11).

Therapist labels Father as IP (F12).

Father (F13) as an intervener and a helper.

Mother:	It isn't easy for me to, after all this time, to, you know, just step back, because for years this is the way it has been. And I had tried with Tommy. I realized a few years ago that I was his alarm clock, his memory bank, and everything else, and I tried stepping back a little then and giving him more responsibility and this is when we started having so much trouble, I think.	*Mother describes herself using the therapist's language. Mother (M8) labels herself as a failure.*
Minuchin:	[To Father] You will need to help her. How can you do that? Apparently, she's saying she doesn't think it's an easy task.	
Father:	She's been keeping me out of it.	*Conflict between Husband and Wife.*
Mother:	Every morning, I get into things. I start getting him up because I feel that's my responsibility to see that he gets here.	
Minuchin:	He's not getting responsible because you are responsible. You started like that when he was 5 years old?	*Mother and Son Complementarity.*
Mother:	Yeah.	
Minuchin:	And he's 15 and you still have that job.	
Mother:	Right.	
Minuchin:	[To Father] She's a foreman. See, you don't need to work because she is a foreman. So talk with your wife to see how you can help her.	
Father:	Well, we talk about this and we've tried different things, right. I am at work and there's nothing I can do unless I go home every day and go back to work, which I can't very well do.	*Father and Mother collaborating in parenting.*
Mother:	You could be back again like I told you before. Be more forceful than you are. Give him a more definite idea of the consequences, like, if you don't get out of bed, I am coming home. And get him out of bed. And this would help me.	
Minuchin:	You're the soft touch.	
Mother:	I don't know if I am the soft touch. I am the one that gives him the punishments and thinking of things to deprive him of and giving him incentive to get up, but it doesn't work. It's not working, because he knows that his dad isn't going to enforce it.	*Wife challenges Husband.*

Minuchin:	You need the wire cutter. She cannot help him to become like you.	*Therapist repeating the same message.*
Mother:	I agree with you.	
Minuchin:	So talk with your husband about how can you be relieved from that job?	
Mother:	Well, the only way I can see is if my husband just takes over.	*Mother and Father reconnect.*
Minuchin:	Talk with him.	
Mother:	And be more firm with him. If you have to hit him, hit him. Even though I don't like it. Just tell me to go get lost or something if you feel you're going to get loud or rough with him.	
Son:	Yeah. I want him to tell me what the rules are.	
Minuchin:	You are a very competent man and you have a klutz. How do you like that?	
Father:	No, I don't like it, no.	
Minuchin:	So begin to change him, and it's your job because you are the model. I like what Tom said: he would like to become like you. That's a hell of a nice compliment.	
Father:	If he wants to be like me he has to get out of bed, huh, Tom? If you don't get out of bed I will pull down your pants and give you a licking. How does that sound? Starting to-morrow morning. Okay?	*Change: Father and Son reconnect in dialogue about competence.*
Son:	Yeah.	
Father:	All right. And your mom will keep out of it. I'll put the alarm in, right? You hear your alarm in the morning, don't you?	
Son:	I hear it. Sometimes.	
Father:	Well, you better hear it tomorrow morning and get up.	
Son:	Okay. I'll be listening.	
Minuchin:	Are you saying to your wife that she should not wake him up?	
Father:	Right.	
Minuchin:	Tell her that very clearly.	
Father:	I'll be home in the morning. All right. Re-gardless, you get up yourself, right?	

Son:	Yeah.
Father:	Nobody's going to call you.
Son:	Yeah.
Father:	If you don't get up, I'll be there, okay? And you will pay the consequences. And I'll tell your mother to get lost. I'm serious!
Son:	Okay.
Minuchin:	Fine. What else can you help him because you see? *[Invites the counselor of the day program, who has been observing the session from behind the one-way mirror, to enter.]* Carl, can you join us? We were talking before with Carl and you did not tell me he was a klutz. You told me he was a bright kid who doesn't mobilize himself. How will you help him to change so he can begin to look resourceful and direct like his father?
Counselor:	One of the things I can think of is getting in touch with you if I'm having some problems, and call you, and maybe Tom can explain to you what some of the problems are that we are having.
Father:	I'll be glad to help, really.
Counselor:	And maybe I can give you a report at the end of the day so that we can tell you what kind of things Tom has been doing with the group.
Father:	That's swell with me.
Minuchin:	[To Tom] Let me tell you what's happening. I think this day program will not help you grow up. What will happen is that your father and Carl will be wired to you instead of your mom, so you will substitute. So the idea is not really to help, because you are like a puppet and you have puppeteers. And mom is your puppeteer and now we are saying your father and Carl will be your puppeteer. The idea is that you need to become a real 15. And you will not be a real flesh and blood 15 if you have puppeteers. But you have a talent. You recruit puppeteers. Your mother has been your puppeteer for 15 years, and we are saying let's not do it for a little while. You know what is the goal?
Son:	Yeah. To grow up.

Father (F14), Mother (M9), and Counselor (C1) are labeled as Tom's puppeteers.

Minuchin:	To kick the puppeteers out. So they are now developing a program that is okay, it means that you will not be a more competent puppet, but the goal is for you to kick these people out: your mom, your dad, Carl . . . Everybody treats you like a puppet. They don't think you have an inner motor. I believe you have a motor inside that you don't need people from outside to move you. Can you move your hand by yourself? [Minuchin gets up and moves his hands like a puppeteer].	*Tom (S10) as a puppet.*
Son:	Yeah.	
Minuchin:	Yeah, you don't need that. You have fooled all of these people. All of them think you don't have a motor. You don't have a soul. How did you manage to fool all of them?	*Tom (S11) as a competent manipulator, changes his symptom into a skill.*
Son:	I don't know.	
Minuchin:	Just luck? Or cleverness?	
Son:	Luck?	
Minuchin:	[To Tom] Okay. You will need to begin tomorrow to convince this man before you convince your father. You will need to convince Carl that you don't need that string. Because it will be easier to convince him than convince your parents. So you will start to convince him. Because you are not so closely wired, so he will be convinced. And talk with Carl tomorrow about some of these things. Have some talks with him about how can he use what he has inside. Begin to change here. I don't even think Carl knows the part of you that is okay. The only thing they know is that you need string. And that is a bad thing for you. They don't know the other parts about you. Not the fact that you're bright, not the fact that you're sometimes helpful. That you're polite, you're considerate, and that you are responsible, though sometimes you're not so competent. See, they didn't see the fact that you painted the bike just the fact that you're a klutz. So you painted the bike?	*Therapist joins with Tom (S12) as a competent resilient youngster.*
Son:	Yeah.	
Minuchin:	What color, gold?	

Son:	Yeah.	*Dialogue about normal tasks of adolescents (S13).*

Minuchin:	Is it a nice bike?
Son:	Yeah.
Minuchin:	What is it, a 10-speeder?
Son:	Yeah.
Minuchin:	What kind?
Son:	I don't know [Looks to Mother and Minuchin gets up and covers Tom's eyes]. It's a German bike.
Minuchin:	[To Tom] And you think your mother is going to pronounce it?
Son:	Yeah.
Minuchin:	Don't use her. We are talking about beginning to change. I accept the fact that you don't know how to pronounce the name. That's fine. You don't need her. The bike is a good bike and you painted it. What did you paint? Did you trim it or did you paint it completely?
Son:	I just touched it up.
Minuchin:	What kind of paint did you use? Is it a spray can?
Son:	No, it's in a jar.
Minuchin:	A jar. You will need to convince your dad that you have inside much more than what he has seen. Then your dad will tell your mom. Then maybe your mom will relax and you will grow up. What about that program? Okay?
Son:	Yeah.
Minuchin:	You will need to do a hell of a lot of convincing, because these people will not believe you.
Son:	Okay.
Minuchin:	It was a pleasure. I will tell you something. It's great that you have a son that wants to be like you.
Father:	Yeah.

Tom left the program two weeks after this session and continued in regular high school. The family continued in family therapy.

What Can We Learn?

This was an unusual session in which the movements of the family members and of the therapist were clearly visible. I felt that I knew the father: responsible, honest, naïve, not very good with children, and I had seen the mother many times in many cultures: responsible, protective, concerned for others at their own expense.

So in the first minutes of our encounter, I felt I could challenge mother's styles, labeling her as an alarm clock and a memory bank, and I knew she would recognize herself in my diagnosis. And later, I could join the father's competence as a foreman and label him an "incompetent father." The son, I thought, was caught between the parents conflictual style of parenting.

From this narrow platform of knowledge of the family, I formulated three as yet unclear goals:

1. Disconnect mother from son.
2. Connect father to son.
3. Join son in challenging both parents.

I did not know how to direct the family members toward this alternative way of relating, but over an hour and a half we conversed and converged toward new ways of being and relating.

My conceptual formulation was that identity expands in different contexts, and my therapeutic maneuvers were directed toward shifting the context in which family members related. To do this, I multiplied the labels, diagnoses, or identities of father, mother, and son, and reconnected them anew under different subsystems, helping in the construction of new conversations and new ways of relating.

I had for didactic purposes counted how many times people were labeled. Father was 14 times, mother was 9 times, and Tom was 12 times. And, of course, I was continuously shifting my interventions, always knowing that when I touched one family member, I also touched, in a different way, the other two. I labeled:

Mother: 1. An alarm clock, 2. A memory bank for Tom, 3. A memory bank for Father, 4. Constrained by her close connections to Tom, 5. Caretaker, 6. Overprotective, 7. Depressed, 8. Mother labels herself a failure, 9. Tom's puppeteer.

Tom: 1. Labeled by the mother as irresponsible and defiant, 2. Loyal to father, 3. Baby, 4. Controlling parents, 5. Challenger of Mother, 6. Competent, 7. Jailor or prisoner, 8. Klutz, 9. Responsible and competent, 10. Puppet, 11. Manipulator of the puppeteers, 12. Competent, resilient youngster, 13. Normal adolescent.

Father: 1. Responsible and competent, 2. Executive, 3. Incompetent father, 4. Role model for son, 5. Jailor or prisoner, 6. Undermining son's competence, 7. Competent as a foreman and incompetent as a father, 8. As a healer, 9. As a teacher, 10. Healer of wife and son, 11. Incompetent and narrow-minded, 12. A symptom bearer, 13. As a helper, 14. Tom's puppeteer.

I was unaware during the session of the many contradictory labels that I, and the family, bestowed on each family member, but I know that identity is not logical, and as the members of the team (therapists included) meandered through content during the session, the moments of confusion challenged member certainty, and healing began in these pauses.

4

DECONSTRUCTING FAMILY ORGANIZATION
Exploring Subsystems

This chapter is focused on family organization. In particular, it highlights the process of therapy that allows therapists to explore subsystems as pathways in the process of change.

Families are social systems whose members have a common history and a complex course of change over time. In order to function well, they must take account of developmental changes in their members, cope with the expectations of their culture, and adapt to new realities. In the relations between generations, for instance, parents are expected to protect, nurture, and control their children when they are young but relate differently when they become adolescents, with changing capacities and needs. They must function, as well, within the realities of their current culture. In earlier times, the roles for men and women were often clearly defined; women carried the "affective" role, while the man was the "executive member" (Parsons & Bales,1955). At least in current Western societies, those roles have changed radically, reflecting not only a broader and more complex conception of possibilities for each gender, but also an increase in the diversity of family patterns. Divorce; shared child custody; remarriage; gay, lesbian, and blended families, and so forth, are now part of the social fabric.

The majority of families that young practitioners will meet have struggled with the symptom and the symptom bearer and they tell the therapist, "We are certain we've tried everything possible, and we are exhausted." Their demand is for immediate attention with a narrow focus. For the new practitioner that demand is felt as an imperative to look in the direction the family indicates. It is a simplistic formulation, however, and a prescription for continuing failure to alleviate the family's pain. Families are complex systems. It's important to see their complexity; to work towards a grasp of the family as a whole, with its resilience and areas of strength, as well as its rigidity and pathology.

In this chapter, we will be describing the early stages of therapy with a family that fits the "typical" description: they came in with an identified patient, a simple definition of the problem, a request to cure their child, and a confession of despair and helplessness. The therapy moves toward a more complex understanding of how the family is organized and how its members participate in the dysfunctional patterns.

As the sessions move along, it will be evident that the process deals not only with the organization of the total family but with the parts that make up the whole. A family system contains subsystems, and those subsystems have subdivisions of their own. The adults in a young family, for instance, relate with each other as "parents" but they are also "spouses," and they function as well in relation to the extra-familial world, making decisions about schooling, finances, and so on. Like all members of a family, they are also "individuals"—subsystems of one person—each with a set of skills, dreams, and needs that change through developmental stages.

Subsystems in a family are aggregates of particular members who are in close relationship with each other; by definition, they have implicit "boundaries" that exclude others. Siblings may have their own world, excluding parents; older siblings may exclude younger siblings; gender may create specific bonds, and so on.

These affiliations can be both a source of strength and a generator of stress; a support for its members, a source of resentment for those who are excluded. Sometimes, affiliations become coalitions, when certain family members join together to challenge or attack others. If cross-generational coalitions appear, they are often an expression of pathology and a source of stress, such as when conflictual spouses recruit their children in a coalition against the other parent, or grandparents enlist children against their parents.

It's important to be aware of the geography of subsystems; it contains implicit directions on how to intervene, how to join, and what roads should not be taken.

FAMILY THERAPY: A CASE ANALYSIS[1]

The consultant in this case (Minuchin) is meeting for the first time with the Boyd family, and their therapist has agreed to be an observer. She has given him the following information about the family: Richard and Mary, the parents, are in their 40s, Whitney is 15, and Joe is 2 years old. Whitney is Mary's child from her first marriage, which ended in divorce when Whitney was an infant. Joe is the son of Mary and Richard. Mary married Richard one year after her divorce, and now they come to therapy because Whitney cannot be trusted. She lies compulsively, and most of the time she's caught in the lie.

What follows is an abridged presentation of the first two sessions. Because the main purpose of this chapter is to demonstrate the use of subsystems for exploring a family and advancing the therapy, the presentation has been adapted for that purpose. The dialogue, which appears in the left hand column, has been shortened and summarized. Numbered headings highlight the nature and shifts of the subsystems involved as the session progresses. Italicized sections are addressed to the reader, and summarize the thoughts and reasoning of the consultant/therapist as he shapes his interventions and evaluates what is happening.

The First Session
When we enter the room and settle down, Mary takes the lead, telling me that "she [Whitney] has lied to us as long as I can remember."

This is clearly impossible, but the problem isn't in the logic of the statement but in the intensity of the proclamation: "as long as I can remember." The family's interaction has been restricted by a story that started at the beginning of time.

1 This case was originally presented in Minuchin, Nichols, and Lee (2007), *Assessing Families and Couples: From Symptom to System*. Printed and electronically reproduced with permission. For a full account, please see this publication.

1. Couple as Parents: Parental Subsystem

Minuchin: Can you tell me more? Could you be more concrete? Remember that you are all familiar with your story, but I am a stranger. Can you talk with Whitney about an incident when she was lying?

Richard: [Takes up the story] We don't know why we thought we could fix it ourselves, but it's gotten worse.

Mary: We had tried everything. We tried to understand why she does it. She lies about the simplest things, and now she lies in school and her grades have gone down.

I have met with a challenge at the beginning of the session: How to join? I need to remember that the family presentation of the problem is always partial, and it is a stop sign that demands hesitation. The inner voice should tell me, "You don't know this family and they are already asking that you should be an expert." I need to remember that I am an "uncertain expert"; therefore I need to ask questions, but to whom? And about what? That's my dilemma. If I join with the parents, I may lose Whitney, and I certainly can't join with their narrow definition of their daughter as the IP. I need to introduce uncertainty, curiosity, and hope, helping the parents to see themselves as the competent and resourceful people they probably are. I ask the parents' permission to talk with Whitney, and I start by saying that I am curious about her life.

2. IP: Individual Subsystem: Therapist and Whitney (Summary of Discussion)

We talk about her school, her friends, her interests. She tells me that she keeps a diary, that she likes poetry, and that she writes poems but doesn't show them to anybody. I ask her if she knows what a metaphor is, and we agree that a metaphor can bring something to attention through calling it by a different name. I say that, in effect, a metaphor is a poetic lie.

I am pleased with this image. It transforms a symptom into a skill, and I'm pretty sure it will appeal to Whitney, who is bright, engages with me easily, and, like any young person, would like me to understand that she's more than just a liar. At the same time, I know that the parents probably feel I've been seduced by Whitney and have fallen for her lying.

3. Family System: Parents Observing Child

Minuchin: [Turning back to the parents] Can you talk with Whitney? I'm a stranger, and you've come to see me about something that's very significant for your family. Maybe you can talk together, and that will help me to know how you deal with each other.

Richard: I can't explain it. That's why we came here.

This intervention of talking with Whitney is contrary to the family members' expectation. They talk with each other at home, and they come to the session to ask the expert; therefore, they are surprised by this turn of events. I know they will probably continue to engage me directly, but it is the beginning of a process in which I introduce the rules of therapy. I am implicitly refusing to take a guiding position, suggesting that

| Mary: | In the beginning, she would just lie to us. Now she's getting into trouble with other people. She never tells us the whole story. She's getting out of hand. | *the healing will require engagement among family members. The challenge to family rules, and my suggestion that therapy is a special context, will not be heard by the family members the first time but will remain as seeding: an idea that will be accepted later.* |

4. Family Subsystem: Child Observing Parents

Minuchin:	[To Whitney] Can you help me to understand what your parents are saying?	*Why do I move to Whitney? I have just asked the parents to talk with their daughter and the parents reject that suggestion. I feel I need a different tack. I go to the IP,*
Whitney:	Well, I'll do something and they ask me if I did it, and I deny it.	*trying something new. I give her a voice; I make her an agent in the family polemics. I also give her a new role as a helper and my ally. All of this is wrapped in a seemingly*
Minuchin:	Can you give me an example?	*neutral request. I also increase her position in the hierarchy by putting her in a symmetrical relationship with her parents.*

5. Parent Subsystem: Father Observing Whitney

| Richard: | [Before Whitney can respond] A week ago she was grounded because of her poor grades and wasn't allowed to use the phone. But I know for a fact she *did* use the phone. | *I continue my challenge to the idea that the problem is <u>in</u> Whitney, but my challenge is invisible. My language is whimsical—it seems as if I am joining with the father, talking about his skill as a detective, but, in effect, it's the beginning of an exploration about the elements of control between the adolescent and her parents.* |
| Minuchin: | How did you know? How did you become a detective? By the way, who is a better detective, you or Mary? | |

6. Child and Mother Subsystem

Minuchin:	[To Mary] Are you afraid she'll get involved in a sexual relationship?	*Here we have another shift in the exploration of the family dance. First, I challenged Whitney's lying, describing metaphors as poetic lies. Then I challenged Father's concern with control, suggesting it is a matter of skill in detecting. Now, I highlight Mother's tense observation of Whitney as dangerous for*
Mary:	I really don't know. Whatever she does becomes a secret.	
Minuchin:	I'm concerned about you. Trying to follow an adolescent child can become a full-time occupation. Are you both equally worried? Or is one of you more worried than the other?	

Richard:	[Glancing at Mary] She gets caught up in it more.
Mary:	It depends on the situation.

Mother's well-being. The initial simple certainty, "Whitney is a liar," is becoming a complex family web, as I introduce confusion, doubt, uncertainty, and, hopefully, curiosity about a new family picture.

7. Therapist and Father as Observers of Mother and Daughter

Minuchin:	[To Richard] Why do you think that happens? What does Mary want from Whitney?
Richard:	She wants her to be truthful. They used to be very close.

The parents' initial presentation was that they are on the same page in relation to Whitney's lying. This is almost never true. The parents have idiosyncratic responses, and I explore the different responses of the parents in this blended family, assuming that Mary, Whitney's biological mother, is more intensely involved than Richard.

Minuchin:	[To Mary] So lying can be a defense. At this point, you and your daughter are hooked together. She's pulling at you so you will watch her continuously. How will you free yourself from her?
Mary:	If I could trust her to do the things she says she'll do, like go to the mall, and really do it. I want to let her.
Minuchin:	[To Richard] Your wife tries to relax her surveillance of Whitney, but then Whitney does something that says, "Look at me!" and Mary is hooked again. They're both caught. Whitney needs Mary to look at her, and Mary is hooked into observing and responding to Whitney. It's a circle. Can you help them? Can you free these two people from this vicious circle?

I separate Richard from Mary and invite him to be my co-therapist; my helper in exploring his wife's relationship with <u>her</u> daughter. I explore the dyad of mother-daughter, highlighting the reciprocal pull of their complementarity. I have moved the label of IP from Whitney to the subsystem of Whitney-Mary, and use Richard as a collaborator in the observation of their dance. I also ask Richard to become an active healer of the troubled dyad.

8. Therapist Recruits Father as Healer of His Wife

Richard: I can see where Mary may overreact. Until a few months ago, when we tried to set up punishments, Mary would holler and yell, but an hour later they'd be going to the mall together. Maybe she would feel guilty and give in.

Minuchin: What did you do then? What did you say to Mary?

Richard: I didn't think it was right. They're close, and then sometimes they're not. I'd say "Let her alone. Let her think about it."

Minuchin: And were you successful?

Richard: No.

9. Therapist and IP as Observers of Mother

Minuchin: [To Whitney] I don't understand your mother. Why is she watching you so much?

Whitney: She doesn't trust me.

Minuchin: And you make sure she doesn't trust you. What are you doing that makes her watch you so closely? How can you help her to release her hold on you?

Whitney: It's not as if I insist on her keeping her watch on me. I don't understand why she gets upset about small things.

Minuchin: Something is wrong when they hold you prisoner and you hold them prisoner. Something strange has happened in a family where the jailers are prisoners, and the prisoners are jailers.

I join with Whitney, increasing her agency in her relationship with her mother and assigning her a healing role.

10. Couple Subsystem: Boundary Making

Minuchin: [To the couple] Do you have spaces that are your own?

Mary: Not as much as I would like.

Minuchin: Who interferes?

Richard: Sometimes it's Whitney's behavior.

Minuchin: Richard, almost any adolescent who is under observation may become a liar.

I will move on now to the couple. I want to create boundaries that will protect the husband-wife dyad by focusing on the way in which the proximity of mother and daughter interferes with the relationship between the spouses.

| Minuchin: | [To Richard] I think you need to help them. Mary spends more time worrying about Whitney than enjoying you. Talk to her about how she can be freer to become your wife. | *Again, I am suggesting a conversation that doesn't include me. By now, however, it seems more natural, and Mary and Richard turn to each other to talk.* |

11. Parent Subsystem

Mary:	[To Richard] If only I could trust her!	*I reinforce the idea that Mary is overstressed, directing Richard to protect Mary from Whitney, and increasing the proximity within the spouse subsystem, as well as increasing the distance between mother and her adolescent daughter.*
Richard:	There are times that I agree with you. I don't trust her, either. We need to establish better limits and rules, without getting caught up in the argument.	
Minuchin:	[To Richard] I think Mary has become a detective, and I'm worried about her. She might be trying to do the impossible. She's overstressed, and she may break.	
Richard:	[To Mary] I can see that your life is consumed, and so is mine. We are always worried about Whitney's behavior. There is no fun for us anymore.	

12. Mother and her Family of Origin

Minuchin:	[To Mary] Where did you learn to be such a worrier? Why do you think that a catastrophe is waiting just around the corner?	*The session ends with the introduction of the idea that Mary must have learned to be a worrier in her earlier life, that the lenses we learn to use as children affect the interactions among family members in the present, and that it will be helpful to explore this in the next session.*
Mary:	I have a friend who also tells me that I'm afraid a tornado is waiting for me around the corner.	
Minuchin:	You seem to be bringing a world from your past into predictions for Whitney's future. I'd like to explore with you where you learned to be like that. Could you have lunch and then return for another meeting?	

Coda to the First Session

Readers, as well as the family, will have a richer grasp of the experience after the second session, but it's useful to review what has been accomplished and what one knows about the family, the therapist and the therapeutic process at the end of this first crucial encounter.

<u>What has been accomplished?</u> Two important goals have been met: a different perception of the identified patient and the establishment of a message that all members of the family are involved in their problems and in the possible solutions. The session has also offered useful information about the process of moving through the first encounter: how the therapist thinks and intervenes, about the techniques he uses, and about the organization of the family.

<u>What have we seen about how the therapist functions, how techniques are used, and how the family is organized?</u> I respond below from my perspective, but it will also be useful for readers to add and discuss their own thoughts about what they have seen.

1. How the therapist functions.

<u>What do I carry into the session?</u> First, I define family therapy as a systemic intervention. When I join the family, I know that the therapeutic system will constrain both the family and myself. I join the family as a whole and in its distinctive subsystems, and as I join I also challenge. I know that the family and their problems are more complex than the narrow description the family adheres to, and that their certainty is an enemy of change. My goal is to create a context where multiple explanations concerning behavior are possible.

<u>How do I move forward?</u> I start by challenging the label of the "Identified Patient," which has summarized her behavior as a product of intrapsychic meandering, and I help family members to see their participation in the maintenance of her symptoms. I conduct separate mini-encounters with each individual and with different family subsystems. In this process, each participant explores aspects of his or her participation in family transactions. My purpose is to communicate that, "You are more complex than you imagine," and to help the members rearrange patterns of relationships within different subsystems.

<u>What is my style?</u> During the session, my function and personal style shift about. I am a leader, but I make clear that family healing requires the participation of each family member as an agent of change. And though I'm a leader, I'm also following. I am both a participant and an observer. As participant, I am proximal and symmetrical with family members; as observer, I function from a distal position that is hierarchical—as teacher, healer, and director of the process.

2. How techniques are used.

I use a variety of techniques: joining; using language as a tool, challenging certainty, reframing labels, enactment; and a mobilization of ethical family responsibility for healing.

I <u>join</u> the family using different aspects of myself. I feel comfortable responding in a variety of ways. With this family I feel protective and concerned, so my style is friendly and frequently funny. I join with individual members for particular purposes, to give Whitney more positive recognition and a stronger voice, to express concern for Mary's difficult situation and, to enlist Richard as a helper in healing the family. I will challenge as the session moves on, but only after I have joined with the family.

Sometimes my <u>language</u> is deliberately confusing, even literally so, as when I call a metaphor a lie, or parental control detective skill, or mother and daughter enmeshment as *prisoners who are jailers. It's also deliberately startling when I describe the family as a judicial system.*

I <u>challenge the certainty</u> of the Identified Patient's <u>label</u> by being generous in assigning many labels. Each member of the family spends segments of the session in the position of the person whose behavior is problematic.

Because I distrust packaged stories, I create situations where family members talk with each other (<u>enactment</u>). I have begun this process in the first session, and in the next session I will highlight the mini-dramas where hidden emotional aspects of the family's story and relationships emerge. I will also convey my conviction, already suggested, that most family members feel an <u>ethical responsibility</u> for each other, and that they will respond to the opportunity to become participants in healing.

3. How the family is organized.

The family comes with a dominant story and preferential styles of interaction. What emerges in the session is a more complex picture of family organization, including the patterns of behavior and interaction that maintain the problems they cannot resolve. The therapist has deconstructed the whole into separate subsystems, and in these shifting contexts the following patterns have become clear:

- Parents' focal concern with daughter's destructive behavior
- Parents' close investigation and control of daughter
- Mother and daughter's distressing proximity
- Husband's passive observation of mother and daughters' liaison
- Husband and wife's diminished interaction via their concentration on daughter's behavior

There is the special feature, in this case, that the family is a stepfamily. The session does not deal directly with this fact, but we know that there are always generic issues in families with that structure. Stepfamilies start as an organization of two separate subsystems: the newly-formed husband-wife system, and the parent-child (or children) system, which has a previous history. In time, these people aim to become one family, and they must be alert to issues of history and balance in their apportionment of loyalties. The Boyds think of and present themselves as one family, but in helping them with their problems, generic questions are still relevant:

- If wife loves her husband, is that a threat to her daughter?
- If wife loves her daughter, is that a threat to her husband?
- Will the biological mother allow her husband to parent her daughter?
- Will the daughter promote conflict and distance between husband and wife?

A therapist aware of family organization will need to explore these tectonic threats.

Prelude to the Second Session:
The second session will bring forth old wine in new bottles. It will be an exploration of the past as a <u>part</u> of the individual subsystem, and in the context of what has already been learned by all participants about family interaction. This is a relatively new feature of my therapy. The traditional psychoanalytic theory in which I was trained highlighted explorations of the past as crucial to understanding the individual, but the systemic theories which

guided family therapy focused on current patterns, rather than emphasizing history and the family of origin, and for many years, as a family therapist, I de-emphasized the significance of the past in my clinical work and teaching. Eventually, and belatedly, I recognized that this point of view robbed the therapist of a valuable tool for understanding the distortions that childhood experience imposes on adult relationships, and I developed a process for exploring the past within the conceptual framework of current family patterns. Once the family and I have come to understand the family organization, I now proceed, in most cases, to what I have described as "a structurally-focused exploration of the past." The details and procedures of this "third step" in meeting a family are presented fully in Minuchin, Nichols and Lee(2007). The second session with the Boyd family begins with this third step, which the therapist has prepared for in his closing comments at the end of the first session.

The Second Session

At the end of the first session, the couple and the therapist have a shared understanding of how the family functions and of how important it is that Mary is carrying a sense of impending catastrophe, especially in relation to Whitney. I have asked Mary and Richard to come back alone for the first part of this session, while Whitney takes care of Joe outside the room. When the couple returns, Mary is clearly uncomfortable. She's preoccupied and doesn't look at me. I'm hoping to change the atmosphere, though without blocking material that may be emotionally laden.

I begin with a comment that moves gently from my general belief that family members are interconnected toward an exploration of the connection between Mary's pessimistic expectations and Whitney's lying. I say that, of course, Whitney lies, but the question is, "Why?" I tell Mary I'm impressed by her fear of catastrophe, and add, "Some people see life through rose-colored glasses, but you. . . ." Mary immediately finishes my sentence.

Mary: I only see things getting worse.

13. Extended Family Subsystem: Mother and her Family of Origin

Minuchin: [To Mary] Yes. I'd like to explore with you who you were before you met each other. You mentioned that you grew up in a stepfamily. How did that come about?

Mary: [Speaking flatly, without emotion] My parents divorced when I was 5. I left home when I was 18. There was a snowstorm. I was supposed to be in by ten o'clock, but I didn't get home until midnight, and so my mother threw me out. My mother has a lot of good qualities, but she wasn't a good mother. I wasn't sure what to do, so I called the mother of a close girlfriend and we've been a family ever since. I never really understood my own mother. I think she was depressed most of

Mary's earliest experience was as a participant in a troubled family, as well as part of a mother-child subsystem that did not protect her as a child and was excessively punitive in expelling her as an adolescent.

I knew from the description and the tone of her telling that we were beginning to learn what had created Mary's uncertainty and fear about what was lurking around the corner.

It was time to go further in hearing about Mary's past, and my next questions moved her toward

the time. She could be cruel. It's hard to talk about. . . . Sometimes it's like water flowing and you would like to dam it but you can't.

later relationships, especially with her two husbands.

14. Past Lenses as a Template for Adult Relationships

Minuchin:　　How did you learn to trust people?

Mary:　　It's always been an issue. It takes a long time, and if the trust is broken, it's hard to repair.

Minuchin:　　How predictable is Richard?

Mary:　　It took me a long time to open up to him. I kept to myself a lot, for years.

Minuchin:　　You were married before. How was that experience?

15. Mother and Ex-Husband

Mary:　　I didn't know my first husband for very long. We married and moved away from my family. I got pregnant, and then I discovered he was addicted to drugs and alcohol.

Minuchin:　　How were you saved from that situation?

Mary goes on with her story. After unsuccessful efforts at rehabilitation for Mary's husband, the marriage ended with a DWI accident, in which Mary and her baby were trapped in the car and then hospitalized with life-threatening injuries. Her husband, who had been driving, disappeared and was never seen again. After their recovery, Mary took Whitney back to their home, and it was there she met Richard.

The story comes out in isolated units, without the emotion such harrowing experiences warrant. Mary has managed to drain her past of affect, probably as a mechanism of survival. I found myself thinking that the effort may have blocked her ability to connect the pain of the past with her prevailing pessimism in the present. Mary may have a low threshold for stress, and I cannot push her too fast.

She will probably need understanding and support before she can hear a challenge.

I turn now to Richard. After hearing Mary's story, he feels peripheral and needs to be drawn in. I say to him, "So you enter the scene. What happens?"

16. Husband Family of Origin

Richard: I was attracted to her and Whitney. It was an instant family. I'm an only son and my parents divorced. I lived with my mother, her husband, and my youngest stepbrother.

Minuchin: And how did you learn to be nurturing?

I am asking each of them to explore a specific aspect of the past that is likely to shed light on the way we know they function in the present situation.

Richard: I don't know. I tried to protect my brother from my stepfather. He had mood swings, and he would threaten to kill me. When I was 16, I left home. Probably, we weren't your average family.

Minuchin: I'm thinking about what you both bring from the past, and how that affects Whitney. How old were you, Richard, when you met Mary?

Richard: Twenty-three.

These people, wounded by cruel and unpredictable families, had found each other, and it was possible that they fit together reasonably well. Mary's fear and mistrust might be healed by Richard's impulse to protect people. I felt protective of them, and moved to offer guidance and support.

17. Forming the Stepfamily

Minuchin: You were a young kid marrying Mary and Whitney. How did you deal with both of them?

Richard: One day at a time. I just stuck it out. I was afraid of getting married. It was all so overwhelming. I had lived alone, and now I didn't have privacy anymore.

Minuchin:	How did you gain her trust?
Richard:	[Hesitates] Once we broke up. She wanted to return to the life she had before.
Mary:	We didn't talk, and I thought maybe it was too much for him—Whitney and me dropping on him all at once. But then we decided to make one last, try. There was a lot of tension. I kept a lot to myself.
Minuchin:	[To Richard] How did you solve it? When did Whitney become your daughter?

18. Stepfather-Daughter Developmental Bonding

Richard:	I always felt her as my daughter. We were very attached. I knew that if we split, I didn't have legal binding with Whitney.	
Mary:	Whitney was a difficult child. If she didn't get her way, she would cry and cry to the point of throwing up. Growing up, she thought that was the way to get things.	*Mary's view of Whitney's behavior carries her traumatic experience with her first husband, and is an imposition of Mary's past onto Whitney's present. Mary is afraid for her daughter. I can see where her fears come from, but it's necessary to challenge the distortions.*

19. Subsystem of Mother, Daughter, and Biological Father

Minuchin:	She was very close to you. Are you afraid she will become a drug addict like her father?	
Mary:	She lies like he did.	
Minuchin:	You're wrong. She lies like an adolescent.	
Mary:	Sometimes, when I look into her eyes, I think she doesn't feel anything.	*After sharing the pain of her past, I feel more ready to challenge Mary's overprotectiveness, and I recruit Richard as a healer of Mary.*

20. Subsystem of Therapist and Richard as Co-Therapist

Minuchin:	[To Richard] What do you think about what Mary said—that she looks into Whitney's eyes and sees the eyes of Whitney's father, whom she hasn't seen for 13 years? And Whitney doesn't know him; for her, you are her father. Mary's fear comes from her past, but that fear makes her see things that don't exist. I think she needs help, and that you can help her. Would she trust you enough to let you help her?	*I bring Richard in as a co-therapist, asking him to challenge his wife in order to protect their daughter. The assignment of healing functions to family members is one of the interventions that help families to change.*
Mary:	Sometimes, I feel like I'm doing it all alone.	
Minuchin:	Richard is a gentle man, and I think you need his gentleness, but you push him back and he restrains himself. Then you feel alone. How do you ask him to enter?	
Mary:	Usually, I'm pretty stressed, but I don't just ask. I have thought about that before.	

After exploring with Mary and Richard some of the experiences they are carrying from their individual histories, I am now focused on helping them to think and talk about the way they relate in the present, as parents. I ask Mary how she can change Richard so he becomes more available. She says he needs to want to be in, and he says he wants that but maybe doesn't respond fast enough for what Mary needs. They both see it's important for them to get past the obstacles—Mary's fear of making demands, Richard's sense that they should let Whitney sink or swim. They need to move toward each other, and they have some sense of what each needs to do in order to close the distance between them, while creating more space between themselves and their adolescent daughter, for her sake as well as theirs.

21. Current Family System

In the last stage of the session, I ask Whitney to come back in, while Joe is cared for by staff people outside. I am reuniting the threesome that has been the core of this family's problems, so that the parents can convey to Whitney what they have been talking about. The father explains to Whitney that Mother is afraid. "We are very protective," he says, "and we are not doing a good job." The mother tells her, "I am going to stop worrying and will try to have some fun." They try to explain to her the content of the discussion that they have had with the therapist and, while this is probably not very clear to Whitney, it conveys the idea that something in the family needs to be changed, and that the problem they're talking about is no longer just about Whitney's lying. Rather, it's about relationships; the relationships of the couple with each other, and the relationships of the parents and Whitney as a family.

As the family leaves, they are thoughtful. They know that something is different, and while they are uncertain about the pathway ahead, they are more connected with each other and more hopeful.

Exploring Family Organization: Implications of the Case

The Boyd family has particular characteristics. They are a stepfamily of four people, in which the young adolescent is the Identified Patient. The goal of therapy focused on transferring the ownership of the symptom from the intrapsychic machinery of the child to the interpersonal drama of parents and child affecting each other. It was also directed toward the realignment of the system: toward creating boundaries to protect the space of the couple as spouses and the autonomy of the adolescent as an individual.

When the Boyds came to therapy they described their reality this way: (1) the parents are concerned with their daughter's destructive behavior, (2) the parents maintain a close investigation and control of their daughter, (3) mother and daughter maintain a conflicting and distressing proximity, (4) the husband observes critically mother and daughter's way of relating but he feels ineffective in trying to change their relationship, and 5) both spouses feel that the relationship has been diminished by the concentration on Whitney's behavior.

This reality has been maintained by years of daily transactions among the Boyds and now it's crystallized and maintained, unchanged and unchangeable, by the patterns of relationship that command their ways of being. It is the therapist's function to help them realize that <u>they</u> have constructed this fortress and they can also create open spaces.

The deconstruction of family and the exploration of subsystems, like the unwrapping of identities in the previous chapter, challenges the ways in which the family members experience their sense of being and belonging. Since identity is contextual, the belonging to a system defines identity; the ticket of entrance in a system is the accommodation to its rule, and through this process we know who we are.

It is this concept that I operationalize in my work with the Boyds. In the two sessions, we (the family members and myself) have participated in at least 19 shifts in different subsystems. And this created an interesting dynamic, because as family members participate in different interpersonal contexts they accommodate to the demands of belonging by shifts in their identity:

When Whitney is under Father's detective magnifying glass,

When Whitney is relating to Mother's anxious and pessimistic protection,

When Whitney talks with the therapist about poetry,

Is Whitney the *same* Whitney?

This process creates confusion, challenges certainty, and expands family member's identities and ways of belonging. The Boyds that we see after the two sessions are the same Boyds, but different.

5

THE THERAPIST'S STYLE

In the previous three chapters, I introduced you to my style of doing therapy and to my explanations of the "why's" of my interventions.

It may be useful for the young practitioner to join me in a short trip along the roads that I traveled through my life, because they are idiosyncratic, much like the roads that you have taken. Maybe my explorations may alert you to look at the resources that you bring to the craft of being a therapist.

I am 90 years old and I started doing family therapy in my late 30s. The year was 1958, not long after Don Jackson had published an article with the title "The Question of Family Homeostasis" (1957). The article dealt with family interaction, family homeostasis, and the implications of conjoined psychotherapy. He described a new kind of therapy, where one sees the patient, the parents, and possibly siblings as a whole group in psychotherapy sessions, and, to my mind, that article was the send-off for a new field.

I think that my memories of the last 50 years could provide relevant views of the evolution of the field and the impact of certain innovations on theory and practice. Like any memories, of course, time has arranged and edited my experience and what seems clear to me now is actually the product of repetitions. Events that first occurred outside of awareness, leaving just a shadow or a vague feeling, came back later as a discovery and with a better sense of what I meant.

As a therapist, for instance, my ideas and point of focus kept changing over the years, but it's only quite recently that I can see and describe the evolution: I see now that during my early years of practice as an individual therapist and psychoanalyst, I gave pre-eminence to my experience as a child, and I thought that the roots of behavior, thoughts, or feelings as an adult could best be understood by exploring childhood. During the decade of the 1960s, however, when I was doing family therapy, my focus fell on the present, and I saw the past as an inconvenient period that disturbed my understanding of conflictual relationships in the present. One or two decades later, I had changed again. By then I felt comfortable with the concept of multiple identities, multiple selves born at different periods of one life, and with the idea of coexistence responses to the demands of life . . . but let me go back and start my story with my early years as a family therapist.

I begin with my work at the Wiltwyck School for Boys in the 1960s, where our team was working with over 100 children referred to this residence by the judicial system of New York. The majority were from African American families, mostly from Harlem, and almost all were from families on welfare. The school was purposefully located at a significant distance from New York, so the children could be free from the pathological environment of their neighborhoods and families.

Wiltwyck was similar to thousands of such schools around the country, and the experience of the children was typical. They accommodated to the rules of the institution and, after a year or so, they were labeled "improved." They were discharged, returned to their previous environment—and, in large numbers, they came back as recidivists.

We knew we needed a more effective intervention and to the group of liberals concerned with treatment at Wiltwyck (Dick Auerswald, Charlie King, Braulio Montalvo, and others), Jackson's article seemed like a great jumping off place for exploring a different process. We declared ourselves family therapists. We opened a hole in a wall, built a one-way mirror, and invited families and their children to come in for interviews.

We developed a three-stage session:

1. First, two therapists met with the family for about half an hour.
2. Second, one therapist met with the children and the other therapist met separately with the parents.
3. Finally, the therapists and all the family members reconvened.

After the session, the therapists and other members of the team who had been watching behind the one-way mirror met to discuss the different ways the family members related to each other at different stages, as well as the style of the therapists in joining the family and their effect on their behavior and their relationships.

What did we learn from all of this?

- That families are <u>complex social systems</u> and that they contain <u>subsystems</u> that may have different agendas from each other.
- That people function in <u>different ways in different social contexts</u>.
- That because of these realities <u>each person has different selves</u>.
- That <u>attachment occurs with different people</u> in different contexts and different developmental periods.
- That <u>family members feel a responsibility and commitment to each other,</u> even in troubled families, and that the <u>therapist should be mobilizing their capacity to protect and heal each other.</u>
- We also learned that the therapist is always relating to only a part of a system and that <u>therapy, therefore, is always partial.</u>

We didn't know that we had learned these things, but knowledge rewards the prepared mind. Those ideas became more evident and useful as time and work went forward.

What of my own style during this early period? I felt responsible for helping families, but I was different from other practitioners because of my challenging style, opening up conflicts and feeling certain that such explorations would produce experiential change. I didn't doubt that families have available resources that would be actualized when needed. This conviction was a natural product of life; an idea I had taken from my reading Borges, the Argentinean poet and writer, who had written that when you come to crossroads, you take the road in both directions. It was a paradox and I understood that it was saying that the road not taken remains available. How did I come to this style? This style is the product of the road I took. I will summarize my early realities that prepared me to become the kind of therapist I became.

I was born in Argentina in 1921. My parents were a typical early 20th century couple: husband the executive relating to the world; wife the affective partner relating to the family. We were a Talcott Parsons kind of family, but Jewish in a small town of anti-Semitic Argentina. I was the oldest of three siblings and as the traditional legacy from my parents, I was the "responsible one." I became responsible for my siblings, my parents, my extended family, and the Jews of the world. In my childhood, that represented the totality of what was known and familiar. Obligation to and for this group marked my first identity: with it came a focus on social justice.

From there, I jump two decades in my story. By then, I was a medical student, and it was the era during which General Peron carried out a military coup and became an Argentinean dictator. I participated in the student uprising against the governmental occupation of the university and was jailed for three months, where, while in isolation, I learned something about sleep deprivation. I was expelled from the university, continued my studies in the republic of Uruguay, and was finally accepted again in Argentina to finish my medical studies. Through this period, I saw myself as an Argentinean Jew, a Leftist, and a rebel, and I felt heroic. My identity was now more complex; on some level dormant but available. I was still the shy child and the adolescent boy, but those aspects now shared space with a different group of reference: the challengers, the ones that see themselves as socially responsible and committed to action in situations of conflict.

In 1948, as I was preparing to open a pediatric office, the UN recognized Israel as a nation and the war of Jewish independence broke out. I felt I needed to go there, and I became a medical officer in the Israeli army. As a doctor responsible for the medical care of my unit, I felt comfortable with being in a hierarchical position while being a caretaker. It should be noted that my sense of who I was changed as my group of reference changed: my attachment to different groups of people supported a different set of responses. In 1949, at the end of the Israeli war, I moved to the United States to specialize in child psychiatry, but what I learned first was what it meant to be a foreigner, not knowing anybody and unable to speak the language. I ate my meals in a cafeteria—the old Horn and Hardart, where you could see the food and take it off the shelf without knowing what it was called. Being a foreigner is an experiment in problem-solving: everything is almost recognizable but not completely. In my head everything now had more than one name. What was a *mesa* in Spanish was *shulhan* in Hebrew, a *tish* in Yiddish, and a *table* in English. Reality was diversity. I was uncertain, frightened, and dependent on the generosity of strangers.

People helped, and I found organizations and institutions where I could learn child psychiatry and the various ways that people in New York were working with children—at the Jewish Board of Guardians, with Loretta Bender at Bellevue Hospital, and through living in a residential institution for disturbed children. This was a period of great uncertainty, where I felt frightened, incompetent, and dependent on people's good will—a very different identity than in my previous experiences.

In that first year, I met Pat, a red-headed, bright, and beautiful psychologist. We married in 1951 and she became part of my dialogues for 60 years. When your monologues become dialogues, reality expands: A new perspective opens and identity shifts. The journey, now taken together, continues to shape my thinking and style as a therapist.

For us, life together was to start in Israel, when we moved "forever." Forever lasted three years, but it was a very rich period in my professional life. I became the psychiatric director of six institutions established by an organization that worked with children who had survived the European Holocaust, and children who arrived from Arab countries without their families. These children had not adapted to life in the Kibbutzim, their original placements, and had required a therapeutic environment. It was there that I began to understand the profound implications of cultural diversity and to think professionally about family influence on the way in which children cope with life, and was confronted with a population whose problems challenged my knowledge and imagination. I knew that I didn't know everything, but I didn't understand that being an uncertain expert was a precious gift. Later on, when I was working with marginalized families, this aspect of my identity helped me to join with the families with whom I was working.

Life in Israel at that time was an adventure, both interesting and difficult. But I had decided to train as an analyst and we returned to the United States, where I had been accepted as a candidate by the William Alanson White Institute of Psychoanalysis. By then, we had one child, Daniel, who was born in Israel. We were very poor, and Pat became our main financial support. My days were a mixture of psychoanalytic studies, fee-for-service work at the clinic (who paid me miserably), a very small private practice, and finally some work that put me in touch with a welfare population. The mix was a breeding ground for contradictions, and I found it difficult to create a coherent set of professional ideas in which I could believe.

As an example: I went to my psychoanalytic sessions three times a week. The focus was on my dependent relationship with my mother and my passive-aggressive relationship with my father. The difficulties of adapting to our new lives in New York became a less and more distant event. I learned much about my early life, but when I described the heroic events I was proud of, my analyst responded: "Salvador, you are a cork on the crest of a wave. You go where the current takes you."

For my analyst, identity was a single event starting at childhood and understood by reenacting aspects of my early life. For me, identity formation was episodic and multiple. I was about 35 years old then and I had lived through many events, struggled with demons, related with a variety of significant people, and developed psychological resources that surfaced in different circumstances. What was collateral for my analyst was central for me and for the small group of people who were my current family.

But I need to jump again. This time to the mid-1960s, when we moved to Philadelphia and I became a Professor of Child Psychiatry at the University of Pennsylvania and the Director of the Philadelphia Child Guidance Clinic. It was not a smooth transition. The two jobs did not follow parallel tracks.

From the beginning, as director of the clinic, I insisted that all children accepted for therapy come in with their families, and that child therapy was family therapy. That was accepted by our clients, but not by the Department of Psychiatry. The Association of Child and Adolescent Psychiatry challenged our training of psychiatric fellows, and the department started an investigation. They finished with a document stating that the training in family therapy for psychiatric fellows was dangerous for the Department of Psychiatry. Strangely enough, I had closed the circle. As in my childhood, where I was a member of a minority group that was rejected, I was again the outsider—the "other."

But the clinic was a different story. We had become a successful institution. We had a very large staff, an outpatient service, an inpatient facility, two apartments where we hospitalized difficult families, and an external training program. In the 1960s and 1970s, the Philadelphia Child Guidance Clinic was one of the main centers of family therapy in the world, with a constant flow of professional visitors from all over who came to learn what we were doing. Between the 1960s and the 1980s, family therapy was the main event in therapy, or so we thought, and we predicted that in the 21st century it would become the most important type of intervention. We were wrong.

Nonetheless, interesting things were happening during that period and after, and I want to describe the different ways in which the field has developed.

During the period I was in Philadelphia, we were working primarily with poor, multi-crisis minority families whose problems included their experience with the established institutions of justice and welfare. It was evident that the selection of these patients required a practice different from that of most family therapists, who were engaged at that time in unraveling the mysteries of psychosis. Bateson et al. (1956), for instance, produced a paper on "the double bind," which postulated that the ramblings of schizophrenics were the result of injunctions by parents who had sent contradictory messages—I love you/don't be near me—along with a third message that the commands must both be obeyed.

While Bateson, Whitaker, Bowen, Wynne, and others were concerned with the <u>meaning</u> of psychotic communication, I was focusing on the patterns of relating among family members, in a population that was struggling with basic life crises and for whom the meaning was in the relationships.

I knew that people must respond to the demands of new and changing social structures by expanding and adapting, and I expected to find that potential in most families. That optimistic viewpoint was challenged again and again, yet it has persisted. Since the time of our first experiments at Wiltwyck with the three-stage session, I have focused on understanding family patterns and exploring possible avenues for novel ways of relating.

Joining the dots that mark my journey from childhood to old age, I discover a map of experiences that have determined the skills and biases of my therapeutic repertoire:

From growing up as a member of a rejected minority, and by belonging to the caste of "the other," I bring an alertness to danger; an allergy to social injustice; a need to defend the weak, the child, the ones who are labeled and unable to defend themselves.

From repeatedly being an immigrant, I have a sense of impermanence, and a doubt about the apparent meaning of things. I know that a shifting perspective changes the meaning of objects, ideas, and relationships, and I have developed a preference for metaphors and poetic images to describe events and encounters because I know that every truth is an approximation.

From working with different cultures, in Israel and in the United States, I have developed a respect for the diverse, a curiosity for learning from others, and the comfort to work in situations of ignorance—since whenever I dare to make an assumption or create a description that is wrong, I'm ready to accept my ignorance and learn from the new.

I am committed to the idea that people in a family are responsible for each other, and are, therefore, responsible for healing and protecting the other. In this orientation, change occurs at many levels. While I accept the significance of meaning in the stories that people tell themselves, I rely primarily on the positions people take vis-à-vis each other—the proximity, distance, protection, support, rejection, love, and so on. People construct each other in relationships, and there is potentially the capacity to use oneself differently when a close person needs us to be different. It is the therapist's task to facilitate this new set of transactions.

Lastly, I want to share with you a strange phenomenon that happens to me when I meet a family in therapy. The world shrinks during the time that we are together or while my attention is focused on them, and I am totally committed to their mystery. We are on an island. Time stops—or is postponed.

I tried to describe this experience in Chapter 1, when I talked about the craft, but I think I was not successful. Since I need to put a name to this experience, I would say that it is a commitment to the process of therapy and, like joining, is an important ingredient that is very difficult to teach.

In writing about the field of therapy, Harry Stack Sullivan (1947), the creator of interpersonal psychoanalysis, maintained that therapy is an interpersonal situation. One may describe an interpersonal situation as though one has been a detached observer, but in actuality one becomes part of the situation—a participant observer. Therapy is a mode of interaction of two or more people.

And you are <u>one</u> of the participants in the process.

THERAPEUTIC STYLE

Now, reflect on your life and the development of your preferential style of interacting, noting both zones of comfort and areas of stress. Jot down both Zones of Comfort and Areas of Stress containing obstacles and biases. Take these notes with you, adding to what you have found as you gain more experience and hone your craft.

6

UTILIZING THE FAMILY THERAPIST'S POUCH

At this point in the book, we want to look back and put together everything we have described. We have presented transcripts of three different family therapy sessions, focusing in each on just one aspect of understanding, such as unwrapping identities, externalizing the symptom, or exploring subsystems. In this chapter, we want to demonstrate how the four main concepts, which also include the use of the self of the therapist, operate in conjunction with one another. We do this by moving through an edited portion of a family therapy session, providing an analysis of how aspects of the therapist's pouch are being applied along the way.

To remind you about what was contained in the therapist's pouch (see Chapter 1) we present Table 6.1.

In the analysis of the session that follows, headings in the text will indicate the subsystem addressed by the therapist in that section. Our analysis of what aspects of the pouch are in use during a dialog will appear in the right hand column, marked with their numbers from Table 6.1. The following abbreviations will be used to refer to the various members of the family: Mother = M; Father = F; Mia = D; Liam = L; Mason = S.

THE CASE: DIALOG AND ANALYSIS

This session occurred some years ago, when Minuchin consulted with a family of five. The Richardsons came with a problem concerning their 16-year-old daughter (Mia), who was being disrespectful to her parents and was regarded as the Identified Patient. The family also consisted of a mother (Emily), father (Benjamin), 14-year-old son (Liam), and another son of 10 (Mason).

When Minuchin entered into this consultation, he did not have a treatment plan and was not attempting to display tools from a pouch. However, he was using some basic systemic concepts, such as family organization and the importance of boundaries and affiliations. As he tends to do in consultation interviews if the family's therapist is present, Minuchin asked the therapist to begin the session so that he could observe family

Table 6.1 The Therapist's Pouch

Basic Principles	Techniques	Working with Subsystems	The Self of the Therapist
1. Joining	4. Challenging • Stroke/kick	9. The individual • Unwrapping identities	12. Therapist distance
2. Families are "wrong" • Externalizing the symptom	5. Exploring alternatives • Enactments	10. Utilizing subsystems	13. Owning expertise
3. Family's certainty is the enemy of change	6. Using content to understand process	11. Unbalancing subsystems	14. Using one's self
	7. Humor and metaphor		
	8. Communicating at different levels • Knowledge • Ethics • Future direction		

interactions.[1] During this portion, Mother stated that she felt like she was living in an armed camp where she and her daughter, Mia, were taking shots at each other. Mia agreed with this metaphor. The verbatim section of the session begins below with the labeling of the subsystem involved and Minuchin's first question.

Mother-Daughter Subsystem

Minuchin:	How does it happen that you and your mom have the same level of power?	*2 (Externalizing the symptom): Begins to shift the family story of daughter being problematic; putting her on the same level as the mother.* *6 (Using content to understand process): Minuchin heard and saw the family interact and used what they said as a path to their process.* *10 (Utilizing subsystems): Begins with the mother-daughter dyad, as daughter is clearly the IP.*
Mia:	We don't have the same level of power.	

---

1 During the session, the therapist speaks very rarely. When she does, the speaker will be identified as "therapist"

Mother-Daughter-Father Subsystem

Minuchin:	Well, that is how I am hearing it. If you are taking shots at your mom and your mom is taking shots at you and your dad experiences the tension and tries to get away it means you have a tremendous amount of power.	(D1) Mia as powerful. 3 (Family's certainty): Challenges the certainty that daughter is a victim and not powerful. 6 (Using content to understand process): There is no talk about what the fights are, but how they are. 9 (Unwrapping identities): Daughter becomes powerful. 13 (Owning expertise): Minuchin accepts his position of listening as an authority.
Mia:	No. I don't feel like I have any power at all.	
Minuchin:	That's interesting. Then the description is, not true. As you describe it you are two lightweight fighters fighting with each other and nobody is winning. [To Father] And you are kind of looking at this phenomenon of these two women in the family fighting. Is that what happens?	(D2) Mia as a lightweight fighter. (M1) Mother as a lightweight fighter. 6 (Using content to understand process): Exploring process rather than content. 7 (Using metaphors): Minuchin changes the armed camp metaphor into a boxing metaphor. 10 (Utilizing subsystems): Father as observer of dyad between mother/daughter.
Mia:	No, because nobody ever wins.	
Minuchin:	Right. That's why I am saying you two have the same level of power, because you continue fighting. In a chicken coop, very fast, the chickens will organize themselves into higher power and	8 (Communication at multiple levels): Communicating at the knowledge level.
Mother:	You mean a pecking order.	

The Whole Family

Minuchin:	And then there is peace. So you don't find a way of being a good chicken coop.	(F1) Family as a chicken coop. 7 (Using metaphors): Uses the metaphor of the family as a chicken coop. 8 (Communicating at multiple levels): Provides a glimpse into a future direction. 13 (Owning expertise): Is an expert at looking at systems.

Mother:	I guess not. I don't feel Mia has any respect for me as a parent. And that is one of the main problems is that I can't teach her anything.	
Minuchin:	Where did she learn that?	2 (Externalizing the symptom): Mother tries to maintain daughter as the IP. This question shifts an individual symptom into a relational conceptualization, which goes against how the family views the situation.
Mother:	I don't know.	
Minuchin:	This learning happened at home. [To Mia] So tell me, who in your family taught you that you can challenge Mom without danger.	3 (Family's certainty): Shifting an individual perception to a relational one. 13 (Owning expertise): Minuchin is the family expert explaining where the transactions occur.
Mia:	I can't. I try my hardest not to challenge her on anything.	

Mother-Daughter Dyad

Minuchin:	Then how is it that Mom feels so powerless with you?	(M2) Mom as powerless.
Mia:	I don't know. I don't understand.	
Minuchin:	Well, let's find out. Because it's clear that Mom feels powerless. And you are fighting with her, and you said you don't want to fight with her, but you do.	
Mia:	The way a fight will start sometimes is if, even if I'm in the, room, if I'm home watching TV she'll come in and say, "Mia, go upstairs."	
Mother:	Oh, I don't say it like that.	
Mia:	You said it like three times yesterday. I don't feel like I have to, cause a challenge, a fight just happens.	
Minuchin:	It means that just by being alive you cause a fight?	
Mia:	That is how I feel.	
Minuchin:	Benjamin, what are your thoughts on this?	

Father: That I am equally challenged by
            Mia and have difficulty carry-
            ing on the simplest conversation
            without some part of that de-
            veloping into an argument or a
            disagreement.

*[We pause now in our analysis. We encourage you to do your own analysis of the ses-
sion to see how aspects of the pouch are being utilized. Label the subsystem, then identify
the relevant numbers from the pouch and jot down your thoughts concerning each unit of
dialogue marked off by the lines.]*

Minuchin: [To Mia] Who is easier to chal-
            lenge, Mom or Dad?

_____

_____

_____

_____

_____

Mia: I don't challenge them. I don't
            know.

Minuchin: Let's find out how you challenge
            them. Find out from Mom what
            she thinks you do that is so
            terrible.

_____

_____

_____

_____

_____

Mia:	What do you think I do that is so terrible?
Mother:	You refuse to do what I ask you, from simple things to complex things, and that is why simple things get blown out of proportion.
Mia:	For example?
Mother:	For example, I hope we don't get bogged down in some trivial thing but I'll give you a simple example.
Minuchin:	Hold it. Your Mom just now expressed powerlessness. Please continue.

[Mother, then Father, then Mother "lecture" Mia for 5 minutes.]

Minuchin:	Is that how it works? That they gang up on you and you stay quiet?

_____

_____

_____

_____

_____

Mia:	Until I can't keep silent any more.
Minuchin:	And then what do you do?
Mia:	Usually I get angry.
Minuchin:	And what do you do then?
Mia:	Yell, and fight back.
Minuchin:	And you feel absolutely in a corner.
Mia:	Yes.

[Here we will pick up with our analysis.]

Separating the Parental Subsystem into individual units in relation to the daughter

Minuchin:	And who is doing that [Minuchin stands up next to Mia and makes like he is choking her]?	7 (Using metaphors): Minuchin's physical action is a metaphor for what is occurring between daughter and parent. 14 (Using oneself): Minuchin is comfortable with physical proximity. He increases the intensity of the room by making like he is choking the daughter.
Mia:	My parents.	
Minuchin:	I think that their style is very different. Mom is more personal. Dad will say from afar "Do that," but Mom is the one that comes at you.	6 (Using content to understand process): Minuchin listened to how the parents each talked to Mia during the enactment and observed a different process of how each engaged her.
Mia:	Usually it's my mother, but sometimes it's both.	
Minuchin:	And why do you keep them at you?	4 (Challenging the client): This challenge is one of connection where people are not victims but active agents in the family's drama.
Mia:	I can't keep them off.	

[_The analysis of the session now shifts back to you._]

Minuchin:	Oh no. I saw just right here there were a couple of times that you could have stopped your mom, but you didn't so she continued talking.
Mia:	If I say, "Mom, that's enough," that doesn't matter.
Minuchin:	So you usually keep silent.
Mia:	Well, not the whole time. Until I feel like I can't take it anymore.
Minuchin:	Emily, what happened with the boys? No problem with the boys?

_____

_____

_____

_____

_____

Mother:	Good relationship with the boys.
Minuchin:	Why? I am surprised.
Mother:	I don't know.
Minuchin:	That means you have a bad daughter and two good sons?
Mother:	No, I don't think she's bad. She's good in many ways and I love her a great deal. But she just never has been one to mind me and I don't know why.
Minuchin:	Why do you go at her for so long? When she keeps silent, what happens to you? Do you feel like she's rebelling and you need to talk longer? Because you kept talking for a long time.
Mother:	I did keep going. She usually doesn't keep silent in my opinion. I think the reason I keep going is to try to make her understand.
Minuchin:	Have you always felt powerless? Do you have other experiences of feeling powerless?

_____

_____

_____

_____

Mother:	No. Only when my mother was dying, but that probably doesn't relate.
Minuchin:	What about with Benjamin? Is Benjamin a very powerful fellow?
Mother:	Moderately, I guess. About the same as I am.
Minuchin:	I am interested in decision-making. Because you see, what I saw happening to Mia is that your experience is absolute lack of power with her.
Mother:	It is. That's true.
Minuchin:	I don't understand from where it comes. So let's find out. I need to understand, why did you begin a relationship with Mia where you expressed that you were powerless. I just want to know in what ways do you feel powerless with Benjamin.
Mother:	I don't usually feel powerless with him.
Minuchin:	You see, that's learned behavior, Emily. It cannot be that it happens only with Mia. It has to be that it happens in other places. So I am looking for where did it start and how is it maintained.

_____

_____

_____

_____

Mother:	There have been times when I have been frustrated in our relationship. Those times have been when I felt I couldn't communicate my feelings. But they are not frequent. And I've never felt it to the degree that I feel with my daughter.
Minuchin:	Okay. I always think that these kinds of things are not two people things.
Mother:	That they involve everybody?

[At this point in the session, we wanted to give one more example of how we understand what happened, to help you as a guide as you analyze the remainder of the session.]

Sister-Brother Dyad

Minuchin:	That they are at least three people things. They may be four people things or five people things. [To Mia] I think that you are probably making Liam's life much easier because if mom is after your ass all the time then Liam is free. [To Liam] Do you thank her?	*3 (Family's certainty): The family was certain that the problem lay within one person, Mia. Minuchin explains how symptoms are at least three-people interactions.* *11 (Unbalancing subsystems): Minuchin focuses on subsystem.*
Liam:	I never saw it that way.	
Minuchin:	Well, she is certainly a lightning rod. So you are scot-free. [To Mason] And you are the baby so you can probably do whatever you want.	*(D4) Mia as a lightning rod.* *(S2) Mason as the baby.* *7 (Using metaphors): Minuchin uses the metaphor of the lightning rod to describe this family's process.* *9 (Unwrapping identities): The daughter's identity changes from disrespectful to a lightning rod; someone who takes the discharge occurring in the environment.*
Mother:	I wouldn't say that.	

Minuchin:	Does he know that you are such a good sister? Does he thank you? Is he pleased with you? Or does he take Mom's side?	*(D5) Mia as a good sister.* *9 (Unwrapping identities): The IP is now termed a good sister.* *10 (Utilizing subsystems): This is an attempt to bring the isolated daughter into stronger relation with her sibling.*
Mia:	I guess it depends on who he talks to. I think he can identify with both of us.	

[*We now turn the analysis back over to you.*]

Minuchin:	He can identify with both of you? That's wrong. He should identify with you. Your dad identifies with your mom. He should at least be in your corner. Aren't you in her corner?

_____

_____

_____

_____

_____

Liam:	I don't get involved in these things that much.
Therapist:	My experience with Liam is that he can move to different corners. He can go to Mia and comfort her or to Mom and Dad's corner and comfort them.
Minuchin:	Why? That means you are the nurturer in the family. The peacemaker.

_____

_____

_____

_____

_____

Liam:	I guess so.
Minuchin:	And when mom and Mia get into one of these very long, prolonged, repetitive, boring kind of things, what do you do?
Liam:	I don't get involved.
Minuchin:	Then you are not in anyone's corner. [To Mia] Who referees your fights?

_____

_____

_____

_____

_____

Mia:	Sometimes my father will step in, but not very often.
Minuchin:	And when he steps in, he will step in in what way?
Mia:	Most of the time on my mother's side. But sometimes, if my mom is repeating herself, like what happened a couple of minutes ago, he will say, "Emily, okay, that's enough."
Minuchin:	So you are alone in this household.

Mia:	Yes.
Minuchin:	So the misery of your life is to have been born in this family.
Mia:	Yeah, I guess.
Mother:	That's a pretty sad statement.
Minuchin:	Let's see who can adopt you. Do you think that's what you want?
Mia:	No.
Minuchin:	I need to understand. You are individually nice people. So how is it that you enter into such a nice miserable road? And how is it that people contribute? You see, I am focusing on you, Emily, because I want to understand why you feel so powerless and how is that maintained. What makes you feel that she is challenging you just by being? [Turns to Mia] Let me tell you a story about a friend of mine. I had once a 16-year-old friend that one day said I don't know why the kids were mad at me at school. I went to the gym and I sat in the middle of the gym and I didn't do anything. And the rest of the people wanted to play basketball. And they began to play basketball and I was just sitting in the middle of the gym. I wasn't doing anything and they were angry at me. And then they called the teacher and principal and I was expelled from the school and I wasn't doing anything. You remind me of my friend.

Mia:	Yeah.
Minuchin:	So there are very nice ways in which you sit in the middle of the basketball court and say, "I am not doing anything." [Turns to mother] And that outrages you.
Mother:	No. I don't get angry at her if she hasn't done anything.
Minuchin:	It's not true then, that she hasn't done anything.
Mother:	Of course she's done something.
Minuchin:	She says, "I don't do it."
Mother:	She always maintains that she hasn't done anything and I violently disagree . . . vehemently disagree.
Minuchin:	But it is your violent, vehement, helpless way of feeling life that I am responding to. It is your helplessness. It is the fact that her minimal push triggers in you something very important. [To Mia] And you feel that mother wants you to give in and be a slave?

Mia:	Not a physical slave, but more mentally. I just feel that I always have to be there to take all the, if she is in a bad mood, the talking stuff.
Mother:	Oh dear, that's not true.
Minuchin:	You think your function at home is to be a lightning rod for your mother?
Mia:	Sometimes I feel that way.
Minuchin:	And you are so good? If you want to be a lightning rod for your mother, then you must be very good.
Mia:	I don't want to be. That's why I'm here, because I want to know what I am doing wrong. I don't do it on purpose but feel like I am always there.
Benjamin:	If she does she doesn't display it.
Minuchin:	People say curious things that sometimes one should listen to. And I am interested in what Mia says. I don't understand it. But it seems as if she is saying she is needed in a particular, peculiar, strange way. That Emily needs her as a discharge of her sense of helplessness. How do you understand that? Do you have a high threshold and sometimes do you go over your threshold?
Benjamin:	I have a high threshold and I think I have crossed the threshold.
Minuchin:	You have a high threshold. And that leaves Emily with a low threshold.

Benjamin:	I don't know if I call it a low threshold. We've developed a conditioned response, where when she responds to a partic-ular situation she'll expound on it and attack it from several dif-ferent directions.
Minuchin:	I don't understand that. It seems to me from what I see here is that you can be out and that leaves Emily with a very high reactivity. I see you as a very low reactive per-son and Emily as a very high reac-tive person. Is that true?

Benjamin:	I think that's true.
Minuchin:	[To Mother] So you are the sheriff?
Mother:	Sheriff? Wow, I don't know. I guess so.
Minuchin:	Well, you are the sheriff.
Mother:	With the children? I suppose.
Minuchin:	Yeah, a left-hand sheriff because you are not very powerful. You are the sheriff, who gave you that job?
Mother:	I'm a parent. I have to try to.
Minuchin:	Were you always a lonely sheriff?

_____

_____

_____

_____

_____

Mother:	A lonely sheriff?
Minuchin:	What about Benjamin?
Mother:	He's very involved, too. He certainly isn't disinvolved in the whole thing.
Minuchin:	When he is involved what happens?
Mother:	It is usually that the three of us will discuss it. And I think at that point sometimes it becomes a situation of the two of us against one. Two parents trying to talk to a child.
Minuchin:	You see, there is a mystery and I am very curious in mysteries. And the mystery is that you three, that seem to be bright people, continue doing something that is very wrong and you continue doing it. And you do it in very interesting ways. It is you two [Pointing to Mother and Daughter] and you [Referring to Father] are an overseer that every once in a while comes to enter into that.

_____

_____

_____

_____

_____

Mother:	But sometimes, they have their own conflict without me being involved.
Minuchin:	Do you let that happen?
Mother:	Sure. I mean, do I let it happen?
Minuchin:	You don't enter?
Mother:	No. Sometimes, I try to enter to support him or sometimes to explain something about Mia. But I am not always there when this happens.
Minuchin:	When you enter, how do you enter?
Mother:	Sometimes, I try to explain better what he's saying to Mia because I don't think she's understanding. Sometimes I try to explain what Mia is saying.
Minuchin:	Is that what she does?
Father:	She may hear about the conflict from Mia's side then she will hear about it from my side. And then she will go back and forth and try to figure out what was going on.
Minuchin:	You are doing a shotgun diplomacy.
Mother:	I suppose. It is not too effective.
Minuchin:	Why does your mother translate you to your father?

Mia:	I don't know.
Minuchin:	[To Mother] You feel the need to protect both of them? Whom do you want to protect?
Mother:	Both of them.
Minuchin:	Why?
Mother:	I hate to see two people talking and not understanding each other. I feel the need to interpret it. If there is something that she's saying that he doesn't understand, I try to interpret it, having been a teenage girl. And I understand where he's coming from as a parent. It's my way of trying to explain, but in this situation it may not be appropriate because it seems to get me into trouble.
Minuchin:	What about Benjamin's way of contacting an adolescent; do you think is faulty? That you think you have to edit, modify, help?
Mother:	Sometimes, I feel he expresses himself in a way that Mia, or all the kids, don't understand, because he thinks deeply, and sometimes when he expresses himself he uses big words that I think maybe Mia wouldn't relate to. And sometimes he is stricter than I am.
Minuchin:	And you want to modify that?
Mother:	Sometimes. But most of the time, I stay out of it.
Minuchin:	[To Father] Are you putting her to be a translator or does she take that job on her own?

Father: I think it is probably a good thing because the times when that has happened when Mia and I can't seem to relate to one another without conflict, Emily's going back and forth leads to it not being the same angry type of communication. I like to see communication made and if that is one way of accomplishing that, then I am in favor of it.

Minuchin: Benjamin likes your job as a sheriff, translator, busybody!

Mother: I don't want to be all of those things. You have to understand, that is not something that I do a lot.

Minuchin: I think that you do that a lot more than what you know that you do.

Mother: Well, that's possible. I am not consciously aware of it if I do.

Minuchin: I think that you are a person that is in a continuous surveillance of your family. And you are tremendously overworked.

_____

_____

_____

_____

_____

Mother:	Well, sometimes I do feel that I have to be responsible for an awful lot. Is that what you mean?
Minuchin:	That you have to be responsible always? All the time?
Mother:	Most of the time.
Minuchin:	Don't you get some vacation from that job?
Mother:	Not very much. But isn't that what being a parent means?
Minuchin:	No.
Mother:	Then I am overworked.
Minuchin:	You are overworked. I see that you are overworked.
Mother:	That I am doing too much? That I am interfering too much?
Minuchin:	Wow. Are you doing too much!! You are in a continual state of hyperalertness. [To Benjamin] Do you think she needs to be doing this?
Father:	No, I don't.
Minuchin:	And you tell her, relax?
Father:	I have.
Minuchin:	And how could _you_ change her?

Father:	I have asked myself that question. I think she has been very intense and very energetic and has bent over backwards, working very hard, especially with Mia, both in disciplinary action and also granting her privileges, to a point that I don't think I can go to. I look at what's happening on Mia's side and say, "Gee, I wish that you could sit where I am sitting and understand all that Emily is doing for you and that it is not all coming down on you."
Minuchin:	But look at all of what Mia is doing for Emily. See, I am interested in this mystery and I know that you are overworking.
Mother:	How do you know that?
Minuchin:	Just from the first three minutes here when I began to hear the dialogue. I saw the level of tension, the level of powerlessness, the level of frustration by which you are responding to all the situations. You started and you took over the session, saying to the therapist, "I am here ready to be responsible."
Mother:	Well, no one else was talking.
Minuchin:	No, no, no. What you said, Emily, is that, "I am going to be responsible. I am going to give you the insights and I will take this family to the green pastures where I want them to be." My dear, this is your function in your family. You are the sheriff, you are the overseer, you are the one that needs to help. You are an overworked lady.

Mother: Well, how can I get out of it then?

Minuchin: You will have to ask Benjamin that, not me.

_____

_____

_____

_____

_____

Mother: [Turning to husband] How do I get out of it? I am overworked.

Father: By cutting off some of the extra tactics.

Mother: Elaborate. I don't understand.

Father: When you speak of something to any of the children, you speak of it once. And then back off and give it time to implement itself.

Mother: What if it is something that has to be done right away and they do not do it?

Father: Then there will be consequences.

Minuchin: See, he is your foreman. That is not a way in which you will work less. He is giving you instructions of how to work differently.

_____

_____

_____

_____

_____

Mother:	But I have to work just the same.
Minuchin:	Yes, absolutely. That was not a change. That was, keep doing it but do it in the way I am telling you. He became your foreman just now.
Mother:	That's not what I want. That will not be helpful to me.
Minuchin:	No, that will not be helpful.
Mother:	So, did I ask him in the wrong way?
Minuchin:	No, you see, you are so responsible that you think that you did wrong. I think that he just sold you a bill of goods.
Mother:	Talk to him about that, then.
Minuchin:	No, you talk to him about that. I think he managed to turn the tables on you and you think that you did something wrong. You didn't do anything wrong. He just handled you exquisitely.

Mother:	Well, I'll ask it in a different way. I feel overburdened. Can you take on some of the responsibilities I am now handling? And I don't mean just doing what I tell you to do.
Father:	Then you become my foreman.

Mother: Well, maybe I do. What if you were to take them over and handle them in your own way, and I wouldn't have anything to do with them and I can rest assured knowing that they would be done? That would relieve me of the burden. If it is me telling you how to do it then, it is ultimately still on me. Do you understand?

Father: I hear you and I hear this conversation but, I am not sure what we are talking about, because I feel that I am heavily involved in a great many of these situations but I do not rise to them in the same way and, therefore, we may start out equal but because you make more noise in this situation you take it on and [Turning to Minuchin] I guess what I was saying . . .

Minuchin: No, no. Go on. We are listening. Continue talking with your wife.

_____

_____

_____

_____

_____

Father: That if you would just back off, we could stay at an equal position.

Mother: Are you saying if I backed off you would take over?

Father: Yes. Or at least carry half the burden.

Mother: Knowing that, if I could feel that you were really going to take the responsibility, then I would certainly back off.

Minuchin:	Emily, do you believe him? It will happen just that easy?
Father:	There is another problem here in that when you see us at point A, you may anticipate that I am going to go to point F to take care of a situation when I have no intention of going past point B.
Mother:	You're saying let me do it my own way.
Father:	Don't take over when I stop at B. Do you understand what I am saying?
Mother:	Not quite. I think you are saying…let me ask you to see if I am right.
Minuchin:	Emily? Are you going to translate him or are you going to ask him?
Mother:	I was going to say back to him, "Do you mean such and such?"
Minuchin:	That means you are going to translate him. Don't. Ask him to work for you. Ask him to tell you that in such a way as it is clear.

_____

_____

_____

_____

_____

We are looking at the ways in which you trick each other. The ways in which you make each other fall on your faces.

[To Mia] The way in which you activate this lightning rod function because you are a part of it. You have a very strong function in your misery. And your mom has a strong function in your misery. And your dad, as well.

[To the boys] And Mia has a strong function in your well-being. Because you are getting much softer parents, because she is taking the rap. Maybe one of the ways of helping her, Liam, is for you to begin to do some mischief.

_____

_____

_____

_____

_____

Mother:	[Laughs] Oh, dear.
Minuchin:	Could you make your Mom's life a little bit miserable?
Liam:	I guess so.
Minuchin:	Could you use your imagination? What do other kids that have trouble in school do? [Silence from Liam] [To Mia] He doesn't want to help you.
Liam:	I just never thought of things that I could do wrong.
Minuchin:	So that Mom will be busy doing her sheriff job and father will supervise her. What about Mason? What kinds of mischief could you do? See, I think you could do all the mischief in the world and your mom would still smile at you.
Mason:	I do.
Minuchin:	Yes. She will smile at you, so you cannot help Mia.
Mother:	He gets in trouble some times.
Liam:	Hardly ever.
Minuchin:	In terms of families, yours is rather traditional. Your mom is an overworked mom. And your dad is very helpful in telling mom in how to do the things better. And your poor mom came here and I feel compassion for her because she is really tight like a drum. You are a very overstressed lady.

———————————————————————————————

———————————————————————————————

———————————————————————————————

———————————————————————————————

———————————————————————————————

Mother:	I believe that. I know I am.
Minuchin:	And you need to go to Benjamin, not to Mia.
Mother:	I don't go to Mia. You mean with my troubles? I try to avoid Mia.
Minuchin:	Mia said something. I am just an observer. I am listening to people. She said something, I don't know, ask her.

———————————————————————————————

———————————————————————————————

———————————————————————————————

———————————————————————————————

Mother:	[To Mia] Did you say something? I didn't hear what you said.
Minuchin:	Before, she said that she needs to be there.
Mother:	Oh, do you feel you need to be there?
Mia:	I can tell that when you're in a bad mood, I'm going to get it.

Minuchin: I will say something that is strange. It is easier for you to discharge your tension with Mia, to feel competent, efficient, effective, or at least try to do that with Mia than with Benjamin. I was impressed with the way that you ask questions to Benjamin. You asked questions from a down-up position. That is what you did here two or three times. I don't know if that is true at home or you just did that for my benefit.

_____

_____

_____

_____

_____

Mother: I don't see it like that.

Therapist: I see it happen a little bit differently. I see you approach him very carefully and gingerly, as if you were walking on a bed of eggs.

Mother: I do do that.

Therapist: And not wanting to crack one on the way to ask him what you need.

Mother: That makes more sense to me. I don't think I approach him as if he is higher in the mountain giving me down the scrolls or something. I think we're a lot more equal intellectually than that. I probably do tend to approach him at times gingerly.

Minuchin: You see, I also think that your therapist is very careful not to let you increase tension. Not to explore the way in which you do not resolve conflicts. What he did just now was a rescue maneuver. For both of you and for me. He felt there was tension developing between us three, and he came to rescue us. Well, I don't need his rescue. I am very comfortable with stress. And I am wondering if you [To Therapist] do not feel very sensitive to how she is with stress and how he is with stress, so you tend not to explore the particular way in which these two people could change and be helpful to each other. You accepted the therapist's expression that you are walking on eggs toward Benjamin. Do you feel she does that?

Benjamin: No, I don't. The way I would interpret that is that she has occasionally been repetitive in her communication, and I have remarked that it isn't necessary and I only need to hear it once. So she has tried to respond to that and is probably being a little more careful in being thorough the first time she explains something.

Mother: I don't feel I do that all the time, although I can relate to that a little bit.

Minuchin: You did it here three or four times. And he works beautifully at this Gary Cooper type of person. He's the lanky cowboy. He is the silent masculine type.

_____

_____

_____

_____

_____

Mother: I know what you're saying, but he isn't always silent. You're saying why do I approach him so gingerly. Do you want me to answer that?

Minuchin: No, I would never want you to answer that. I am interested in both of you. See, you are working too hard. Benjamin, don't let her work so hard. Take over.

Father: I have tried.

Minuchin: No. You are very relaxed.

Mother: Why would he be reluctant, do you think?

Minuchin: You see how hard she works. [To Mia] Your poor Mom, she works tremendously hard. Continuously. And I want your dad to help her by just saying to her, "Relax, my dear. I will do things." He's such a nice smiling silent type. But he comes to the rescue when it's necessary. Does he come with a white `stallion or a black stallion? Do you cry so that he comes?

_____

_____

_____

_____

_____

Mia: Yeah, usually, I'd be crying. But not to rescue me.

Minuchin: Would it be better if he didn't need to rescue Mom? [To Father] So Emily is the explainer, and you are the silent type.

Father: Much more so, definitely. I have cut way down on my explaining because it hasn't borne fruit. So I have become much more silent than I have in the past.

Minuchin: So Emily makes you silent in the same way that you make her overworked.

_____

_____

_____

_____

Father: I am not relating to that. She can be out of the house and completely gone, and in my communication with Mia I have tried to explain things to Mia and it has been totally ignored. So rather than keep explaining I have decided to bide my time. I think at one time Mia expressed a feeling about existing in the house until she went away to school and things would be much better, and I think I have kind of fallen into that same trap where I am waiting for that to happen. And rather than enter into conflicts, I have tended to be quiet.

Minuchin: But Benjamin, you see, Mia now became a lightning rod again. Because what I want to ask you is if you can help Emily. See, I am not talking about Mia. I am talking about Emily. I am asking you, can you help Emily?

_____

_____

_____

_____

_____

Father: Well, other than the times that I have stepped in and tried to have her relax I'm not sure what to do.

Minuchin: I think you are right. You don't know what to do. Isn't it time for you to learn?

Father: Past time if that's what it is, certainly.

Minuchin: Can you two begin to learn how to do things differently so you will not have a wife that is so tight? I think that unless you help her, she is so tight that she is discordant. A drum that is so tight, if you play on it, will not produce good sounds. She produces discordant noises.

Can you help her? Because instead of talking and dealing with Emily and her need to develop a language with you, both of you are involved with Mia.

_____

_____

_____

_____

_____

Father: That's true.

Minuchin: [To Mia] And you are handicapping them getting to know each other now after 17 or 18 years of marriage.

_____

_____

_____

_____

_____

Mother: Do you think we don't know each other after all this time?

Father: [To Mother] I've talked about this with you. When I was away at work and was coming home, I would have so many positive thoughts of talking with you and spending time with you and doing things, and you've had a battle with Mia and we'd get all embroiled in that, and by the time we get through with that it's time for bed and we don't have any time to talk to each other.

And we're exhausted emotionally; just blown up. And I get very angry and very frustrated with that.

Mother: I do too. I get very exhausted.

Minuchin: [To Father] I know that in your family, Mia will expect Mother to be over-alert and over-responsive. Your children, and you, expect Emily to do it. You will continue in a tempo that is interrupted by her tempo. And she finds it difficult to intersect with you, so she intersects with Mia. Because your silence is powerful. In this family, this under-functioning is very powerful. The result of this pattern is that at this point you are having an unnecessary miserable period, in which Emily does not know how to ask you for help. And you don't know how to give it. She takes over instead. And when I use the word under-functioning I use this word advisedly. Emotionally, she is over-functioning and you are under-functioning, and it is two sides of the same coin. It is a complementary coin. It is a yin-yang. Both of you are a unit and what happens is that when I ask you a question, she answers. And why not, since you are one unit. But that leaves her and you in a spot. So I will stop now and will say that it is up to you, Benjamin, to begin to see in which way you can help your wife, because she is overburdened. And as long as she is overburdened, she will continue producing sounds that are discordant in your family.

_____

_____

_____

_____

_____

WHAT CAN WE LEARN?

The family came to therapy presenting Mia, the Identified Patient; as being in conflict with distressed, powerless parents. After the session, we found ourselves with a different scenario: at least three family members were seen as involved in a perverse triangle that makes them unhappy.

What is the territory that the family covered in the session?

Family members found themselves challenged in their view of themselves and in their sense of belonging. Over the course of 1 hour and 30 minutes, they became participants in a variety of subsystems. Each of the changing contexts imposed a different reality on family members and demanded different ways of relating with each other.

Throughout the session, the therapist was moving in different directions: joining with first one then another family member, challenging at other times the ones he had joined, exploring old and new narratives, highlighting diverse possibilities, and teaching, confusing and confirming in the interest of creating change.

Part II

Teaching and Learning the Craft

INTRODUCTION

In the first half of this book, we have laid out for you some general principles of systemic therapy and described a therapist's pouch of tools for challenging the certainties a family brings to therapy and for eliciting change. We illustrated these ideas by exploring the sessions of a master family therapist, and considered what could be learned from the sessions. Now we shift to the process of learning the craft, and the experience of students engaged in this process.

As we begin the second half of the book, we hope you have become familiar with the concepts and assumptions a family therapist is making as she/he meets with a family. They can be summarized as follows:

- A <u>family's</u> view, usually, is that they are coming to therapy with an individual symptom bearer whose problems are intrapsychic. They are certain that they have done all they can to alleviate the situation, without success, and they expect the therapist to solve their problem. The <u>therapist</u> believes that the problems are part of an interpersonal context, and that the family has resources for healing that they are not aware of and have not explored. Because of this difference in mindset, the therapist and family are in a conceptual polemic about the focus of the therapy.
- The therapist must challenge the family's certainty, on their behalf, and must help the members to question their assumptions and explore alternative pathways for the way they are organized and function. The therapist will facilitate the expansion of individual identities, so that family members see themselves and each other in different ways, and will help them explore new and more positive ways of connection with each other in the family as a whole and in various subsystems.
- The therapist will function as an expert, but will be aware of personal style and biases, acknowledging that his or her work is always partial and that the ultimate goal is to cede healing functions to the family itself.

These are useful guiding ideas but, as we have noted from the start, we believe that the best way to learn the craft is by doing; that is, through an inductive method in which the practice of therapy by those who are learning is supervised, explored, and expanded. In this second part of the book, therefore, we focus on what you can learn from others who also have been learning the craft; students who brought their work to the Friday consultation sessions with Minuchin. In presenting this material, we move from a zoomed lens to one that is wider, bringing you in to the intimacy of our Friday sessions and back out to the therapy room.

The first two chapters of this section (7 and 8) present our conversations with the student therapists, rather than case transcripts, since this stage of learning principally served as a tool for the supervisor to gain access to the therapist's style. As you read these chapters we hope you can gain a sense of the common challenges that new therapists face, as well as some cues for thinking about how to improve your craft.

The next three chapters (9, 10, 11), written primarily by the student therapists, provide a view from their perspective of how each one understood and utilized supervision to expand as a budding family therapist. As we watched portions of the videotaped sessions and provided these therapists with feedback, we were supportive of both their efforts to help the family and their growth in the development of their craft.

After each case was presented and discussed, Minuchin conducted a one-time consultation with the family as a way of contrasting how a novice and a master therapist utilize craft. Segments of these consultations are presented within chapters 9 and 10. The whole of the third consultation is presented as a chapter of its own (12). In reading these consultations, be aware of the consultant's dual aim. First, he is working with a family to help them move toward their goals. Secondly, he is working with a therapist to enhance her practice and style. Be aware also that just as a therapist needs to be different with each family, depending on how it is organized and what issues it is addressing, the consultant/supervisor needs to be different with each supervisee. They are each asking and requiring something different from him.

As we bring the hands-on experience of our students to the reader, we remind you of an earlier reference in the book to a "homunculus"—an imaginary self that observes, thinks, and raises questions. The students were learning to carry this idea into their therapy sessions, and to keep track of such basic questions as the following:

1. How can I shift the presenting complaint from a story that most likely includes only one individual to a story about relationships?
2. How can I expand family members' identities so that they view themselves and each other in alternative ways?
3. How can I explore greater nuances of family organization than the restricted view of subsystems that is initially presented by the family?
4. How can I understand myself and my personal style while exploring each of these questions and moving toward the therapeutic goals?

These questions are continuously in play during therapy sessions. The answers come through the therapist's growing skill in applying the craft, his or her style of relating to the family, and the family's capacity for change.

We asked our students to go beyond their comfortable styles, taking risks in the therapy room so they could expand their use of the craft. Just as a therapist's job is to show the family they are richer in resources than they think they are, it is the supervisor's task to help his/her students understand and expand their possibilities. In the coming chapters you will see the students struggle to develop their craft.

7

ANGELA AND THE WAY TO ASK QUESTIONS

What's a good question in a therapy session? It depends, of course. A question is good if it's useful for your purpose at a particular moment of therapy with a particular family. A therapist needs to know how to ask questions that will help in joining, gathering information, challenging a set story, bringing other family members into participation, or opening new perspectives. What beginning therapists need to learn is how to keep track of what they are trying to do in asking a question. And they need to work on the parts of their personal/therapeutic style that make some kinds of questions difficult to ask.

We present Angela's case in this section because the issue of how to ask questions has been an important stumbling block in the development of her therapeutic style. Angela is working with a couple, married for many years, who present themselves as harmonious and loving. As they see their problem, they're overwhelmed by financial issues, especially about helping other family members. Angela wants to challenge their peaceful narrative, but she struggles with how to ask questions that will disrupt the couple's story and their sense of unity. Her style of therapy is basically supportive, and she finds it difficult to rock the boat of this family's loving presentation. Supervision, in this situation, focuses on the multiple features of useful questions and actions that will further her therapeutic goals.

The setting for this chapter is a meeting of the family therapy student group with Minuchin, the supervisor. At the start of the meeting, Angela plays the first half of a family session tape. When the tape is stopped, Minuchin, Angela, and the group embark on a discussion, followed by the remainder of the tape and further discussion after it. The discussions are presented below, through verbatim sections and commentary. They move back and forth among (a) dialogues between student /therapist and supervisor, (b) discussions between the supervisor and members of the group, and (c) additional commentary to the reader. In order to distinguish the discussion that occurred at the meeting from comments to the reader, the latter appears in italics and is in the right-hand column.

THE SUPERVISORY SESSION: DIALOGUES AND COMMENTARY

After everybody has seen the first part of the session, Minuchin begins by asking Angela to supply a broad context for the discussion, to talk briefly about the issues already highlighted as central concerns of this book, the therapist's style; challenging the symptom, the organization of the family; and so forth.

Minuchin:	So, today we have Angela, who is presenting her first session with a couple. We'll look at Angela as a therapist, what she thinks about the family, and at aspects of her work. Who are you as a therapist? What is your style? What are your biases?
Angela:	I think my style as a therapist has been a work in progress. I bring my personal self into my work as a therapist, in that I'm very giving and I'm very self-reflecting. I think I'm an active participant as a therapist. I've had to work to hone my skills to sit back and allow my natural curiosity take the foreground, and not be so quick to try and fix things. I think that I have a tendency to be a fixer, wanting to do too much, and I think that has thwarted my efforts. I find my progression as a therapist to be exciting. What informs me now is that I find, when I can remain calm in the room, I have all this information of the family therapy models and what I've learned in the Master's program. I'm somehow able to synthesize that information and let myself be present in the room.

Minuchin: Angela is describing herself in a nice, very beautiful, flowing narrative. How that expresses itself when she's in a room with a couple, we don't know. However, what she presented was too perfect, and I mistrust perfection. I want to look at this tendency that she has of responding. She says, "I'm very giving," and then she says, "I'm quick to respond." So that's one of the things I will look for: how able is she not to respond. How able is she to be decentered, because a centered therapist always breeds biases. When she's working in "zoom" she probably does not see peripherally.

What else? What can you tell us about this couple?

Beginning therapists, like families, tend to have a restricted view of themselves and their possibilities. One of the roles of a supervisor is to expand the therapist's alternatives and ways of being. As Minuchin tries to get a sense of the therapist's style, he begins the process of unwrapping this identity by commenting that he mistrusts perfection.

Many people come into the therapy field because they are caring individuals who want to help others. The more they try to fix a family, the more central they become. Working in close, with a zoom lens, they tend to miss the wider view. They have difficulty seeing outside the family's narrative and beyond the periphery of family transactions.

Angela: The couple has been married for 30 years, and the only thing I knew going in was that they were going through a life transition. They're recent empty nesters, and I was told that he's like the caretaker of the whole family. The impression I got was maybe there wasn't enough money to go around. He works in the construction business, and perhaps because he was taking care of so many people he wasn't able to meet his own obligations and everybody else's. That's as much as I wanted to hear from the referring person because I was really trying to go in without any bias.

What I learned about the couple once I was in the room was that they are very loving. They sat very close to each other, touched each other, and described themselves as soulmates. Both of them were telling me about all the ways in which they take care of all the people in their lives. They have two sons, 21 and 22, and the last one just went off to college. They're very excited about being empty nesters, because they're best friends.

Can I say something about me?

Minuchin: Go ahead.

Angela: I wanted to be with them and to have this experience with them. They really wanted me to know who they were and I felt honored by that. At the same time, I was still actively trying to listen for what was the problem, because I couldn't really hear a problem, and I didn't want to push anything on them. That was the first half of the session; listening and asking questions. I was thinking, "I'm delighted that this was so wonderful, but this was such a perfect picture and they were not bringing up issues."

Minuchin: You know, Angela has presented the first half hour, in which she has a question mark: "What's the problem?" She says they didn't bring any up. What she says is untrue. It's not that they didn't give it to her. It's that she doesn't know how to ask questions with confidence. And she told us before that this is an area where she has difficulty . . . difficulty with confidence. She is nice and sweet,

It's never true that therapists are seeing the family "as it is." When a client or family enters the therapy room, they're transformed, as is the therapist. The two subsystems come together to form a therapeutic system. In this case, the therapist played a role in maintaining a session that was nice but did not bring forth a direction that could lead to difference and change.

and they are nice and sweet. Two nice and sweet systems do not collide with each other, so there is no information. When the family presents themselves as, "We are loving, respectful, and fun," Angela needs to realize that something is fishy. But she doesn't. So what is she doing? She continues talking with them, but in such a way that they find it difficult to present themselves in great detail. They're formal with her. So again, the question is how to listen.

A critical listener doesn't listen for what is said, but for what's not said. Angela is describing a system, but she describes it as if it's not a system; as if she's an objective observer of a couple. But you're not an objective observer; you're an observer with bias. And your bias is that you like calmness and harmony, which prevents you from challenging their presentation. The first half hour is a time in which they need to present you with a story you can penetrate, and that didn't happen.

Minuchin:	So, can you present us with the second half?
Angela:	I would like to show you the second half, because the second half is where I was poking around more. I think I was looking to unravel everything that they said.
Minuchin:	Tell us, and then we'll see it.

Angela:	What you'll see, after the consultation break, is that we had left off where the husband was beginning to really open up, to say what it felt like to have the weight of the world on his shoulders. I asked his wife how she felt while he was saying this and she began to share how concerned she was for her husband, that she was worried, that all these people came to him, and he didn't have a means to vent.
Minuchin:	And what did she say?
Angela:	I asked her what she was feeling. I wanted to see if she was thinking the same things as him. She said she was worried about him; that he didn't have anyone to vent to and that somehow he was going to get sick. She was very concerned about his well-being.
Minuchin:	And your thoughts?
Angela:	I was thinking, "Okay, we're getting somewhere now." I felt this was not the rosy picture I had been seeing. It was starting to open. And then I had more questions. Like, I wondered where he learned to be the caretaker of the family.
Minuchin:	Good. Tell us the whole session before we see it.
Angela:	Okay. So we came back into the room, and I talked to him about the weight on his shoulders and what it felt like. I got up and pressed down on his shoulders.

One of the main goals of a family therapist is to externalize the problem; to move from focusing on an individual who exhibits the problem to the perception of a relational system that is helping to maintain it. Angela describes a technique she used to heighten intensity and gain depth into one person's understanding of himself. Minuchin, instead, is focused on the relationship between husband and wife, as well as the therapeutic system of husband, wife, and therapist.

	I made a comment about how big they were, and that I wondered what it felt like to feel the weight of the world on his shoulders.
Minuchin:	[To group] So what are your responses to that?
Student:	I actually was uncomfortable with that idea. I mean, it may work for other people, but I don't know that I would be personally comfortable.
Student:	I liked it.
Minuchin:	Okay. You see, I'm a family therapist. I don't like it. Why don't I like it? Because it's an individual approach, in which Angela is taking the road of exploring this man's experiences. Her question is not relational. That is, she got up and put her arms on his shoulders, which is something that can be okay or not. For some people that's a perfectly good approach, and for some people it wouldn't be. But that's not what concerns me. What concerns me is that she's not getting the wife to do something. It's an individual exploration between the therapist and the man, with the wife as an observer. At this point, the wife and Angela have isolated him as the "Identified Patient." That's perfectly okay if Angela knows that she's taking a narrow road, and that she will expand it later. But I don't think she knows that. Did you know that?
Angela:	Mmmm-hmmm.
Minuchin:	You did know? And so what do you do to change?

The dialogue here is about the therapist as a tool. If Angela can only push for harmony, she has limited herself. Just as her goal is to expand the couple's options, she has to expand her own options for how to move forward. Beginning therapists have a tendency to move people away from conflict. This interchange suggests that a movement toward conflict, even in peaceful seas, is a useful avenue of exploration.

Angela: I guess it would have been better for me to use her in that situation, but that didn't occur to me. But I made sure that I paid attention to both of them, because I believed that it was both of them creating a situation where the whole family was coming for their help. So, I asked her also.

Minuchin: Okay. Continue describing.

Angela: I asked her what it felt like to have all of these people to take care of, and how it impacted on both of them.

Minuchin: Angela is sweet. But what she has done is a Libra act. It means she keeps symmetrical; if she explores him, she explores her. But she doesn't say to the wife, "Margaret, what do you do when Peter takes all this responsibility?" She doesn't ask a question that opens an avenue for the exploration of conflict within the couple, rather than between the couple and an external system.

(to Angela). You don't have a small Angela in your brain that's looking at you and saying, "Angela, at this point you're not paying attention to how you can explore their disharmony." Clearly, being harmonious is a value for these people. They are loving, and they think about other people. You should ask yourself, "Why not?" They come to you because "why not" is the issue. The issue is that, in some way or other, that way of being serves them. You don't know in what way. So you're exploring, and the exploration needs to be one in which you feel comfortable with proceeding until you see dissonance. For me, I would say "conflict." For Angela, I say "dissonance," because Angela still has difficulty entering into conflict, but dissonance is okay.

The first approach when you meet a couple is to say to the couple, "Your truth is partial. What you're presenting is a particular way of being. I want to understand more." And that means that the function of the therapist is not a harmonious function. The therapist introduces tension, doubt, and questions. You look to me like a very nice lady, and I'm wondering if you can fight.

Angela:

Yes, I can fight! Later in the session, I asked how their past histories had formed them. He started talking about being abused as a child. He opened up about his father and how he became the caretaker of the family, protecting people from getting hit and abused. She shared some of her feelings about that experience for him.

I remember thinking, at the end of the session, that we had unwrapped some things, but I was still wanting to challenge them about whether they have enough money to take care of everybody. I wasn't sure if I should, but finally I just went for it. I said something like, "You know, this may be an

The therapist views herself as being able to bring forth tension, but she doesn't quite see that she still has difficulty challenging the harmonious picture the couple has painted for her. She touches on the possible tension between the couple and other people, but doesn't explore what may be happening between just the two of them.

out-there question, a personal question for someone who's only known you for 45 minutes, but you talk about wanting to enjoy this empty nest time. Is there enough money to go around?" I thought it was a bold question, but I thought that's kind of what I was there for, and if it wasn't they could dismiss it and maybe it would bring something else up.

Minuchin: They will come next session?

Beginning therapists tend to be nonintrusive. They do not view themselves as experts. This therapist has not exerted her authority to explore disharmony, so the session does not go beyond information gathering. Her questions have been benign and not allowed her to challenge the couple's presentation of themselves. At the end of the session, both the therapist and the couple are confused about why the couple is there.

Angela: You know, I'm not sure.

Minuchin: She spent one hour with these people and doesn't know if she likes them or not.

Angela: No, that's not true.

Minuchin: Because if you were sure, you would have said to them, "Come." She doesn't know if she will be useful or not. She doubts her usefulness to help these people with a problem they do not have.

Angela: Okay. Got that.

Minuchin: You see, the session finishes with a question mark. Angela didn't carry the narrative to a point that

Students learn how to ask questions without realizing that their questions are biased. But any

was interesting for the couple so they could think about what to do. They came in to Angela saying something is new, and we don't know what to do in this new situation. And there it stays. (To Angela). I'm talking about your style of curiosity. It's a neutral curiosity; what you do is gather information. My curiosity is never neutral; it's related to what the family wants from me. Your style is respectful and minimalist, and that style finishes a session without opening up the peripheries, the marginal aspects, of these people.

question is informed by what is important to the person asking it. If the therapist believes that family history is important, questions will explore the family of origin; if it emphasizes hierarchic organization, questions will highlight structure. The basic point is to challenge a therapist's style, in the interest of developing a broader repertoire.

Minuchin: You need to do something that says to both of them that you're dealing with the issue of the complementarity of the couple. And you need to have in mind that, as a couples therapist or a family therapist, you are not the one who must do these things. You're the one who directs people to do things. You're not the savior. I like what you did with the man. It means you introduced proximity, you introduced a kind of friendliness, and it's nice. And they feel, "Okay, she's a nice person." But it's between you and him, and you're the one that does the moving. At this moment, a yellow light should come on in your head signaling questions you want to ask yourself: "What can I do to involve his wife? Can I ask him to ask her how she feels? Or to ask her 'How often do you feel I'm too rigid, or lacking control?' or 'Do you feel I'm a schmuck?' This is where I want to introduce tension, thinking

This is a moment of combined "stroke/challenge" in the supervision. Angela's way of joining is acknowledged because it's nice and reassuring for the couple, but it's not thoughtful enough to move toward her goals. She needs to develop a style that tends more toward "nice/and." She can be both nice and challenging.

that I could also say directly to her: 'Do you think Peter is unable to stop being a nice guy?'"

The point is that you are not ever working with just one person. You are always working with two or three. Your movements are nice, but they're not thoughtful. You have the thoughtfulness of a person who is curious—but not as a curious couples therapist. A couples therapist isn't curious about the inner motivation of one of the members, but of the way in which what is happening mutually impacts them.
Am I being too harsh now?

Angela: No. So, then I asked him where he learned to be the person that carries the burden. And he said he learned from his father's mistakes.

Minuchin: Stop! You want a dialogue between the husband and wife, so you can understand. You're there to see the things that they don't see. You asked the wife what she thinks about his situation, and she said she thinks he needs to find a way to vent. That she tries to talk to him, but doesn't feel he has the opportunity to vent.
And what does she mean?

Angela: That he takes care of all these people but who does he release to? How does he let go of the tension that he absorbs from the family?

Minuchin: She's saying that they come to him and he just gives. So she's saying to him that he's a schmuck.

The previous point is picked up and extended. If Angela had initiated an enactment, getting husband and wife to have a dialogue with each other instead of creating a dialogue between therapist and husband, she could have widened her lens. The shift to a relational view allows access to areas that are not present when looking within individuals.

Reiter:	Isn't he being a schmuck on two levels? He's being superman to these people, but he's also not allowing her to help him.
Minuchin:	Absolutely. He's exploiting the nuclear family, and she resents that. She has years of resenting that, and she's critical of him.
Angela:	There was one thing that I didn't mention earlier; that she does what he does, too. She gives to the family. She does a lot of what he does.
Borda:	They also do it sort of behind each other's backs, in some ways. I'm wondering if he created that person in her too, as "the giver." Because, that's the way he set it up in his world. He was set up to be the caregiver in his family. When she joined him and they became a family together, all of a sudden she had to participate in that giving as he gave. So I'm wondering whether she is resentful toward him; that she has to caregive, as well.
Minuchin:	You see, I would say this information is correct but not useful for Angela. Because I really want to criticize Angela. I think that she has a perfectly nice and ineffective style.
Angela:	Tell me how you really feel.
Minuchin:	I'm sorry. I think you should realize that to me it's essential to criticize you if I respect you.
Angela:	Thank you.

Here, the supervisor is modeling something analogous to the situation between therapist and clients: As the expert in the room, you can convey your connection and respect for others through your freedom to challenge and criticize to help them change.

Minuchin: Because the idea is that I like this fact that she gets up and puts her arms on the man's shoulders. That means she has the ability to use herself. It's unnecessary, but when she does it I like it. And you [To another student] don't like it.

Student: I just felt it was very intimate for a first session, that it was mothering, and like it felt too active for me.

Minuchin: All of that is correct, and therefore you will not personally do it. But therapists have different styles. And it worked with her because she can work with intimacy in such a way that she doesn't feel she's seducing. Maybe if you did it, you would feel it's too seductive.

The craft of family therapy is idiosyncratic. There's no one specific way of being a therapist. People have their own ways, which will most likely shift over time.

What I see now is that I don't need to see the end of the session. I know the end of the session will be as ineffective as the first part, because she finishes not knowing why they came to her. And that's not the fault of the family. The family came with the certainty that they need to keep harmony, and that the right way of being is to keep conflict at the lowest level. The family came and they leave, and they haven't got the sense that the therapist is helping them with something.

Student: Are you insinuating that sometimes conflict in a family allows them to move forward in different ways?

Minuchin: I'm not insinuating that. I'm saying that.

The meaning here is not only that the members of the couple should feel uncomfortable, but that the therapist should be uncomfortable, as well. The more people stay in their comfort zones, the less need they feel to expand

and the more restricted their sense of what alternatives and possibilities are available.

Student: Okay. So in this case, that conflict would be something healthy for them to explore?

Minuchin: Absolutely. She needs to be comfortable enough with a man she's been married to for 32 years to say to him, "Did it ever occur to you that you take it out on me?" And for 32 years she has had that thought and she never said it.

Student: They're prisoners. She's like a prisoner.

Minuchin: They came with a certainty that it is a prison. And it's a function of the therapist to say, "You have alternatives." That's what a therapist does. The therapist says, "You have alternatives to that style." So, I want Angela to be uncomfortable.

Student: So, it seems like you're saying that in every interaction the therapist should be attending to the couple as a twosome. We shouldn't be seeing them as individuals, where you balance things out between them, for instance, by giving them both an equal amount of time to talk.

Minuchin: Yes and yes. I think that you need to be able to do both things at different times. What Angela did as far as the man's childhood is very good, and her talking with the man was very nice. But she needs to have a yellow light that says, "That's enough. Now I explore the same thing with the wife," or "I ask the wife to comment about that," or "I ask her? 'How did it affect you?'"

There's no such a thing as the right way of doing therapy. It's a very complex set of transactions. So, I'm saying that first you need to develop a mindset. The techniques, the craft, will be varied, multifold, and good for some people but bad for others. I teach all of them in terms of the things that are more comfortable for me. But the mindset is generic. The mindset is that you are always exploring the way in which a couple affects each other.

The idea that conflict is useful is interesting, because I come from a culture where conflict is resolved with knives, and so conflict with words is minimal. If I have a couple that comes and they continue fighting, I say to them: "You know, you're very funny. For the last three minutes you have been doing exactly the same thing with exactly the same result. And that's amusing. Do you have any other way of doing it?" I challenge in a completely different way, using humor. We need to use a variety of ways to relate to the family and fulfill our function. The function of the therapist is to expand the family's style. Angela's couple leaves without expanding their style.

In the first session, you need to find out who the "Identified Patient" is; then you tell them, "You are wrong, the IP is not that." To do that, the first thing you need to ask is, "In what way do you want me to help you? What is it that you want?"

Okay. I think I've been too critical—but that's how you made me feel.

Angela: Just so you know, I'm not as fragile as you think I am, so it's fine.

Minuchin: No, I don't think you're fragile, but I think you prefer not to ruffle the waters, and I think that's incorrect as a therapist. I think that's nice as a parent. Very nice as a spouse. But as a therapist, that's incomplete.

Minuchin: [To group] Angela needs to find the spot in which she can think. Because she's too proximal she cannot do that. As a therapist, she will need to find a way of decentralizing herself. The moment you're not required to do anything is a special moment for therapists, because then you can think, "Okay, how could that go?" And then you try it before you're absolutely certain that it's correct. If you're certain it's correct, you're incorrect. The point is that whatever you do is partial, so you don't need to perfect the answer before you ask the question.

Novice therapists think they must know what to say and do before they do anything. That mindset restricts them; it's an impossible goal. Therapists make mistakes, and that's both expected and acceptable. You need to be flexible enough to see the other roads that can be taken. As for which road is correct, any or all could be!

Minuchin: [To Angela] So it's a question of what techniques are available to you. You have a large repertoire, and you selected for this family one set of skills that was incorrect. It will be incorrect any time you want to be a family therapist. But you have among your skills the ability to see a large system. You can function with attention to complementarity, to conflicts, to multiple encounters, all of it. They're necessary, for family therapists.

Here, the point is about personal style. Angela has other, hidden resources; they were available to her but not utilized. The point is general, applicable to all members of the group, but the repertoire is unique for each person.

Minuchin: [To group] When you look at Angela, you will see a minimalist. Somebody that is very respectful. I am disrespectful. I start with the idea that families come with a certainty, and that, in itself, is generally incorrect. Families create a set of certainties, and we grow up carrying those certainties with us.

So I would say to this couple, "You've come to me to say that you're uncomfortable, now that you're empty nesters. That's very interesting. You are certain that harmony is the best and only way of being. But that's partial, and therefore incorrect. Let's travel together for the next ten hours to see how much richer you are than you think." I'm respectful, I'm nice, I bring hope, and I'm saying, "You are wrong." I believe that this family, in 32 years, created certain norms. The norms represent a certainty that their way of being is the way they described themselves. My function is to say to them, "You're wrong, you have more possibilities than you think. Join with me in a trek of adventures; in a trek through alternatives. I believe you have internalized the norms you created in 32 years of marriage, and your story will be different if we challenge the certainties." Yet when I do this, I will smile. The function of a systems thinker is to say to people, "You are richer." And that can be done in a respectful, fun,

challenging way. You can be polite and say to people, "You know, I don't agree with you. What you said is nice but it's wrong." I think Angela is very rich. I think she doesn't know how to use that, so in this session, she was poor. It means she doesn't know how to use other aspects of her self. I was hard on her today because I want my voice to go with her.

What Can We Learn?

We present this chapter to you because we think it very important for therapists to be comfortable with uncertainty, discord, and challenge. Our ultimate goal is to help the clients who come to us looking for more harmony. However, even in harmony there is discord, and both are normal and acceptable. As we saw with Angela, novice therapists try not to rock the boat and create waves; they feel comfortable in a calm sea.

Angela's questions were designed to extract information, mainly benign information. These questions developed a context for an interview, but not a family therapy session. A therapist's questions should be purposeful. They should be designed to challenge the family's presentation of themselves, and to bring forth differences and alternatives. A therapist's job is to explore those aspects of the family they may not be aware of, those underlying processes that lie below the surface.

Angela stayed on the surface of calmness and harmony with this family. Her style as a therapist did not allow her to hear and observe areas of tension between this husband and wife. She did not think she should or could challenge them as a happy couple. They had carried their tension into couples therapy, but did not know where the tension was rooted, and they were not comfortable bringing it to the surface. Because their therapist did not know how to ask questions that would explore the strains in their relationship, they left therapy in the same situation that had brought them in.

What we've seen in this case is that Angela does a very good job of joining and a poor job of challenging. Like many people, she tends to see challenge as creating disconnection. The discussion in this chapter highlights the idea that it's possible to challenge a family while still maintaining a connection—with a smile, with focused curiosity, with an attitude of exploring more satisfactory alternatives on their behalf. What we have suggested, also, is that a therapist who wants to challenge a family effectively may first have to move beyond his or her own zone of comfort.

8

OLIVIA AND BECOMING A SUPERNANNY

In the first years of learning, it's difficult to enter a therapy room thinking like a family therapist and carrying that orientation into practice. It was easy for our students to see each person in the room as an individual, but it was harder for them to remember that these individuals were connected with one another in ways that impacted each person's behavior, and that the network of relationships was the crux of working with the family to explore better ways of living together.

In this chapter, we present the work and supervision of Olivia, whose natural therapeutic style has been formed by the experience of growing up with a single, overburdened parent, by her work with troubled children, and by her individually-oriented professional training. Her difficulties as a young practitioner were partly typical of most students and partly specific to her particular style as a therapist.

The family that came to Olivia for help consisted of a single mother and two young children. The older child, a boy almost 5 years old, was the Identified Patient, and his troublesome behavior was described as the problem. As Olivia describes her response to the family and her way of working with them, it's clear that she accepted the problem as presented and was trying to be helpful. Olivia understands systemic concepts, but in this arena of action she invoked a therapeutic style that drew on her experience and felt natural. She focused on the child, she was protective and nurturing, and she created a comfortable situation. She assumed that this way of working would be helpful to a mother who felt overwhelmed and was relying on Olivia to solve her son's problem.

Beyond the problem of the individual focus, however, there is a particular aspect of Olivia's style that hampers the effectiveness of her work and the accomplishment of her therapeutic goals. We are presenting this case under the title "Becoming a Supernanny" because, as the session went on, Olivia was demonstrating that she is a more competent parent than her client. She found herself wearing various hats—firefighter, referee, teacher, motivator. Essentially, her style is more about being a Supernanny than about functioning as a family therapist, and the supervision is about helping her to expand.

In this chapter, the verbatim section of the dialogue between student and supervisor is taken from the beginning of their discussion, before presentation of the tape. Olivia's description of her background, and of her problems when she tries to function as a family therapist, shapes the supervision from the start.

DISCUSSION: STUDENT AND SUPERVISOR

Olivia: I did not grow up with my father, and I value the relationship a father has with his children, and a husband and wife have. So when I encounter clients that come from traditional families, I tend to value and honor it and think it's wonderful. I've had clients who are single parents, and I guess I empathize with them. I understand that my mother worked really hard, and some days she wouldn't even eat because she had no child support. So, I guess I would empathize with that.

In this case that I'm seeing, the mother has recently divorced from her husband. She has two children from this man. The boy, the IP, is 4 turning 5, and the little girl is 3 turning 4. The mother was referred by her pediatrician to seek counseling services from a play therapist and child psychologist, but because of her budget she came to my internship site. When she came, she had the idea that, "Okay, you can handle my son and I'll just take a step back." She specifically said that, "The counseling is really for my son." So upfront, I knew what her expectations were.

[Speaking to Minuchin] I have a problem. Sometimes I feel like I need to perform for the client. You've talked to us about how the therapist gets put in a position where the clients come in and say, "Okay, fix me." And I tend to feel the anxiety of that very easily. So it's almost as if I have a bag of tricks and I start just trying to fix things. "What about this? What about this, no, no? That doesn't work? Okay, okay." I feel like I have to perform because they are coming to me for advice. They are coming to me to fix their family and their problem.

Minuchin: Did the mother come with just one child?

Olivia: At first she came with just him. After the second session, she came with her 3-year-old daughter, as well. I saw them for seven or eight sessions.

Minuchin: What can you tell us about your eight sessions?

Olivia: I attempted to do a lot of play therapy. I would try to connect with the child and my purpose was to try to make the child feel very comfortable. I would say to him, "Is it okay if I ask you a question?" "Is it okay if I talk to your mom?" I kind of made the child have more power in the session, because I felt that was the mother's expectation of what play therapy was. We did a lot of self-esteem building, where we would draw pictures. I'd say "What does Chris like? Oh, he's good at basketball? Draw a basketball."

I realized after viewing the videotapes that a lot of my approaches were very scattered. When I would try and talk to the mother, the son would come up to me and show me a bubble or something and I would pay attention to him, while the mother would just kind of sit there, and then I would go and jump right back in. So it was like I was turning off, turning on, going with the son, and then going with the mother. I tried to keep in my mind, "Wait a minute, this is family therapy and I need to engage both at the same time." So, randomly, I would say, "Wow, isn't that great that your brother did that, Penelope?" and "Mom, what do you think about that?"

Then, of course, I would go back into individual therapy. When Mom reported that Chris did his homework and went straight to bed, and that was something she was struggling with, I said to Chris, "Can I write that down? That you did your homework with Mommy, and you wrote a letter to your teacher apologizing for pushing her?"

Olivia's description of the family moves quickly to an account of her anxiety about what to do in a session, about the demand she feels to be helpful and her erratic search for what might work. She's asking the supervisor for help, but he doesn't respond directly to her discomfort. Instead, he moves their discussion toward the details of her session. Supervision is about the therapist and the family as an interactive system. It will be most useful to discuss Olivia's problems and possibilities in that context.

Minuchin: If there were a caption or title to this session, it would be *The English Supernanny*. Therapy is very complex and whatever movement we do we need to know it's partial. So Olivia is now engaging in conversation with the child. It's perfectly okay. It's not bad, but very incomplete and skewed. The chaos is part of what happened in her brain. She sees so many things and she answers to all of them, so she can't organize her thinking in hierarchical units, saying, "I don't need to answer that, I don't need to answer that, but *that* I need to answer." So what Olivia has created is two mothers for two children, and the two mothers are continuously busy with what the children do and what the children don't do. Olivia is hyper-alert. She's never decentered.

There's now a lot of information about how Olivia was thinking and acting in her session with this family. The supervisor begins his comments by providing a title—a clear image—that captures Olivia's constant activity in the session. "Supernanny" is a useful image to carry with her as she develops, reminding her that this way of functioning that comes naturally to her creates problems in family therapy, where the goal is to help the family members to function more effectively.

Minuchin: Before Olivia does anything, she needs to think hierarchically about what is important to do. She needs to think about what the family asks her to do for them in order to be a more harmonious family. What is the problem? What do they need? And what can be my intervention? She needs to be able to say that in this family there is a loving and inefficient mother, and the fact that she's loving—or not so loving—doesn't take away from the fact that she is inefficient. She has two children that she is continuously monitoring, and she is exhausted. So she becomes—or may become—punitive, because she doesn't have a sense that she is in control. Olivia needs to see that and say, "What should I not do? I am not the Supernanny."

Olivia has become a supplement. She is a rescuer of the mother and enters to do what the mother doesn't do. The therapy is a therapy of the child. So at this point, she is not really thinking as a family therapist. She is thinking as an individual therapist, and as an individual therapist maybe she's helping the child, but that is only if she plans to adopt him.

The central problems in Olivia's work include her focus on the child, in what is essentially play therapy, the fact that she is so involved in everything she sees that she has no time to think or plan, and the further fact that because she is never decentered she doesn't organize or control her interventions. The suggestions for change highlight the value of creating distance, so she can organize her understanding of what she is learning about the family and ask herself the basic questions about what the family wants, where the issues lie, and what possibilities she has for useful interventions at a given moment.

Olivia: Part of that is true. I described before how the anxiety to perform and to be completely attentive to everyone in the room so that everyone feels happy and light and has fun brings a lot of anxiety for me to perform in a certain way. So when I am thinking of things going on and how I can be helpful to everyone, I lose my ability to organize and to focus. I have learned that pacing myself, or just slowing down and taking a step back and staying with their story for a little bit longer, might have been useful for this family. But the first thing that Mother told me was that she wanted play therapy, and she said to me "I want it to be fun when Chris comes here. I don't want him to think that he's being analyzed or observed." So I think I kept that in my mind the whole entire time. I wanted him to enjoy coming, because I know therapy can sometimes be scary for a child, especially at that age.

Minuchin: You see, you are cluttered by too much information. And I want you to be poorer, not richer. It's a strange thing to say, but I want you to get control of what is involved. You don't have a map, so you are traveling through many territories.

The mother comes and says Chris is the problem. Now, for some reason or other, you accept that. The first thing that you need to do is to challenge her certainty. The assumption that Chris is the problem is wrong. The *family* has a problem. If Mother is certain that the oldest son is a problem, I know that her presentation is correct but partial. When she says Chris is a problem, she's saying, "I have a problem with Chris." So the first step is to take the IP label away from Chris and to make it a matter of mother and child having a problem. The problem now is not in Chris, not in the mother, it's between Chris and the mother. At this point, you are having a different conceptualization of what is the target. And then, if you want, you say to Chris, "What is the problem?" in your nursery school voice, then do so. You'll see that Chris sees the problem in one way and Mother sees the problem in another way and you have a narrative—more information. My concern is that you accept information that they give you and you don't question that information.

If you ask questions, you can be nice; you're curious and you are exploring. And you are free. The important thing for you is to be free. You diminish your freedom in this session by responding to every demand placed upon you. You should enter there not as a Supernanny but as an exploratory person concerned with the human condition. It's a very different way of thinking. You need to think, and then you will access more information.

You are tremendously rich, Olivia. Yet, you don't use it. You have experience as a musician, as an actress, . . . but you accept a very narrow story, and that doesn't give you access to your intuition.

This is the basic concept of family therapy: that the problem is relational, that families usually do not understand that, and that the therapist's task is to challenge their certainty about problems and solutions. A developing therapist can learn to challenge in acceptable ways, using what is available in themselves as well as the techniques of the craft.

WHAT CAN WE LEARN?

From Olivia's presentation of her case, two things are clear: the centripetal pull of the therapeutic system and the limited power of knowledge.

When Olivia, or any therapist, joins with a family to form a therapeutic system, certain things inevitably happen. First, the therapist influences the family, imposing his or her point of view on its members. As a profession, we have become alert to this process and concerned about controlling it. Second, the therapeutic system curtails the therapist's freedom to think and act. This process, less visible than the first, is not so frequently addressed.

In Olivia's case, as you will also see in Roseann's case (Chapter 10), the therapist has become ensnared in the family dynamics. Olivia feels the mother's helplessness, she accepts the primary concern with the boy's troublesome behavior, and she is transformed—almost against her will—into a family helper. She becomes a Supernanny. This stealthy process occurs in spite of Olivia's knowledge. There is a clear disconnect between her understanding of systems theory and her automatic response to the family's needs.

9

LEARNING FROM MY MISTAKES

Sarah A. Walker

I was 23 years old when I saw my first client. At that time, I had completed three family therapy classes, which I loved. The passion of my professors was inspiring and contagious. But like many first-year students, I was terrified at the prospect of seeing my first client. Thankfully my classmates and I had "training wheels" in the clinic at our university. There was a live supervisor, a team of classmates, and a one-way mirror. An additional security blanket was being able to watch several of my classmates in the therapy room before having my own client.

One Tuesday, the call came with the news that I had been assigned a client. This was not just any client, but a mother referred by the Department of Children and Families, as her children were removed for neglect. My first response was dread. "Is the universe playing a trick on me?" I wondered. How could my first client be a child welfare case? My supervisor asked aloud the same question that I asked in my head: "This is such a tough case. Why would they assign it to a first-year student therapist?" She called the clinic director, who felt confident that my supervisor could handle it, due to her experience in the field.

And it turned out that they were right. As soon as I sat across from my client and began our session, I realized that I could listen, be present with her, and realize that her experience was far different from my own. We had five sessions together, which were valuable to us both.

During my Master's program, I was trained in postmodern therapy; primarily in solution-focused and narrative models. Within a month of graduation, I was accepted into a Ph.D. program for Marriage and Family Therapy and was hired full-time at a community mental health agency, working in the child welfare system providing psychoeducational support for children and their families. These two influences led me to see how parents could help their children to grow. They simultaneously blinded me from seeing how I might be different with families to help them change in other ways. Part of my emerging vision can be attributed to my time with Dr. Minuchin and our supervision group.

Minuchin pointed out to me that I tend to rescue. I did not see this at first, though with a little reflection it makes sense, since I became a therapist because I wanted to help people. This limited my effectiveness with the family I present here. In this chapter, I will try to convey to you what I learned through a supervisory relationship with a master family therapist that has spanned over three years. This relationship has not only changed what I do in the therapy room, but how I view myself outside of it.

I think about myself at the time I first met Dr. Minuchin: a 24-year-old female Master's student in her second year of training to become a family therapist. The first Friday of my initiation into this group, I walked into his home, drank the strong coffee, ate the grapes, pastries, and cheese I was offered, and sat on the wooden kitchen chairs gathered in the living room. He greeted the group, introduced himself, and addressed us by asking, "What are your questions?" At the time I did not have any or think that I knew enough to ask the "right" questions. I have since learned that this search for being right has hindered my work with families. Often, there is no "correct" intervention or question to ask, only possibilities with unknown consequences. One area of my struggle and growth that I hope comes through in this chapter is that sometimes taking risks is the best thing you can do for yourself and the families you work with.

I knew I was taking a risk when I signed up to be part of the supervision group, as Dr. Minuchin was going to push me out of my comfort zone, as he had done for 50 years with the families he worked with and helped. At that first meeting he did something that he told us he did not like to do, and in over three years of working with him, I have never seen him do since; we role-played. He may believe it is not a good teaching tool because it is simulated, but through it I learned my first lesson.

LOOK AT YOUR LEFT FOOT

It was absurd, and yet so simple. I have never forgotten it since, although, as you will see, there are times when it is difficult to do such an easy endeavor. Somehow I was chosen to be the therapist and my classmates the family. One of my colleagues was acting out the part of a father who is distanced from his wife and two children. The "husband" was demanding my attention, begging me to be on his side, and Minuchin stopped me.

"He hooked you."

No supervisor had ever told me that before. What did it mean? Supervisors in the past helped me formulate a version of the miracle question, assisted in designing an intervention, questioned my use of assigning homework, and challenged me to "respectfully interrupt."

"He hooked you," Minuchin continued. "He is saying, 'Listen to me. Like me. Be on my side.' And while you are so close, you don't have time to think about what you will do. And so, if I were in the situation, I would look at my left shoe. Your shoes are very nice, and so you should look at them, and not at the family. You need distance from them, to have them talk to each other, so that you can watch them and think, 'What will I do now?'"

I had been taught that as the therapist you are supposed to listen to the client in front of you, be attentive to what they say, and be empathetic to their experience. This suggestion of looking at your left foot was a completely foreign concept to me. While for Minuchin this is a metaphor that may be taken literally or figuratively, and is so simple to understand, it should not be mistaken for something easy to do, as it is complex and extremely difficult for the unseasoned therapist to implement. In session, all your instincts push you to be one of the major actors in the family drama in the therapy room. At times this may be appropriate, but at others, as we learned from Dr. Minuchin, the therapist has more freedom by taking a step outside the family to allow them to be and to allow yourself to think. I thought at the time that I could do this easily; however, in the role play, Dr. Minuchin showed me otherwise. This has been a struggle for me, one that I want to present to you to help normalize your potential struggles, as they are something that we all experience and all can learn from.

Last year I had the opportunity to attend an intercultural exchange to China to share research and practice between American and Chinese students. Each student who participated in the exchange presented their best work in areas such as couples therapy, internet addiction, and psychosocial rehabilitation. One Chinese student, however, was quite courageous, which provided a unique opportunity for dialogue and growth. Instead of sharing a case in which everything went well, she presented a case that was considered a failure. This is something that I found immediately to be brave and valuable, because it helped each of the 20 students realize that failure also provides a pathway to the possibilities of learning.

I attended many of Dr. Minuchin's Friday consultations. Throughout our meetings, I engaged in conversations where he spoke about externalizing the symptom so that the Identified Patient shifts from the individual to the family, unwrapping identities so that people realize that they have more possibilities than they present, and a therapist posturing him or herself to anticipate the demands that family organization makes. We discussed the self of the therapist, and how the therapist uses aspects of this self as an instrument when working with families. All of this and more was swimming around in my head as I held two sessions with the Rodriguez family. So why was it that none of this came through in my work with them? In reflecting on my two sessions with the Rodriguez family, I can see opportunities that I had in each of these areas that I did not take. As a result, the sessions that I present could be conceptualized, like the Chinese student I mentioned, as a failure.

In the third session, Dr. Minuchin consulted with the Rodriguez family. He was able to view and engage the family from each of these parameters. What were the differences between his actions and mine? This chapter will explore how a well-intentioned therapist equipped with the intellectual knowledge needed to succeed might not do so. My hope is that through my presentation, reflection, and analysis, you can learn from my mistakes, so that you can more smoothly translate your understanding of family therapy into your practice.

THE RODRIGUEZ FAMILY

The Rodriguez family includes Caroliña, her 8-year-old daughter, Christina, from a previous relationship, her husband of five years, David, and their 2-year-old son, Daniel. The family was referred for Christina's behavior problems. Caroliña reported that her daughter was having issues with rage, anger, and depression. She had concerns that her child may have ADHD and was acting out because her father was released from incarceration a month ago, after being in jail since Christina was 2.

Three sessions were held with the family. The first two with me as the therapist, and the third as a consultation with Dr. Minuchin. I will present portions of my first session, where I began with good intentions but was unable to accomplish what I hoped. At times, I will reference ways in which Minuchin was able to accomplish what I hoped to do, or how he took the family in an entirely different direction. I am not including portions of my second session with the family, as the process was similar to the first.

I was nervous going into that first session. I knew that this session was being filmed for showing to the supervision group and, even more anxiety-provoking for me, to Dr. Minuchin. I was opening myself up for critique. Just the fact of being observed likely restrained how I would view what was happening and what I might do. This was likely my first mistake. Here I had the opportunity to take risks, as ten people, one of them being one of the foremost family therapists, would view my work so that I could get feedback. But instead of loosening up and expanding, I was restricted. Therapists, like clients, are susceptible to retreating to what they know when they feel stressed or under pressure.

Upon hearing that I was a student and seeing that I was young, the mother questioned my competence. This put me in a position where I felt defensive, and that I had to somehow prove myself. Yet, feeling that I was being challenged in my position as "an expert" limited and influenced the ways in which I felt I was able to work with the family in challenging their certainty. Even before the day of the session, I had been experiencing some "performance anxiety," which I believe also limited my effectiveness, because I put pressure on myself, knowing that my work would be scrutinized.

This issue of my age is one that I have struggled with throughout my career, because I am an unmarried female therapist in my twenties. Clients have asked questions such as, "How old are you?" "Are you married?" "Do you even have children?" This is something that you will invariably encounter as you begin your practice, and I will let you in on a secret . . . *It has nothing to do with you.* It is about the client's own assumptions and biases related to their insecurity of having a problem that they are unable to solve themselves. The clients are trying to be as certain about you as they are about their understanding of themselves and their problems. This is one of the demands placed on the therapist by the family organization, and you must challenge it. Here is how Minuchin addressed this quite easily in his introduction to the family.

Minuchin: My name is Minuchin and I am quite old. I am a professor of psychiatry and a teacher. I am going to be with you an hour, hour and a half, and will try to be useful. So that's the best that I can do. Maybe we can start by asking you why did you come here.

Minuchin immediately established his position as an uncertain expert, but an expert nonetheless. I could not introduce myself exactly as he does. He is more than 60 years my senior and can engage the family as a grandfather. My entry, probably like yours, will need to be different. As my university training has taught me, I am not an expert on how the family should be, but on developing a context in the therapy room that illuminates pathways to change. In my consultations with Minuchin, we discussed subtle ways of establishing an expert position; for example, by having the client call me Ms. Walker, rather than Sarah. I had never before thought about this small distinction in creating maneuverability, where I would be able to be more than a student therapist but, rather, just a family therapist. Thus, my entry into the family, will have to be different than Minuchin's. Yet we can both be useful to the family as we both have something to offer the family: a different viewpoint—a systemic viewpoint—that may open up pathways that they had not previously seen.

Although my initial approach to beginning the therapeutic dialogue was similar to the end of Minuchin's, I handicapped myself from the get-go, which would hold for the two sessions I met with the family. Although I view myself as a family therapist, I had not realized until we did a thorough analysis of my work with this case that my training as a child therapist would play such an integral and underlying role in my viewing of the situation, my interventions, and even the questions that I asked. This is how I started the session:

Therapist: I kind of wanted to get an idea from you both about what's been going on and what's been leading up to coming to therapy.

I addressed myself to the parents here, and framed the question this way, to elicit a narrative and jump right into the presenting problem. I later ask for the child to share her understanding of why she is in therapy. However, from the very beginning, my opening maintained the child in the Identified Patient position, rather than exploring a story of relationships. By first addressing the parents, I unwittingly aligned with them in agreement that they were separate from the daughter and that they would give me information so that I could help her. Instead of starting with a focus on family process, the session started off focused on "the problem child."

Caroliña: I feel that Christina needs help learning how to understand her feelings, and to properly express her feelings. I feel she has a lot of anger, mixed emotions inside of her that cause her to react from one extreme to another. She's either very loving, very happy, or throwing a temper tantrum. When she was younger it was worse, to the point that they kicked her out of daycare because of her temper tantrums and flying off the handle because she didn't get her way, which that has not been the case since then. But she still gets very angry or very emotional, and likes to tell fibs, and is sneaky. Some of the stuff is just common for most kids, but I feel there's certain areas where she may take things to a further extreme. I want her to learn how to express her feelings so she's not so angry and upset and that she can vocalize what she's feeling and learn how to deal with them differently. [Turns to David]

David verbalizes something undistinguishable, gestures with head nods, and makes some movement of his head, which seems to be less certain than Caroliña.

Therapist: [To David] I saw you nodding your head some and then some, like [Copies the uncertain head movement back and forth].

David: I agree. I just think she's young, so certain things you just have to expect that. But maybe just not at times to the extreme that it is.

I interrupted the long narrative of the mother bringing in a laundry list of complaints about her child. I brought attention to what was being said not through words. This is an area of importance as a therapist, to not only listen to what the family says, but also to see what is happening in the room. It is an area I have needed to work on in terms of growth, because I have often acted in the past as if hearing was the only sense that I possess as a therapist. However, one of the things that I still need to work on is connecting one person's nonverbal communication into a relational message rather than an individual characteristic.

Here, if I were to do the session over again, I would want to highlight the differences in the viewpoints of both of the child's parents. Her stepfather normalized the behavior some, while the mother criminalized it. I would want to challenge the assumption that they were a united front, which would have opened up different possibilities for the remainder of the session. Coming from my psychoeducational and solution-focused background, it was difficult for me to challenge what, on the surface, seemed like harmony. I think I was working from the notion of ensuring that mother and father were "on the same page," which would then lead them to being able to implement joint parenting strategies.

Instead of sticking with my initial interruption of the problem narrative, I privileged what was being said with one voice, which was incorrect but more comfortable for me. I was seduced into their certainty, a type of "group think," partly because I was not able to gain enough distance. By being too proximal I was not able to intervene in a way that introduced change. Instead, I was joining in their certainty.

Perhaps my hesitancy in challenging their viewpoint came from just having been challenged myself as to my credentials. My lack of confidence in myself as an authority in the room pushed me to accept more of the parents' position, rather than being able to see what they might not have. This was an example of the family as an organism that makes demands of the therapist. Below is a portion of transcript where the same "we" talk occurs with Minuchin, and how he addresses it to open up possibilities.

Caroliña: She started to understand more that we were on her side, and we wanted to do things to help her. It wasn't that we were trying to be mean or anything like that. We needed to come up with a solution.

Minuchin: Caroliña, I know because I have been married for 60 years that when my wife talks and when I talk we are two different voices. You're talking about "we" and that means that I am sure you are different. There's no question about that, so I know that. [To David] So when she says "we," what does she mean?

I had seen this same pattern and tried to make a distinction between the parents from the first session. However, I was unsure of how to do this. Even worse, I eventually began talking with Christina from a "we" position that included the mother, the father, and myself (together in a coalition that maintained Christina as the IP). Minuchin was able to use himself and his 60-year marriage to separate the husband and wife's viewpoints, letting them know that they are two distinct people. This opened the door to talk about their process, which cannot be done if they are considered as one entity. You can find ways that fit who you are to let the family know that you truly believe they are distinct entities, yet are entangled with one another in a relational web. This is the first step the therapist takes in expanding the identities of each member in the family, and how they see one another.

David:	For the most part, it would happen more with Caroliña than it would happen with me because I work longer hours, but then I would get home and see the notes from school and try and have a conversation with Christina about it. She would be on defensive mode, become very angry, and start to cry. So it kind of went really sour or downhill very fast.
Minuchin:	And who is the disciplinarian at home?

Sitting in the chair next to Minuchin during this session, I wondered, "Why had I not asked them this question?" It is a clear demonstration that Caroliña and David have different ways of operating that impacts Christina. This may have led us to a road where we could have more clearly seen possible difficulties based on family organization. Instead, I had viewed the parents as one disciplinarian entity.

David:	Well, for the most part, Caroliña is. I don't like laying hands on Christina.
Minuchin:	You are more even-tempered than Caroliña?
David:	Yes.
Caroliña:	He makes a joke out of it. He makes more of a joke out of it where I get angry.
Minuchin:	And does it work better for you to use humor when you talk with Christina?
David:	No. I kind of do it to soothe the situation. I don't want her to feel like we're against her, but that she can come to us and talk to us.
Minuchin:	Again, I will remind you that I don't believe in the "us." I believe that you are different people. I am sure you are. And I am sure you have different tempers. So if we can during this one hour, can you speak with single voices?

It is clear that Minuchin is comfortable in his position of authority as the therapist in the room. As a new and young therapist, this is a position that seems to be in the future for me, rather than the present. But when I have this viewpoint I know that I limit my options, taking out the option of being the leader of the therapeutic conversation. I still hear the postmodern explanations of "no truths." Yet, even postmodern therapists are authorities in the therapy room, as they have a view of how to manage a session (rather than what the client should do).

David:	Sure.
Minuchin:	Let me tell you from where I come. If Christina has a temper tantrum, she is responding to something that happened. That is a mystery but I am a detective who loves mysteries. So let's find out what makes you, [To Christina] that has such a lovely smile, have a temper tantrum. Because if you say now things have improved, then it means that there has been a change in the atmosphere at home? Or you are more relaxed. I don't know. Tell me a little bit about what happened at home.
Caroliña:	Part of the problem is her birth father and the relationship she had with him. He got out of jail in October. He was in prison for the past 6 years. She doesn't visit often.
Minuchin:	You are 8, Christina? [She nods] How old was she when David came?
Caroliña:	She was 3. He has been in the picture 5 years.
Minuchin:	So as far as she is concerned, you are the only father that she knows.
Caroliña:	She knows her birth father, but she doesn't have a good relationship with him.
Minuchin:	But you said that one of the things that has changed is that he is out of jail.
Caroliña:	Now that he's out, she's seeing that he's not the person she imagined him to be.
Minuchin:	Oh, that's interesting. Tell me a little bit about that. What did she imagine?
Caroliña:	I think like most little girls—he's gonna be a hero, spend all this time with you.
Minuchin:	Save her from your temper?
Caroliña:	Just save her, in general. Not even from my temper, because I don't think my temper is that extreme, but she just thought he was going to come and do all these things with her and be this imaginary figure she had in her head.
Minuchin:	Caroliña, can you talk with your daughter? She will respond to you and not to me. So I would like you to talk with her so that I know how you talk.
Caroliña:	[to Christina] What do you think is the reason that you have changed and are doing better?
Christina:	Because you used to be so mad and stuff, and now you calmed down.
Caroliña:	That's why you're doing better in school and that's why you calmed down?
Christina:	Well, you've just been nicer and stuff. Not been yelling at me.
Minuchin:	That's interesting. So she thinks that your temper is not so even.

Halfway through the session, Minuchin had explored areas with the family that I had not gotten to because I was so focused on making sure that the parents knew that I was on their side. Here he had opened a door to focus on mother instead of daughter.

In returning to my first session with the family, when they were trying to tell me how Christina was problematic, I did not externalize the problem. I could have explored how this was a three-person system by asking, "Who is she more 'playful' with? Caroliña or David? What does David do when Christina and Caroliña engage each other like that? What does Caroliña do when it is David and Christina?" These questions would have helped move us out of the notion that Christina's behavior is separate from the relational dynamics of the rest of the family. By not challenging their view of the presenting problem, I provided them with validation that Christina was the problem. Caroliña then picked this up.

Caroliña:	She's very sneaky. If she knows I won't allow her to do something, she'll try to go to David, her grandmother, or somebody else. Try to say, "They told me so." Even if they tell her no she'll say, "They said yes, so do you say yes?" And, which I think is common among kids.
Therapist:	You told her that you would be coming here today?

Here I wanted to interrupt the problem-talk, as the entire conversation had been the parents talking about the child. I wanted to bring Christina into the conversation so I could be more of an observer of the family process, and to ascertain the child's ideas about why her parents brought her. However, I could have challenged the mother's view that this is a willful act from a child by asking a relational question such as, "Who did she learn that from, you or your husband?"

Caroliña:	Yes, she knows.
Therapist:	Can you talk with her about her understanding of why she's here?
Caroliña:	Do you understand why you're here, Baby?
Caroliña:	shakes her head "No."
Caroliña:	Remember me telling you that we're trying to fix things in our home so we can all be better? I know when I talk to you, and say, with your homework, "Oh, this one is wrong," you get angry and start crying and we get frustrated and start arguing with each other? But I didn't want it to be like that anymore? That I wanted you to learn how to talk about what you feel? Also at times, I see that you're crying a lot lately. I want you to be able to tell us why you're crying or feeling a certain way. That we are here to help you. We're here because we love you more than anything, want to make sure you're happy. I want you to learn how to deal with all these different feelings that you're going through. You're going through a lot of changes, right?

Caroliña has laid out the framework for why they are there in therapy. I had the knowledge in my head that when families come into therapy they are wrong (in that they think they know what is wrong, they think the therapist can fix it, and that they are not aware that they are richer than they realize), yet for some reason this knowledge was unable to escape my brain to manifest into an intervention. Instead, I succumbed to the family organism's demands on the therapist; I jumped along with Caroliña's position through my questions as well as my silence. Here I could have used a relational understanding and asked Caroliña or David about their relationship outside of Christina. I could have asked about the context of what happens before the anger outbursts, to see what Christina may be reacting to, or how her behavior may serve a function in the family.

This was also my first attempt in the session to introduce an enactment. Enactments allow the therapist to see the family process, but perhaps more importantly, to think about what is going on in the therapy room (including what is happening between the family members and the family members and the therapist). It is the point where the therapist is able to look at her left foot and think. But I did not look down. I looked straight ahead. As a student therapist, I had an impulsive need to do something rather than nothing, and that was a mistake. Yet Minuchin's dictum of looking at one's foot, what seems to be a statement of "do nothing," is actually a prelude to doing something; something that is more thoughtful than the reactive engagement I had been involved in with the family.

Here, I set up an enactment to allow the family to communicate these things in an effort to be "influential yet decentered."

Christina:	[Timidly] Sure.
Caroliña:	Do you understand what she just said?
Christina:	She said I need to say what I am thinking.
Caroliña:	Very good! So what are you feeling?
	[Silence]
Caroliña:	What do you think? What do you feel? No matter what you say, nobody's gonna get mad at you. Like right now, this is like a safe zone. You're free to say whatever you're feeling, so you can be able to talk about it, and we can be able to help each other to understand better.
Christina:	[Quietly] My dad.
Caroliña:	Well, what do you feel? You can't just say your dad. That's not telling us very much, Baby.
	[Silence from Christina]
Caroliña:	What are you thinking in your head right now?
Christina:	I don't get to see my other sisters and brothers.
Caroliña:	What about the fact that you don't get to see them? How does it feel, the fact that you don't get to see them very much?
Christina:	[Tentatively] Sad.
Caroliña:	It makes you feel sad? And what happens when you feel sad?
Christina:	I get mad.
Therapist:	So when she gets sad and mad, how does it affect the rest of the family? [To parents] What do you do?

My attempt here was to shift Christina's anger (the presenting problem) within the context of the family. However, I did not accomplish this. Although I thought my comments were relational, and they were to some degree, it still kept the focus of the problem inside of Christina. Yet now, she became a further burden on the family. Her anger became an inconvenience to the other members of the family, rather than all members of the family maintaining the symptom.

Caroliña: I think honestly, it makes us mad, 'cause we see her crying, and we see her upset, and that builds anger in us, 'cause she shouldn't have to go through it.

Therapist: And you almost feel helpless.

For the family to be helpless over this situation is much less pathologizing for Christina, and allows the parents to be supportive of her, rather than criticizing, and for them to take ownership of their own emotional response. Again, I thought I was working within the world of relationships, yet underlying it was a sense of individual components. My response to Caroliña was a perfectly good empathetic response. But it did not change the family story of Christina being the IP.

I was able to initiate an enactment, but forgot that enactments are done for several purposes. First, they allow the therapist to sit back, observe, and think. The observation that occurs is about the processes occurring in the room, between family members and between family and therapist. I was getting swept up within the content of their conversation, which allowed me to be empathetic. However, I missed out on being able to ask about the family process that was occurring. This would have allowed me to start to externalize an individual problem into a systemic issue.

At this point in the session, I thought I was doing well by having them explain what they thought was going on. I thought I was still outside of their process and objective. Although someone might say, "Be aware of getting sucked in," it is not that easy to realize when it is happening and then to do something different.

Caroliña: Why do I usually end up yelling? I ask you things, and you don't answer. Or you tell me lies, and I tell you to tell me the truth. And you keep lying to me. And then I turn into the crazy lady, right?

[Laughter in the room]

Caroliña: I don't want to be the crazy lady anymore, so we're here trying to fix things, because Mommy needs to be at peace just as much as I need you to be at peace. I need us to be able to communicate so we don't have to scream and yell and become crazy people. Right? You know when you get angry and you have a temper tantrum. You know how you feel inside? When you lie to me and don't talk to me and don't tell me the truth, that's how I feel. Mommy doesn't want to feel that ugly feeling. So that's why we're here, so we don't have to get to that point. Does that make sense? [Christina gives a weak nod] That's good. Because we want to be happy, right? [Christina nods more weakly] These are the things we've been talking about lately. [The baby had become active at this point in the session]

Therapist: Is your little one always such a mover and shaker?

Caroliña: Yes, both of them. This is like the most still I've seen her in a long time.

Therapist: I was going to say, Christina seems to be doing very well.

Caroliña: In school she's an honor roll student. She's very intelligent.

One of the difficulties of coming from a child welfare and psychoeducational position is having a focus on "the problem" itself instead of being able to view "the problem" as a relational circumstance. When Mother says that Christina's lying eventually leads her to be the "crazy lady," I had an opening to explore where that was coming from. Where is that anger coming from and how is it that it seems to be heightened with Christina's behaviors? This would have been a huge step for me to pose these types of questions to Caroliña. She might have taken it that I was blaming her for Christina's behavior. Yet my systemic training had told me that behavior makes sense in context, and I was not unfolding that context.

I noted several times when Christina helped her younger brother. When I began praising her, the mother stated that Christina was being manipulative because she knew she was being watched. Both Caroliña and David stated that Christina is an observer of others. I also made connections between how Christina is an observer, or a people watcher, much like David. Caroliña told a story of how Christina was a manipulative person. She stated that this went back to infancy, where Christina would watch people from her crib and calculate them to determine how to get them to do what she wanted. I sought to reframe and challenge her certainty by stating, "So you gave birth to a genius?" The family agreed, which I thought was strange that a child so young could have so much influence. The relabeling as genius stuck, and David used the term a couple of times during the remainder of the session.

I attempted to expand Christina's identity from a problem child to someone who is relationally aware (and thus a genius). However, Caroliña and David vetoed my reframe and made it into something that was problematic. In being too respectful of their certainty, I severely limited my capabilities. Here we will pick up with Dr. Minuchin's session with the family. The mother had just made a similar comment to where my last section of the session began, but as you will see, it went in a very different direction, for very different reasons.

Minuchin: You think Christina is that bright?

Caroliña: Oh, I know she is. She is very bright.

Minuchin: Oh great! I love bright kids. I am bright also. I am a child psychiatrist for 60 years so I know a lot of children. I know if she had a temper tantrum and is a bright 8-year-old something happened to start the temper tantrum. I am looking at you for information.

Caroliña: When she was 4, her temper was really bad, to the point that she got kicked out of school because she would flip out and beat up other kids. She's had an issue with anger for a long time, and I think a lot of it does result back to when she was younger and to all of the things that she would witness in the home and a lot of it dealing with my anger and her father's personality and him being in and out of the picture.

Minuchin:	Caroliña, I am an absolute stranger and you are talking about things you know a lot about. Can you give more detail? Bring me into your home.
Caroliña:	When she was younger, before David was in the picture, she witnessed her father physically abuse me, choke me, smack me. So she witnessed that.
Minuchin:	Do you remember that Christina? Do you remember your father hitting your mom? [Christina shakes her head no]
Caroliña:	I've never talked about that in front of her, either.
Minuchin:	So you never tried to protect her? Do you remember that she tried to protect you?
Caroliña:	Yeah. It didn't happen too often, because once the abuse started, I got out of the picture very quickly after that, but I was holding her in my arms and he had me pinned up choking me and she was punching him in the chest telling him to stop.
Minuchin:	Christina do you remember that? [Christina shakes her head and says, "No"] No. But you were kind of a heroine. You must have been a very strong little girl trying to protect your mom. That's very nice. So she did that. And then you left your . . .
Caroliña:	I separated from him.

My attempt to expand the identities of the clients, including Christina being a genius because she could "read" people, was shot down by Caroliña and David by them thinking that it was just a manipulative ploy she was using. As I watched Minuchin light up when talking with and about Christina, it was clear that he was genuinely enchanted by her. Instead of being an angry girl, she had now become a heroine, trying to protect her mother from an awful situation.

Minuchin:	David, how did you become Christina's father?
David:	I came into the picture and it just happened.
Minuchin:	No, no, no. That's not true. That's never true.
David:	What do you mean that's not true?
Minuchin:	It's a process. It's always a process because Caroliña and Christina are close. You enter. You're attracted to her, but she has a child and that starts a process. Can you bring your memory to that period and see . . .
David:	When she would actually let me go to her home and from that point is when my relationship with Christina started to build a bond because it became a regular process.
Minuchin:	Is Caroliña very apprehensive?
David:	At times. With things that she is strongly passionate about.
Caroliña:	What do you mean by apprehensive?

Minuchin:	You know, as she describes her relationship with her first partner, people that have that kind of violence become very observant, afraid that tragedy can happen at any time.
David:	Correct.
Minuchin:	They become hyper-vigilant.
David:	Right.

During my two sessions with the family, I had been looking to expand the scope of the problem so that it is out of Christina. Yet I was trying to be very respectful of the family's position. I had forgotten Minuchin's teaching that when you come from places of joining, you are freer to challenge. I had joined with the family, which was correct yet partial. I think in some ways I saw my joining as a tenuous thread that could be easily snipped if the parents did not like something that I said. Here, Minuchin shifted the IP from an "angry daughter" and recontextualized the system to include a "hyper-vigilant mother." He did this as a person who cares about the family and was therefore able to challenge. This has been a clear lesson for me to learn.

Minuchin:	Okay. So my expectation is that Caroliña developed some hyper-vigilance and I am wondering how hyper-vigilant you are with Christina.
Caroliña:	Yes, I'm very observant.
Minuchin:	We're getting to know each other. [Minuchin's cane falls to the ground and Christina moves to pick it up] [To Christina] Thank you, my dear. Do you want a job? To pick up . . . I am kidding.
Christina:	I am already used to it, because Mommy makes me clean around the house.
Caroliña:	She's my helper.
Minuchin:	Excellent. Does she help with Daniel?
Caroliña:	Playing and bottles. She helps me a lot. I have chronic fatigue syndrome and other health issues. I have a lot of pain, and the medication does not help.
Minuchin:	This is a very difficult illness and the way in which it's treated is with a lot of pills, and that's a problem. So, are you sometimes very irritable?

I had known that Mother had chronic fatigue syndrome and was in pain, and though I touched on it during our first session and hypothesized that her pain was an organizing feature of her interactions with her daughter, I did not return to this territory. As I sat and watched Minuchin's compassion for a mother in pain, I made some important connections for how to address this in my own sessions.

| Caroliña: | Yes. When I'm in a lot of pain, I'm very irritable. |
| Minuchin: | And what happens with your relationship when she's irritable? Is she short-tempered? |

David:	Yeah.
Minuchin:	[To David] How do you handle that?
Caroliña:	He ignores me, because he knows I'm in a bad mood and stays away, for the most part.
David:	I don't try to avoid her, but I stay out of her way because I know she can kinda snap.
Minuchin:	What happens with Christina when you help her by being out and she is irritable?
David:	No, I don't go anywhere. I'm there.
Minuchin:	You had learned that it's helpful to be out of her way when she is in pain.
David:	Right. In another room, or downstairs watching TV while she's in the room upstairs.
Minuchin:	Is that helpful?
Caroliña:	Yes and no.
Minuchin:	Yes and no. Tell me the no.
Caroliña:	No, because when I don't feel good I want him to be there and cuddle me and show me some love, so it can be frustrating and very lonely.

This was a moment when I was able to see a true master at work. It was something that I knew in my head and struggle with crude and clumsy efforts to make a reality in my therapy. I saw that when you keep asking relational questions and really see family members as interconnected, you develop a family rather than an individual story. Minuchin was asking about functions. It was clear to me at that point that if David maintained his distance when Caroliña was in pain, she needed a substitute.

Minuchin:	What's Daniel's function there? Is he very loving?
Caroliña:	Daniel is very affectionate, very loving. He's a Momma's boy, where Christina is more a Daddy's girl. He's very mellow.
Minuchin:	Okay, so you see what I am doing is being a detective. I am trying to find out the context, because I don't believe in anger issues. I believe that anger at her age is direct and this is not just inside. It's directed towards somebody. So I am asking in order to know what happened when you are irritable, what happened with David, what happened to Daniel, what happened to Christina? Because if we know what happened, then we can try to fix it. As long as you have pain, you will be irritable, your threshold of focal attention diminishes. You become less available. You know these are things that you need to understand that when that happens to you something happens to Christina. If Christina is feeling better, I would hypothesize that you are feeling better as well.

Caroliña:	No, actually, I've gotten a lot worse.
Minuchin:	So I was wrong.
Caroliña:	Yes. I've gotten a lot worse, where I haven't been able to work in 4 months. Since I've gotten worse, I think Christina has stepped up to the plate. She's matured a lot over these last 6 months and she has become more of my helper. I think we've developed a better bond since I've been sicker.
Minuchin:	Beautiful. So she's your helper.

Sitting in the chair next to Dr. Minuchin, I was pleasantly surprised. I knew that one of my hesitations of making more drastic interventions than getting parents to discipline differently was knowing that I might be wrong. However, Minuchin was able to simply admit that he was wrong. Yet the mother did not challenge his underlying assumption that there was an invisible connection between all of the family members, that when she was in pain her husband got out of the way of her irritability, and her daughter became activated. This was a dynamic that I had been searching for, but was unable to clearly lay out. I was too focused trying to rescue the child, getting her parents to help her to not have tantrums or lie. I did not see the front end of her outbursts and how they were connected to mother's emotional and physical condition.

One of my goals, based on my time in Minuchin's supervision group, was to expand each client's identity. In my two sessions with the family, I was so focused being on a rescue mission, on helping the parents help the daughter, that I did not see how Christina was helping her parents. This beautiful frame was another way Minuchin helped shift her out of the IP role.

Caroliña:	Yeah.
Minuchin:	And this lovely girl is compassionate. What happens with your mom when she's in pain? Does she cry?
Christina:	Sometimes. Almost every single time.
Minuchin:	My goodness! I see how hard it must be for you! So let's gossip a little bit about your mom. When she is in pain, does she cry because she's in pain?
Christina:	Well, like if it's worse pain she will cry, but usually it's not bad or worse pain.
Minuchin:	She cries with tears or she cries with words? She says, "Aaah, I'm in pain"?
Christina:	She says, "I'm in pain."
Minuchin:	And what do you do when she's in pain?
Christina:	I ask her if she needs any help or anything.
Minuchin:	So you will grow up with a very big heart. Does she ask you to do things?

Christina:	Yeah. I ask her does she need a cup of water, something to drink, and if she says yes I just go downstairs and get water.
Minuchin:	You are 8. And you are learning how to be helpful.
Christina:	Yeah. Like when she goes downstairs and forgets something—like her phone or her keys—upstairs, and she tells me to get it and I just go and get it for her.
Minuchin:	You're lovely. You are so lovely. And do you do something for this handsome man [Referring to David]? Does he need you in any way?
Christina:	Sure. That's a harder question.
Minuchin:	I ask hard questions but you can answer easily.
Christina:	Sometimes he needs . . . well . . .
Minuchin:	What do you do? Is he good at playing with you? There are some people who are very good at playing with children and some people who are really very dumb.
Christina:	He's a person that, like, when I ask him if he can, like, play with me, he says yes.
Minuchin:	So you learn how to read people? Wow. So she reads both of you.
Christina:	Like if he's sick or anything, I am just going to ask him if he needs water, something to drink. Usually if Mommy feels sick, I give her love.
Minuchin:	You are lovely. How are things in school? [Christina is silent and looks at her mother] You know, my dear, whenever I ask you a question and you don't know the answer, you look at your mom.
Caroliña:	She's used to Mommy coming to the rescue.
Minuchin:	But she doesn't need any rescuing. She's very, very smart. I am so glad that you came because you gave me an opportunity to fall in love with your daughter and that's very nice. I think you're wonderful. And your problems with her have diminished now?
Caroliña:	They've gotten a lot better.
Minuchin:	Do you realize how much she's responding to you? And how much when you are in pain, she's in pain, also? So that as you become less able when you are disabled, she's disabled when she is in emotional pain. Are we talking the same language?

At this point in the session, I wanted to stop time, put the movement into a frame, and name it a masterpiece. It was absolutely beautiful for me to witness this family's revelation of how connected and wired they were to one another. This seemed to be the movement to real change for them. They were able to see each other in a new light. Another part of me was in complete awe in acknowledging my raw and unrefined state. I remember in my first painting class being unable to paint with color because my professor wanted me first to become acquainted to the nature of the oil paint, my painting knife, and my brushes. I realize that while I learn, I am still "painting in grayscale" until I understand my medium, my tools, my subject, and how to make my intention with all these aspects a reality.

For the three years of training, Minuchin was clear that he was hesitant to show students his tapes as a learning tool because they could not engage in his style of therapy; they had to find their own. At this point in my career I have a murky sense of my style. I know that one of my strengths is my calm, soothing demeanor. This can be helpful in some instances, but it leaves me unrefined when I need to be more tenacious. It is an aspect of myself that I need to develop to counter my tendency to try to rescue my clients.

I continued to watch as Minuchin focused on the connections between people.

Caroliña:	I believe so.
Minuchin:	Okay. So she had found that she has become a people watcher, she watches you, she knows when you are in pain. She responds emotionally. That's nice.
Christina:	I don't really know when she's in pain, but when I look at her face I can see like she's feeling sick or something's wrong.
Minuchin:	That's wonderful, and that means you are growing up with a kind of view of how to see people. You know I am a psychiatrist and that's what psychiatrists do—they look at people and they try to understand people, and psychologists do that also. That's our job, so you are growing up into a very interesting lady.
Christina:	[Looks to mother]What is it?
Minuchin:	Look at David when you have a question. Don't look at Mom. Look at David.
Christina:	The thing that he said I don't know how to say it.
David:	A psychiatrist?
Christina:	Yeah, what is that? What kind of job is it?
Minuchin:	Beautiful! She is sharp!
David:	Well, they go to school. They are a doctor. It's just a different form of doctor. And it's to understand people and, at times, be able to help them and their situation.
Christina:	Oh. So like here. Like somebody comes over and somebody's frustrated and that . . .
David:	Right. And that was the point of us coming here in the beginning, because a lot of the times you were lying, you were not doing good in school, you were giving both of us a lot of attitude and we noticed that something was bothering you but we couldn't figure it out. So we came to the doctor to try and figure out what is it that's going on. So that's pretty much where they come in. That's what a psychiatrist does. They try and figure out how can they help the situation to make it better.

Minuchin: Christina? Did you see that your dad can answer questions as well as your mom? You can ask him instead of asking her? You know, I will give you an idea that sometimes when Mom is in pain and you need something, you should ask him.

I know I can make this type of intervention, as I had it in my head during my time with the family to make sure that I highlighted that Caroliña and David were different. Perhaps my eyes are not as open as Minuchin's, because when I saw nonverbals, which were meaningful to me, I saw them more as an individual behavior. Minuchin, in this instance, saw the nonverbals of who looked to whom as a relational message. Christina was tightly connected to her mother. His intervention frees her up to not have to be so worried about how her mother is feeling, and allows her to connect with her stepfather.

Caroliña: She does.

Minuchin: Christina, I really was impressed with the way in which he was able to tell you what my job is, because that's exactly what it is. I will pretty much finish. I got to know you and like you a lot. Because you are very smart, you have a very nice way of being with people, and I like your smile. And the question that you are feeling so much for people, it's nice up to a point. It's up to a point, because it's temporary. So think about that when she has a temper tantrum. Think that sometimes she takes upon herself the job of being a healer and that's too young to start this job. Sweetheart, I loved to meet you.

I sat in this session and was amazed that in this short hour it was possible to witness that a therapist's "way of being" with this family I had worked with moved Christina from the position of the problem child who has anger problems to a loving and caring daughter who is trying to be a healer. His reframe moved her from the IP (a lying girl who had temper tantrums) to an integral position in her family (a loving daughter who was too connected to her mother's pain). These were the goals I had in mind yet was handicapped from accomplishing. Minuchin also challenged the parents to find a different way of operating. As he said, Christina is too young to be a healer for her mother, which implies that wife needs to turn to husband for the support she is receiving from her daughter, and husband needs to be more alert to how he can be helpful to his wife.

CONCLUSION

For two sessions, my hesitancy to really challenge the adults in the family, combined with my unconscious urging to rescue Christina, led me to be ineffective. I had many goals in mind that I had learned in my trainings with Minuchin: externalizing the symptom, increasing people's identities, and exploring greater nuances of the family organization. Not only did I not accomplish these goals, I unwittingly decreased identities and maintained the symptom on the Identified Patient. Yet after this session, we sat and processed all that unfolded during our time together in the room. I was struck by many themes Minuchin often spoke of and demonstrated during the short 50 minutes: complementarity, mutual responsibility, the family healing one another, enactment, stroking, and kicking, and the therapist using him (or her) self as an instrument. The thing that really brought it all home for me was that I had been the therapist in the room with this family myself. I had probably learned more experientially in those 50 minutes than hours listening to explanations on other cases and lectures of theory.

In many ways, my journey of becoming an "uncertain expert" or a "decentered but influential therapist" has been about learning to perfect the technique of looking at my left foot. The first couple of times I attempted to have the family talk with one another rather than myself, I forgot to look away, to make myself smaller, to focus on something other than them, and my attempts were unsuccessful. Or, I would set the events in motion and interrupt too soon, not giving myself time to think, or freedom to intervene by doing nothing. Yet, as I grow as a clinician, I find that I have what Minuchin calls the homunculus, or the "little self," tell me that I am too proximal, that I need space to see and not just to hear.

I am unsure when I will gain the confidence in myself as a therapist to move past what my age or appearance might be, and to take the risks and challenge the families in ways that make sense to me. But I know that I need to, and perhaps that is one of the greatest strengths I can have, to be able to see where I need to see.

I have provided you with a discussion of a case in which I believe that I "failed" and in which I learned. I have the knowledge, and know that there are areas in which I don't know, and now realize that I can also take more risks than I thought I could. Through my work with Minuchin, I have grown in many ways. One of my misconceptions at the beginning of our work together may have been that I would learn to execute Structural Family Therapy perfectly, but this is not the case. I learned some valuable tools and concepts from Minuchin that I can apply in my own ways, and in doing that I have become a more versatile and less narrow therapist. I have learned to trust more than my sense of hearing when I am in the room with a family, to see and to evaluate the system that elicits behavior and patterns and interaction, and to observe myself and how I impact those in the system. I have learned that the only skin I can be comfortable in is my own, that I do possess an expertise that is uniquely mine in the perception that I bring, and that when I believe what I am saying, my voice is powerful. I learned that asking relational questions takes work, but that the result is worth the effort of developing the skill. Above all, the experience has helped me to become a better systemic family therapist, and that is a risk worth the taking. I hope that the things I learned in the analysis of my "failure" in contrast to Dr. Minuchin's "success" provides you with a new way of looking at yourself and your work with families.

WHAT CAN WE LEARN?

This chapter provided a comparison between a young novice therapist and an older, very experienced therapist. Each was attempting the same goal: to move a family from being stuck in their problem to the experience of more harmony. One therapist succeeded, while the other did not. In this section, we will look at each of our generic questions and describe the differences between the therapists.

The Therapist

Walker attempts to join the family, yet is undercut even before the session begins by the mother's challenging of her age and her credentials. However, she also handicapped herself by doubting her abilities and exhibiting performance anxiety before the session.

As such, she lost her maneuverability, as she was not able to take on an expert position. Instead of the "uncertain expert," she was just "uncertain." From this hesitant position she did not trust herself to challenge the family's narrative. She was also not cognizant, at the time, of how she viewed things on more of an individualistic than systemic manner.

Externalizing the Symptom

The Rodriguez family presents the daughter, Christina, as the Identified Patient. They hold that she has temper tantrums, sadness, behavior issues, and even when she is nice it is really manipulation. Walker knows that she wants to challenge this presentation. However, she is unsure how. Her primary attempt, which is to talk about Christina's observance of and ability to get people to do what she would like as being a "genius," is obfuscated by the parents as being the actions of a manipulative and troubling child. The therapist's difficulty in externalizing the symptom comes from her narrow view of the connections between people. She is very good at being empathetic to individuals. Yet, family therapy demands the therapist understand a family's process.

Minuchin quickly begins to deconstruct the family's narrative by connecting Christina's behavior with the atmosphere of the home. He informs the family that if there is an improvement in Christina's behavior it is because something in the house has changed. Implicit in this is an understanding that child and parents are connected to one another. Later in the session, Minuchin discovers that Caroliña was in an abusive marriage, leading him to hypothesize that part of Christina's behavior, was as a protective measure for her mother. He then, after finding out about Caroliña's physical illness, discusses how mother and daughter are connected. This again shifts what seems like an individual problem into a symptom that serves a function with a system.

Layers of Identity

During the sessions with the Therapist, there was not much movement in each person's identity, including the Therapist's. Even before the first session, she and the family viewed her as a nervous young student-therapist who was not an expert. The Therapist could not figure out how to enhance the way she viewed herself, which would have helped the Rodriguez family to see her differently. This may have opened up possibilities in the therapeutic relationship. The Therapist did attempt to shift Christina's identity from an angry child to a smart person. However, this move was undermined by the parents. During her sessions with them, there did not seem to be an attempt to change either parent's identity.

Throughout the consultation session, Minuchin was able to utilize himself and his multiple layers of identity to help move the family toward a different experience. He entered the session as an older professor of psychiatry. The family viewed him as a teacher and family therapist, which put them in a position to be ready to listen to him. However, Minuchin played with this identity by presenting himself as an uncertain but hopeful expert who was a detective who loves mysteries. This encouraged the Rodriguez' to join him in exploring the mystery of their family's dilemma.

While, the Therapist was not able to enhance Christina's identity as the problem child, Minuchin was able to take the presented characteristic of her being a people watcher and made that into a strength. He moved Christina from being a behaviorally problematic child with anger issues into a very bright young girl who was big-hearted, compassionate, helpful, socially observant, and a protector of her mother. This allowed the family to see Christina in new ways.

Minuchin enhanced David's identity, shifting him from an aloof husband who is even-tempered to a (step)father that Christina could go to (instead of her being so connected to her mother). With Caroliña, Minuchin distinguished her from David (the shift from a "we" to two distinct people). He was able to connect her positions of being a disciplinarian, a rescuer, and a sufferer of pain to demonstrate how these aspects of her self were connected to the other family members.

Family Organization

The Rodriguez' are a family of four, yet they have multiple subsystems. A few of these include mother-daughter/imprisoned father; mother-husband/daughter; mother-daughter/husband; mother-husband-son/daughter.

The Therapist primarily stayed within the subsystem of mother-father in a hierarchical position to the daughter. This limited view of the multiple subsystems of the family kept the therapist trapped in working within the established perspective of the parents. She was not able to move outside of this and see the opportunities for exploration.

Minuchin, from the first minutes of the session, challenged this limited view of subsystems. When the mother made a comment about "we," referring to herself and her husband, Minuchin quickly discussed how he and his wife have two different voices, and that Caroliña and David have two different voices, as well. This separates the parents into distinct entities, which allows him, toward the end of the session, to talk with Christina about being able to go to David rather than Carolina.

Two Families with Similar Family Organization (Commentary by Minuchin)

As you finish reading about Christina and her family, I invite you to visit the Boyds, who you met in the fourth chapter of the book. These two families have structural characteristics in common. Both are stepfamilies in which the mother brought to the second marriage a daughter from the first, and now there is a younger child from both parents. When I described the Boyds, I said that the therapist had deconstructed the family into separate subsystems.

When I separated the whole into different subsystems, the shifting contexts made the following patterns clear:

- Parents' focal concern with daughter's destructive behavior
- Parents' close investigation and control of daughter
- Mother and daughter's distressing proximity
- Husband's passive observation of mother and daughter's liaison
- Husband and wife's diminished interaction via their concentration on daughter's behavior

The generic questions, then, to consider in working with stepfamilies are these:

1. If wife loves her husband, is that a threat to her daughter?
2. If wife loves her daughter, is that a threat to her husband?
3. Will the biological mother allow her husband to parent her daughter?
4. Will the daughter promote conflict and distance between husband and wife?

As you can see, when I came to work with the Rodriguez family, I had a previous map that guided my work with both the Rodriguez and the Boyd families, since they share certain characteristics. But "Minuchin" is a different Minuchin. While I follow the same map, I am guided by the different contexts and, after more than 10 years, I am a different person with a different style of working.

In my first challenge to the family—"challenge the symptom bearer"—with Whitney (the Boyd's daughter), I joined with an adolescent and engaged with her in an intellectual exploration of meaning or the meaning of metaphors. Later, I invited her to explore her mother's responses to her behavior and a self-exploration of her participation in their distressing proximity.

With Christina, I joined spontaneously in play with a young, bright child, and I was explicit in my feelings of pleasure with our encounter. Working with a young child, I use my spontaneous pleasure without being concerned with meaning.

Working with the Boyds, I positioned myself in an intermediate position of distance. I was deliberate, I developed strategies that were (in the beginning) invisible to the family, like when I called the father a "detective," but I challenged control. I played with language and used humor and irony, and in general I felt like an old man protective of this young couple and empathizing with the mother.

With the Rodriguez family, I am more spontaneous and proximal. I use myself as a teacher, exploring with Caroliña the nature of her physical pain and the consequences of her pain on her caretaking behavior. I direct the child to talk with her father and block her access to Caroliña (her mother). I think that the fact that I am a supervisor of Sarah Walker influenced the nature of my response, since I feel I am a teacher of the therapist and of the family. Besides, as an older person, I allow myself more spontaneity and less intellectual restraint.

I want the readers to look at the fact that it was the same "Minuchin" that was influenced by the family organization, but being in a different stage in his life, he is a different responder. Also, consider the importance of the homunculus on my left shoulder and how he shifts in different stages of life.

10

TOO CLOSE FOR COMFORT

Roseann Pascale

While a Master's student of marriage and family therapy, I was fortunate to be invited to take part in the weekly consultation group with Dr. Minuchin. From the brief overview of Structural Therapy I received in my Introduction to Theories course, I knew that Dr. Minuchin's method was a more directive, confrontational form of therapy than the postmodern therapies I was learning. I was not entirely sure the model would fit my sensibilities, but I could not pass up the opportunity to study with one of the field's founding fathers.

During this training, Dr. Minuchin often spoke about the importance of being a self-observing therapist and the ways in which our life experiences help shape our therapeutic strengths and blind spots. He encouraged us to remain aware of the roads taken and the roads still available to us. The learning process ultimately is one of doing, not talking.

As a beginning therapist, my therapeutic style and approach is still in development. A native New Yorker of Italian ancestry, my impulse is to be straightforward and direct. Contrasting that, I have been told that I have a calm, down-to-earth demeanor, which seems to put clients at ease. Still green behind the ears, I have only seen a handful of clients at this point in my training. However, I have a fair amount of life experience that influences me as a therapist. I am a woman, daughter, ex-wife, single mother, artist, co-worker, and friend. I've lost a parent, moved far from home, faced a life-threatening illness, and am now approaching my mid-century mark and the silence of an empty nest. After two decades as a producer in the television industry, I've set my foot upon a new path and am following a lifelong ambition to put my energies into helping others. Through this chapter, I hope to be useful to fellow students just starting out on their path, who might find themselves confronted with similar challenges when working with therapeutic issues, particularly those related to proximity.

THE COUPLE AND THE REACTIVE THERAPIST

While participating in Dr. Minuchin's consultation group, I worked with a young couple, Lydia and Carlos, who came to therapy to address domestic issues related to gender roles, power, and privilege. My personal objective in working with these clients was to see if I could be effective working within the principles of structural family therapy I had been learning. At the same time, many other family therapy models were fresh in my head and my ability to be particularly competent with any approach was questionable. In the therapy room, I often felt perplexed. I wanted to follow my instincts and actively help my clients define the hurdles I saw before them. Yet at the same time, I longed to be more elegant in my work, and understood the ineffectiveness of imposing simplistic solutions on them. I struggled to find my voice.

During one consultation session, as a group of us sat sipping coffee, Minuchin uttered a most provocative statement: "All families that come to therapy are wrong." A collective gasp could be heard in the room. Non-normative, postmodern colleagues reading this might be relieved to learn what followed this pronouncement. This is where Dr. Minuchin's sublime and seemingly confrontational methods reveal themselves to be among the most empathetic and respectful; a sheep in wolf's clothing. Yes, "The client is always wrong"... but they are wrong "because they are richer than they think they are, and have alternatives available that they are not yet aware of."

The same, Minuchin informed us, is true for us as beginning therapists. My experience has been that although I have learned various theories and interventions, when I get into the room I inevitably act from who I am, while grasping onto one (or more) theoretical approaches to guide me. When I begin to act instinctively, I tend to lose my cognitive path and find myself drawn into the family drama. Due mostly to these issues of proximity, it is often difficult for me to identify the available alternatives.

A common error that I made as a new therapist was being too eager to *do* something. In fact, I felt *obligated* to do something. I found that sitting back and doing less with clients who are demanding my attention and seeking solutions is a challenge. I wanted so much to help my clients that my eagerness caused me to become entrapped, as they were, in their struggles. As a beginning therapist, I believe becoming more competent in this area will have the greatest impact on my effectiveness in the room and my ability to be of use to my clients.

In the case of Carlos and Lydia, I was presented with an ambitious and assertive young wife and her genial and compliant husband. They were parents of two young children from Lydia's previous marriage and a 6-month-old infant from their own union. Lydia initiated therapy to address conflicts primarily related to equity and initiative in their relationship. Common domestic concerns such as responsibilities for childcare and the distribution of household chores topped her list of complaints, beyond which were the more complicated matters of finances, co-parenting, and lack of intimacy.

Lydia was frustrated and exhausted by the demands of spending her days in service to three small children. She admitted she could be "harsh," but insisted her abrasive tone was out of love and concern for her family. Lydia directly identified Carlos as the Identified Patient, the person in need of change. Carlos, for the most part, took a passive yet defensive position. He enjoyed the autonomy granted to him by virtue of his gender and cultural norms. He attempted to have influence, but found himself out-talked and out-thought. His responses fluctuated between full-out defensiveness or tempered compliance. He was placed in a double bind—Lydia would say she wanted him to take the wheel, yet insisted he not deviate from her prescribed path.

Minuchin taught us that the preferred therapeutic stance is to be active, but decentered—to maintain a meta-position in relationship to the family. At first, I did not understand how I could be active without being central. Eventually I came to see that I was looking at the concept too literally. It is not a matter of a therapeutic style; rather, it is a question of how central a role I have in the dynamic between family members. Are they talking to me instead of each other? Am I explaining to one partner what the other one means? If I am doing anything like this, I am too central. Minuchin's lesson, that it is appropriate to stay active and enter the family system to provoke, direct, and help them see alternatives, was a very difficult lesson for me to learn. In the transcripts that follow, you will see me be too central in this couple's dynamic, where I unwittingly maintained the therapeutic process in which they looked to me for approval, rejection, and, ultimately, solutions. Rather than a family therapist, I became at worst a judge and jury, and at best an advisor or counselor.

This one concept, a cornerstone of Dr. Minuchin's teaching, has proven most difficult for me to put into practice—one of proximity. The inconsistency with which I am able to maintain detached concern sabotaged many of the interventions I attempted and limited my and the client's possibilities for change. Through reviewing my sessions with Minuchin, I came to realize how I was drawn into their relational dynamic, helping to maintain the symptom and keep the clients locked into their limited definition of self.

Following are session excerpts in which I wrangled with issues of authority and proximity. I will share my attempts at transversing the slippery slope between joining this couple and being swept away in the avalanche of their complaints. My comments to the reader about what I was doing and why, at that particular point in the session, are italicized in the right hand column.

SESSION ONE: ROSEANN'S INTERVIEW
Getting Connected . . . Too Connected

Carlos was late to our first session. I made the mistake of having Lydia join me in the room while we waited for Carlos. During this time, she provided me with a laundry list of his errors. In retrospect, I should have waited for Carlos to show up to begin the session, especially since this was our first session. What I got from these minutes without him was the content of Lydia's frustration and anger, which tainted me to view her as overbearing. Having a sense of the one up/one down complementary pattern of their relationship from this conversation, in the first moments of our session I addressed myself to Carlos and used humor to join with him, while playfully challenging his submissive position.

Therapist:	So, Carlos, why did you come here today?	
Carlos:	Lydia said we had to come here.	
Therapist:	Do you do everything she says?	*I took note of his willingness to speak from a submissive position and challenged this presentation of self. I was*

		smiling as I said this, which helped him accept it, even as he experienced it as a challenge.
Carlos:	Well, I'm trying to.	
Therapist:	Will you do anything I say?	*Seeing that he was earnest, I continued to playfully provoke him, while still challenging his position.*
Carlos:	No. Of course I want to be here too, to work on our relationship.	
Therapist:	Was it your idea to come to counseling?	*I know it was Lydia's initiative, but I wanted to explore how they make decisions and how he responded to my challenge.*
Carlos:	To be honest, I think we both agreed on having counseling.	
Therapist:	Can you tell me what the issues are?	
Carlos:	It's as simple as me being late here. It's nobody's fault, right? She told me to be here at two o'clock. I was on time coming. But I got caught in traffic and in unanticipated school zones. I got a haircut before I came, it usually takes 20 minutes.	
Therapist:	Sounds reasonable. [I look to Lydia]	*I know from her comments prior to the session that Lydia is not okay with him being late. I offer an accepting perspective to challenge her certainty and demonstrate another possible interpretation.*
Lydia:	Well, I don't think it's reasonable, because I think that the way you treat something shows how important it is to you. I also had things to do.	*At this point, I wanted to have them relate to each other rather than both talking to me, to try to keep some distance, and not get engaged in the content.*
Therapist:	Talk to each other.	

Lydia:	I feel like you got your priorities mixed up today. You left work, which is earning your money, while getting a haircut is spending your money, and you still allowed getting your haircut make you late to our appointment. You should've gotten up and left because this is more important.

Therapist:	So is that how it usually goes between you?	*Not wanting to fall into the abyss of content, I bring their attention to a focus on their way of relating, expanding the IP from Carlos to their way of relating.*

Carlos:	No, this is pretty smooth.
Lydia:	This is actually very mild compared to the way it usually goes.
Therapist:	How does it usually go?
Lydia:	It gets loud.

I had spent enough time learning from Dr. Minuchin to know that having the clients talk to each other provided me room to sit back and think. And I thought that was what I had done. However, in looking back at the transcript, I intervened much too quickly in this initial attempt at an enactment. I knew I did not want to get caught up in content, however, I did not allow enough of their interactions with one another to get a better sense of their process. I then had to ask them to describe their process rather than me being able to observe it. My eagerness to intervene, as well as my quick sense of familiarity with this situation, led me to be too proximal and central.

During our consultation sessions, Minuchin encouraged us to express how our clients impacted us, as this has an influence on what we do in the therapy room. I could sense my frustration with this woman, thinking that she was too overpowering in the relationship. While I thought my conceptualization was systemic, I was engaging in the same process the couple was—they brought an IP to the session (Carlos' aloofness) and I brought an IP to the session (Lydia's aggressiveness). I thought that Lydia's suppression of Carlos' voice in their relationship was the core problem that needed to be addressed. I felt that until Carlos took his place beside his wife, rather than under her, the relationship would continue to deteriorate. However, my focus on expanding his identity from passive/submissive husband was not matched by an equal effort to expand her identity from that of overbearing/controlling wife. The reason for this is that I was internally reactive to her manner of speaking, which brought me too close to her, and this limited my ability to see beyond the self she was most accustomed to presenting.

AT THE CENTER OF THE CONFLICT

In the following excerpt, I began an effort to expand Carlos' identity from the incompetent person Lydia had determined him to be, to the competent employee his employer and customers see him as.

Therapist:	[To Carlos] Are you good at what you do?
Carlos:	Very good at what I do.
Lydia:	I'd hire him to work for me.
Therapist:	How do you know you're good at what you do?
Carlos:	I have recommendations from clients. They call my boss to give positive feedback from the job.
Therapist:	So you're a competent person.
Carlos:	Very competent.

Therapist:	So as such a competent person, how have you managed to get yourself into a situation where your wife feels she has to speak to you like you are a child? How do you think that happened?	*This is my attempt at a "stroke & kick." I acknowledge his competence, while addressing his active role in creating his wife's way of relating to him.*
Carlos:	Well, maybe if you think she speaks to me like a child, you should ask her why she does that.	*He gets defensive and rejects any responsibility for creating her way of relating to him, which was okay with me, because I wanted to unbalance and challenge his role as passive victim.*
Therapist:	I'm asking you.	

Carlos:	Well, if she speaks to me like a child, that's her choice. That's how she figures she has to communicate, and that's fine.	
Therapist:	That is just my perception. Do you feel like that's not accurate?	*Seeing he was not willing to directly address Lydia's way of speaking to him, or his role in it, I back off and take the position of the uncertain expert.*
Carlos:	You know it can be for good causes, for good reason.	
Therapist:	Sometimes she's right?	
Carlos:	Yeah, sometimes she's right.	

Unfortunately, because I did not effectively manage my reactivity to Lydia's manner of communicating, and because she was so certain she knew what was needed, I could not see or address the complementary nature of their conflict. Most sessions were so accusatory in nature, I continued to relate to her as the dominant, demanding self she presented. This went on for a few sessions, with occasional moments of empathetic conversations directed at easing the demands she placed on herself as well as on Carlos. I failed to really challenge Carlos on his part in this dynamic, because I viewed him as the victim in the sessions, and therefore, did not help them to explore how he was contributing to their explosive dynamic. Instead, I ended up defending him.

BACKING OUT BUT STAYING IN

During one of the supervisory consultations where I showed parts of previous sessions, Minuchin reminded me that I could not sit between them—that that position was too central and would not lead to change. In my next session, I tried to extricate myself from their conflictual back-and-forth interchanges. In the following excerpt, the couple is once again blaming the other for the misery that they experience as a couple.

Therapist:	I'm going to take a stop, because you're both talking to me, but I'm not in a position to tell you who's right, who's wrong. I'm not a judge. I'm not going to give you a verdict.	*They are in a state of high conflict and demanding my attention. I state my position, but it has little impact on their desire to continue to blame each other.*

Lydia:	As far as our relationship is concerned, the bottom line is I'm fed up. I am fed up with always having to be in the house with the kids, and that's why I act out in various ways, okay? I act out! All my life, I've had to bear the burden and now that I have a partner, I'm still bearing the burden! Why do I always have to know everything? Why do I have to be a master planner?	*After many more minutes of this bickering and several unsuccessful attempts at interrupting, I see an opening where the conversation can take a relational turn.*
Therapist:	Very good question! I think you would both benefit from asking yourselves that question.	
Lydia:	Because if I don't, everything is going to go to hell in a handbasket, that's why! I want to see the attributes of a successful person. You know we only have one or two mornings where we have a few allotted hours when we could do something . . . get your ass up!	
Carlos:	Why don't you get your ass up?	
Lydia:	Why do I have to say, "Get up, get up, [Banging the tissue box on table] come on, get up!" Look at Roseann's face. Can you read her body language?	
Carlos:	You read it!	
Lydia:	I'm not the one that's running my mouth and she just said be quiet! Because she doesn't feel that she can get in a word, and neither do I.	

| Therapist: | It's not that I don't feel like I can get in a word, although clearly I can't. It's that you two will just continue this. I could probably sit here for hours and just do the same dance and I don't have a magic wand to say. . . | |
| Lydia: | [She interrupts me] Because there's core issues. We each have core issues, okay? And we need a third party, which would be you, to actually say to Carlos, "There's a big red flag that your wife has been waving!" | *Here she takes a symmetrical position to me. She attempts to instruct me on what I should do and the role I should play. This is an obvious case of how the client makes demands on the therapist. It is also an indication of how much I have entered into their system, that she relates to me as she does to Carlos.* |

It was not only the power struggle between the spouses that I had to be conscious of, but also the power struggle between my clients and me. At one point, Dr. Minuchin suggested that I had a problem with being an authority. He noted that I confused being authoritative with being an authoritarian.

Put in the position of expert, I struggle with how to be an authority without being overbearing. In looking back at my transcripts, I see that I often asked questions of Carlos when the content was meant for Lydia. Other times, I couched my comments indirectly, hoping the clients would catch my meaning.

I have since come to see that I was not relating to Lydia and Carlos as individuals, or as a couple, but as archetypes. It had become a feminist quandary for me, although not one addressed by the primary principles of the feminist critique. I did not have a female client who needed support and encouragement to find her voice, or develop a sense of agency. Lydia was quite capable of expressing her anger directly and asserting her needs and wants. Having grown up in America, Lydia thought she had entered into an egalitarian relationship with Carlos, only to realize that the grooves of traditional gender roles superseded even the most honorable of vows and intentions. She still found herself bound by the inescapable duties of motherhood and lack of economic resources.

Throughout my work with Lydia and Carlos, I struggled with becoming symmetrical to her. Her demanding presence felt like a vortex of energy that threatened to swallow up not only her husband and children, but also me. Although I was able to maintain a relatively convincing appearance of detachment, it took all I had to manage my reactivity to her within each exchange. As Minuchin later pointed out to me, my frustration with Lydia tempered the way I viewed what I should do in therapy; restricting me from being able to see the couple in a different way—one where they mutually influenced one another and each contributed to their misery.

None of this is to say that I hadn't joined with Lydia. I believe I was in fact too joined with her. Our dynamic was a sisterly one, me being the elder, trying to illuminate the ineffective and contrary way she presented her needs. But my focus was her as the IP, and that was ultimately a fatal flaw in my work with this couple.

Seeing the box I was in, Dr. Minuchin lifted the lid. He told me I did not respect the husband. I was confused. Of course I respected him. I was coming to his defense! But Dr. Minuchin pointed out that I was not *respecting* him, I was *protecting* him. This was an "ah-ha" moment that began the shift in my vision of this case.

In my attempts to assist the husband by challenging the wife, I was reinforcing his position as a man who needed a woman to speak for him—I was mothering him. During our consultation, Carlos spoke of being ill as an infant and having a mother and step-mother both caring for him. And now, as a 35-year-old man, he had managed to create a similar dynamic between his wife and myself.

In further contemplating this single piece of enlightenment, I again considered gender. How can I, as a nurturing, motherly figure, use myself in the room in a way that was authoritative and considerate yet respectful? Particularly in relationship to the hier-archal paradigm of Structural Family Therapy, what is my personal stance as a woman in the room—toward the wife, toward the husband? How could I incorporate the wis-dom and authority of the mother figure, without treating my clients like children? And how did my gender affect how they each related to me? If a male therapist had a similar approach as I, how would his gender affect their perception of his challenges?

The hurdle that I could not clear was one of proximity. I was too invested in helping this couple, and that limited my ability to use myself in a way that might have produced significant change in the way they perceived each other. Although my clients reported some improvement after seven sessions, they were as prone to their relational standoffs as they were in the first.

What did not occur to me at the time, because of my reactivity to Lydia, was how Carlos, although he protested otherwise, may also have been content in his position, however uncomfortable he found it. Later on, when reviewing the tapes of my sessions, I saw how often Carlos would recruit me to see his perspective and then, when I was fully engaged in the effort to help him deliver his message to Lydia, he would retreat.

After the presentation and discussion of my interview, Dr. Minuchin conducted a consultation with the family. It is presented below as the second session. The italicized comments in the right hand column, and the subsequent text of the chapter, are written by authors of the book and are directed to the reader.

Prior to this consultation, Dr. Minuchin asked me what I wanted from the session. I told him I wanted Carlos to rise up and stand on level ground with Lydia. I felt this was ultimately the only way this couple would be able to withstand and conquer the myriad of conflicts and challenges experienced by new parents and remain intact as a couple.

SESSION TWO: MINUCHIN'S INTERVIEW
Connected Yet Unconnected

Minuchin continually impressed upon the students in the supervisory group that one of the therapist's primary responsibilities was to challenge the client on behalf of their possibilities, to criticize in a way that will expand them. Following are excerpts from a consultation Minuchin had with Carlos and Lydia, where he challenges Lydia and Carlos in a way that expands their sense of themselves and each other. He connects husband and wife into a mutually complementary relationship where they each help to create the other person. These excerpts begin approximately midway through the consultation session after having explored aspects of each of their childhoods.

Minuchin:	Do you think that I didn't hear you?
Lydia:	Do I think you heard me? A little bit, yeah. But I think you disarmed my approach. Like it's hard for you to get a full read on me.
Minuchin:	Oh no, my dear.
Lydia:	No?
Minuchin:	You are very easy to read. You are not a complex person. You're an intelligent person. You're a talented person. But you are not a person that is difficult to read. You are relatively simple, because you don't accept complexities. Everything needs to be reduced in complexity, and then you accept it. So, I know you. You are not a complex person and I understand why and I accept the reasons and I understand that. Now it's much more difficult to be your husband, but it's not difficult to be your therapist. It just is a question of helping you to understand that complexity is good.
Lydia:	Is it?
Minuchin:	Yes. But uncertainty is necessary. That when you find a crossroad, maybe both are

Rather than seeing Lydia's rigidity as self-serving, Minuchin sees her as trapped by it. He redefined what Roseann saw as her bossy manner as an inability to work with uncertainty and complexity. He stroked her by saying she was intelligent then kicked her by suggesting that, unlike her husband, he himself did not think she was wise. At the same time, Minuchin told her that uncertainty is good and called upon Carlos to help her learn to accept uncertainty. In this way, he enlisted Carlos as a competent husband, able to meet his wife's needs.

In moments when Carlos defended Lydia from Minuchin's pointed perceptions, Minuchin reframed Carlos's right. And so you want to reduce Carlos to simple parameters. [To Carlos] In order for her to accept, you need to be very simple, so she can observe you. You are a very complex person, you live a complex life, you come from a different culture.

Lydia: [To Carlos] No, I can't give you any more time. I told you I wanted something in black and white of where we were going to be staying. I left that up to you to decide. . . .

Minuchin: Lydia?

Lydia: Yes.

Minuchin: You talk a lot.

Lydia: I do. I talk a lot. Repetitively.

Minuchin: Do you know that if you talk a lot, he talks much less? That he constructs you? Do you understand the concept? You construct his silence.

Lydia: Maybe.

Minuchin: You see, I am an observer. You constructed his silence. Because you talked, talked, talked. . . .

Lydia: Dr. Minuchin, this is like the 10th time we have had this conversation. Ten times.

Minuchin: I just observed this time, so I don't know.

desire for harmony as a strength. When Lydia tried to enter the dialogue from a symmetrical position, Minuchin addressed her rigid thinking and defined the primary relational issue between them, that she constructs his silence.

Although people realize that they are connected to one another, they usually are not aware of how much what they do informs how the other person reacts to them and how this then informs how they respond. This notion of mutuality, of circularity, is a systems idea that shifts individual action into a relational paradigm. In the previous excerpt, Minuchin lays the foundation that Lydia and Carlos are ultimately connected to one another and in a continuous process of creating how each other is in the relationship. Since they each create the other, they can change to create a different other.

Lydia:	Ten times.
Minuchin:	Hold it a moment. Do you like this dialogue?
Lydia:	No. I don't.
Minuchin:	Do you want to change it?
Lydia:	I don't even want to have it!
Minuchin:	I'm just asking you if you don't like it, do you want to change it? Change the dialogue, I mean.
Lydia:	Yes.
Minuchin:	It's easy.
Lydia:	Please tell me how. Please tell me.
Minuchin:	I'm telling you. You don't listen.
Lydia:	I'm listening.
Minuchin:	No, you're not listening. I did tell you.
Lydia:	You said stop talking like this.
Minuchin:	And give space.
Lydia:	How much space?
Minuchin:	No, give space.
Lydia:	Dr. Minuchin.

Minuchin:	[to Carlos] Wait. Wait. Wait. And answer. Answer in such a way that she hears you. Go ahead. Do you feel controlled by her? Do you feel she's a very controlling person?
Carlos:	I don't feel controlled by her. But she is controlling.
Minuchin:	You feel she tries to control you?
Carlos:	Sometimes, yeah.
Minuchin:	You're not hearing her. You both are very similar, and an issue that is very important is that when she needs something, she needs it now. You belong to a culture in South America that would say "tomorrow." I know your culture. I am from that culture. Lydia cannot understand that, because tomorrow can be....
Carlos:	Too long.
Minuchin:	Too long. So when she is acting like that and you feel like she is trying to control you, your answer is correct. You said, "You don't control me." But she's not trying to control you. She wants to have security. It's a need. She's not trying to control you. She tries to control her anxiety. Can you reassure her? She needs your reassurance. "You, husband, loving husband, do something for me." That's what she said. She's saying it in a very bad way, but that's

Whereas Roseann tried to change this couple through an abstract challenge (change, but I am not telling you how you are connected to each other), Minuchin found a way to help them to be healers of one another. Although he expressed that Lydia needed to change, he did so through talking with Carlos about how he needed to be the person to make sure this happens. They were two individuals, but two individuals in a complex drama.

	what she means. Now I'm a translator of people like your wife, so I am translating her for you. Can you tell her, "Trust me"?
Carlos:	Yeah.
Minuchin:	And she's not controlling. You are satisfying her needs, but you are not allowing her to control you, because you don't like that. Can you understand me?
Carlos:	I understand. It's just that if we take that time out and we take a few moments to rethink instead of just react and speak, it probably would go a lot better. Maybe I would see that she is right in what she's saying.
Minuchin:	She's telling you, "I need." But instead of saying, "Carlos, I need," she says, "Carlos, you are wrong and I will control you." And you don't like that. You are right. It's not nice.
Carlos:	Okay.
Minuchin:	Can you help her?
Carlos:	Sure, I can help her.
Minuchin:	You have a big job. You have a job of providing her with a cane. You are going to be a cane.
Carlos:	A cane?
Minuchin:	Yeah, she needs you to lean on.
Carlos:	She can lean on me.
Minuchin:	She doesn't know that. That's your job. She needs to feel that she and her three children can lean on you. Mothers

Roseann's attempts at challenging the couple, especially Lydia, were borne out of her frustration with and distaste for what she viewed to be Lydia's assertiveness. Minuchin found a different way to connect with them, as he did not view Lydia's behavior as an affront but as an aspect of herself in relationship to others.

Carlos: Absolutely. I agree. She wants to know she has security. I know in my heart that there is no way I am going to let the children suffer. And if the children don't suffer, she doesn't suffer, because she's the mother of the children.

Lydia: I'm suffering.

Carlos: If the children don't suffer.
. . .

Minuchin: Wait a moment. When she said that, you did not acknowledge it. Let me lend you a word.

Carlos: Okay.

Minuchin: Ask her, "Why are you suffering?" Ask her that. Just know that I am lending this to you. You can borrow that.

Carlos: Okay.

Minuchin: Ask her why.

Carlos: Why are you suffering?

Lydia: Because I'm worried.

Minuchin: Isn't that interesting? You know she will be very hard to reassure. You need to know that.

Minuchin: (To Lydia) So, sometimes you are incorrect. And you don't accept uncertainty. He is immature and so are you. So you both have a lot of growth to make. A lot of growth.

(To Carlos) You will need to learn what is very, very hard for her: To relax. Just to relax. She's tight wound. She's very tight. And so it's nice that you have found a way when you are fighting, you are saying, "Okay, I will talk louder because I don't want to fight." But you need to understand that she does not want to control you. She wants to control life. She can't. She can't control life. How will you help her?

Carlos: Well, I'm going to try to help her. I think what she needs is that the things we can control let's take care of it. Some things we cannot control. I can't force her to change.

Minuchin: Yes, you can. Husbands and wives change each other, always. Continuously. I have been married for 60 years.

And so I know that my wife changed me a lot. And I changed her a lot. In this session, we have been one hour and you have changed. You have been very flexible. You have told her that you will do things to satisfy her. You talked about the fact that if she needs something, to relax, you will provide for her. That was very nice and that happened in one hour. You did that. I don't know if you noticed that. But I did notice. Did you notice?

Lydia: Mmmm-hmmmm.

Minuchin: You had noticed?

Lydia: I did.

| Minuchin: | Because you became more flexible than him. You did it. So, good for you. |
| Carlos: | You saw that flexibility, but I was thinking I need to do more and do things on time. |

One of the primary tools therapists use is reframing. In this section, Minuchin has reframed control as being tight, and spouses are then able to help one another relax. He has also, without bringing resistance, brought out the complementarity of the couple. The wife does not just act upon the husband, but she engages in behaviors because the husband prefers these actions. Husband and wife are together in a dance that maintains the symptoms of the couple. At the end of the session, Minuchin has brought out from them how they are mutually reliant on each other.

Minuchin:	Okay. Wonderful. She's a tight lady and you need to help her to relax. It's not that she wants to control you. You can relax about that. She cannot control you. She cannot control life. So you need to accommodate to her for a little while and hope that she will grow. She needs to grow up.
Carlos:	Yes. You need to grow up a little bit.
Minuchin:	Now you see the truth is that you don't want her to change so much, because you like the way she does things for you. You know that you like that she should take care of you, that she should do things for you. You know you like that.
Minuchin:	So I understand why you selected Lydia. Because you need somebody to protect you.

Lydia:	And I do.
Minuchin:	You do that. I know that.
Carlos:	I don't need anybody to protect me.
Minuchin:	I think you do. You see, she is a very protective person.
Carlos:	She is. She needs somebody to protect her.
Minuchin:	That's true, also.
Carlos:	I will protect her. But she does not accept protection sometimes.
Lydia:	That's true. That's true, Dr. Minuchin.
Minuchin:	Do you think you have learned something from me?
Carlos:	Absolutely. I believe I think I have learned something from you that is going to give me the opportunity to be more attentive and be a better listener. To be more open to hearing instead of just looking at a picture while she is trying to control me.

WHAT CAN WE LEARN?

This chapter explored the concept of proximity, how close or far a therapist is from their clients. While Roseann wanted to be decentered, her emotional reactions to the couple's dilemma, especially to the wife's behaviors, led her to lose her distant and wide lens, and become swept away in the anxiety of the couple's conflictual relationship. Minuchin, on the other hand, was able to join with husband and wife, yet remain decentered.

As a therapist, Roseanne made a mistake at the beginning of the meeting, perhaps because she was nervous about needing to do something. She started the first session without waiting for Carlos to attend. This allowed Lydia to express her frustration with Carlos and did not allow the therapist to see their interactions. Instead, she was focused on what looked like an "angry" individual.

Minuchin joins the family on a dual level. He lets them know that he is old, but he is also a professor of psychiatry and a teacher, which puts him in a hierarchical position. He is the "uncertain expert," because he tells them that he will "try to be useful" and that is the best he can do. He does not give them promises, but he is hopeful and has an expectancy that something will come out of the contact.

Externalizing the Symptom

When they first entered therapy, the couple offered up Carlos as the Identified Patient. His lack of engagement in decision making and timeliness in getting things done was presented as the problem. The therapist's difficulty in externalizing the symptom came from her proximity, where something about Lydia's way of dealing with her environment (what the therapist viewed as her controlling personality) narrowed the therapist's ability to view Lydia and Carlos in alternative ways.

Minuchin knew, from supervising the case, that Carlos was viewed as the Identified Patient. What he does in his session is focus on Lydia's childhood, where she experienced many losses and did not feel secure regarding who she lived with or where she lived (material not included in the consultation excerpts, due to space restraints). Minuchin explained to the couple that people with Lydia's type of childhood are anxious, so he actually begins by pathologizing, rather than his normal process of depathologizing. He took an idiosyncratic characteristic and transformed it into a label of who she is as a person. However, this was a prelude to shift the focus of where the problem was located. As Minuchin explained in his supervision of Angela (see Chapter 7), conducting an individual exploration between the therapist and one member of the family is acceptable as long as the therapist knows that this is a partial exploration and will expand it to include the other family members.

Carlos was initially the IP by being, in many ways, out of the loop in the family. Minuchin's individual focus with Lydia was a push to change her from an over-demanding wife to a woman in need. He told her that she needs to change by becoming able to have alternatives. In essence, he informed the couple that Lydia's narrowness defeats her, which is an individual orientation and makes her an IP. Minuchin then turns to the husband, saying that his wife needs him and that she cannot change unless he changes and becomes a healer. This strategic move shifts Lydia from being a controller to being in need of Carlos, and her illness is because he has not been a healer. The therapist wanted to move Carlos into a level of power equal to Lydia, but did not know how to do this. Minuchin knew that by helping the other person you become more of an authority.

Through the session, Minuchin worked with each person as an individual self, demanding an expansion of this self. After this individual exploration they are each expected to go home and work on being different. At the end of the consultation, Carlos is no longer seen as the IP but as the potential healer of his wife. Lydia's attempts to control have become her weakness, with which she needs her husband's help. The message that comes through to the couple is that they construct each other, and it is, each of them changing that will ultimately change the partner.

Layers of Identity

The Therapist lets us know about who she is through the narrative she presents in the beginning of the chapter. This includes her being an Italian New Yorker who is a mother and is finding herself in a new career. As we saw during the case, her identification with what was happening in the case became a constrictive lens. Being informed by feminist ideas focused her attention on a limited drama. Like many new therapists, she is not comfortable in using herself as a tool to push the family toward change.

Minuchin entered into the session as an expert, utilizing this position because he believed that Lydia needed someone in her relational field to be certain. Here we see quite a different Minuchin than we saw in previous chapters where he entered as the uncertain expert. With this couple, for strategic purposes, he is not uncertain. As he tells Lydia, "So I know you. You are not a complex person and I understand why and I accept the reasons and I understand that." Given his position and authority, this is an intervention that the younger therapist would not have been able to do. She would have been countered and the intervention would have most likely failed.

The session started by Carlos being viewed as disengaged and someone who could not be relied upon. Through the metaphor that Carlos needed to be Lydia's cane, he was shifted from being her burden to being her support. The session ends with Carlos becoming Lydia's protector.

Lydia's identity changed from an aggressive, demanding wife to a woman who had a difficult childhood to someone who has difficulty handling complexity. This shift, while in ways containing a pathologizing viewpoint, is a challenge for her to accept uncertainty. Whereas Lydia presented herself in a very strong position at the start of the first session, by the end of the consultation with Minuchin her attempts at control, seen earlier as aggressive, have been transformed into a need and call for help.

Family Organization

Roseann and Minuchin both made a critical mistake when it came to this case. They operated as if this was a twosome—Lydia and Carlos. However, this family was a fivesome. By not including the children in the sessions, both student and teacher restricted their view of the family system. Although the children were quite young, having them present in the room would have allowed the therapist to observe the parental system. They might have noticed patterns of who is most responsive to the children, who the children turn to for support, and how the parents negotiate duties with one another. As it was, they were only able to view the marital subsystem and potential pathways of movement were not available.

Reflection (Commentary by Minuchin)

One of the techniques in working with couples engaged in symmetrical escalation may be difficult for young practitioners, because it involves the creating of an unbalance in the couple, giving one of the members of the couple more influence over the other. It is also a technique that is unfair, because, temporarily, the therapist sides with one member against the other. But the crisis that this technique engenders challenges the symmetry of the couple and introduces complementarity, making Carlos, in this case, the healer of his wife. This change offers alternatives to the spouses' style of relating and it opens an avenue for new therapeutic interventions that can support the wife and reintroduce therapeutic neutrality.

11

SIX LESSONS FROM DR. MINUCHIN

Helen T. M. Reynolds

One day Dr. Minuchin placed a statue on a table in the center of the room and said, "When you begin thinking like that, you will be therapists." Staring at the metal figure on the table, I wondered how this single object could so completely encapsulate what we were trying to learn. The statue was and wasn't what it seemed: a metal figure of a man on horseback carrying a shield and a flag. The horse's head was made from the head of a hammer welded onto a length of thick chain that made up the spine and tail. Its legs were made from two pairs of bent pliers, which cleverly suggested the movement of a galloping horse. The rider had a bolt for a head, blacksmith's nails for feet, and carried a shield made from a flattened spoon. To learn to see as the sculptor had seen, explained Dr. Minuchin, was to see that a hammer could also be the head of a horse, a fork could be a flag, and a metal cable could be a rein. To learn to see a family in multiple ways would make us therapists.

This chapter describes how I came to understand Dr. Minuchin's metaphor, and thus began to see families through multiple lenses. I am a 35-year-old woman in the second year of a Marriage and Family Therapy Master's program. When I began receiving supervision from Dr. Minuchin, I had been studying family therapy for one year. I was seeing clients in our university clinic and had begun to develop some basic therapeutic skills that enabled me to join, ask open-ended questions, and generate useful metaphors. I was learning the techniques, tools, and concepts of a variety of theories, and I was doing my best to maintain a relationship-oriented perspective. However, I knew that in many ways I was at sea, an enthusiastic sailor rowing my little boat through the waves. My rowing technique was improving, but I didn't know if I was headed for land or going around in circles.

I had been told by numerous professors that one of the fastest and best ways to learn the art of therapy was to watch the tapes of my sessions, but I had avoided doing so for fear of how unpleasant it would be to watch myself fumble. In supervision with Dr. Minuchin, not only was I expected to watch my tapes, but to transcribe, annotate, and present them, as well. The experience was arduous, but it caused me to embark on a detailed analysis both of my therapeutic style and of my influence as a member of the

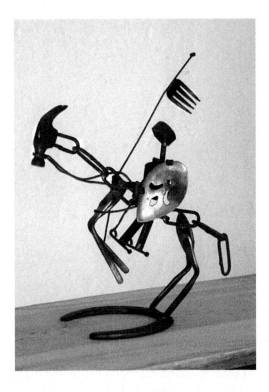

therapeutic system. Whether I go on to practice therapy that focuses on solutions or problems, family structure or emotional congruency, relational ethics or differentiation, the process of becoming a self-observing instrument has prepared me to be a much better therapist.

This chapter describes how the frequently nerve-wracking, regularly bewildering, and endlessly exhilarating experience of receiving supervision from Dr. Minuchin helped me to grow as a therapist. He once described the *homunculus* that he envisions sitting on his shoulder—a tiny version of himself removed from the action and observing everything that happens in his sessions. Luckily for the rest of us, Dr. Minuchin's homunculus is available for hire, and he now sits on my shoulder every time I enter the room with a family. I am still very much a beginner, but the time I spent with Dr. Minuchin has transformed how I approach therapy. I learned so much through his supervision that it will probably take years to fully integrate his teachings. In this chapter, I describe six of the most meaningful lessons I received from Dr. Minuchin, and I hope that they will be beneficial to other new therapists as they embark on their own careers.

THE WILSON FAMILY

While receiving supervision from Dr. Minuchin, I saw the Wilson family for nine sessions over the course of two and a half months. Lori Wilson had been in individual therapy since her divorce 6 months earlier, and she was worried that her two daughters were not coping well with the fallout from the breakup of her marriage. Natalie (aged 15), normally a very good student, was struggling in school, obsessing over random thoughts, and showing signs of depression. Jocelyn (aged 11) was very emotional and suffering from frequent nightmares. When I first began seeing the family, I quickly adopted Lori and the girls' version of the family narrative in which the girls' father, Ken, was cast as a villain: an overbearing, controlling man who had bullied Lori and her children for many years. From this perspective, the children were "damaged" individuals.

However, through Dr. Minuchin's supervision, I began to expand my understanding of how the family was currently functioning, and I gradually learned to see how the children's symptoms were being maintained by the family system. It seemed that long ago, Natalie and Jocelyn had become caught up in the middle of their parents' marriage.

Jocelyn had taken on the role of her mother's defender, and Natalie had become so highly attuned to Lori's needs that at times she could barely function. Even though Lori wanted only the very best for her children, somewhere along the way she had turned to them for emotional protection, and when the marriage fell apart and her emotional needs intensified, so too did the burden on Natalie and Jocelyn. Natalie herself eventually described with simple eloquence what had happened from her point of view: "*I think it started when I was 6 or7. I thought, who shall I side with—Mom or Dad? Because there is no such thing as neutral. Because sooner or later, you're going to side with somebody.*"

LESSON ONE: INCREASE THE COMPLEXITY OF YOUR VOICE

Every week, we met in Dr. Minuchin's living room to discuss the videos of one another's sessions. After watching a few minutes of each recording, Dr. Minuchin would pause the video and ask us to describe what we had seen. Whenever we limited our observations to the behavior of the family, he reminded us to widen our lens to include the behavior of the therapist. How had she entered the system? How was his presence in the room altering how the family related? As I watched I saw that, more often than not, the behavior of the therapist reinforced rather than interrupted the relational patterns of the family.

As a beginner, I was still learning to translate from the individual to the relational and to see how problems were maintained by systems. It felt like an extra step to recognize my own participation in a problematic family dynamic, particularly in the midst of a session. Nevertheless, in order to become useful to my clients I had to accept the challenge to observe myself in the room. A surgeon cannot walk into an operating theatre and expect her scalpel and forceps to repair a damaged lung irrespective of how she wields them. Nor can a therapist expect the theories and techniques he has studied to be helpful to a family regardless of how well he has learned the craft of therapy.

The first step in becoming a self-observing instrument came as something of a shock. When I began my training, I already had a lot of experience working with children, and I had a warm, empathetic manner. As I began seeing clients, I naturally relied on the skills that I already had, and I was rather surprised when Dr. Minuchin declared that my strengths would actually impede my development. As long as I continued to do what I was already good at, I would remain a specialist and my range as a therapist would be narrow. To expand the possibilities of what I was capable of meant that I had to abandon my competence and take a risk. As Dr. Minuchin put it, "You need to learn a language in which you are a stammerer."

I found it highly counterintuitive to sit down with people who were suffering, who had turned to me for help, and to hold myself back from doing what I did well. If I hadn't trusted that it was ultimately going to make me a better therapist, I doubt I would have been willing to stretch myself as I did. However, by watching my tapes and paying attention to the ways I interacted with clients, I soon perceived that the parts of myself that were always center-stage were keeping other parts of me in the wings. As Dr. Minuchin demonstrated in his session with the Smiths (see Chapter 3), every individual is also multiple. As a therapist I had to learn to increase the complexity of my voice, to say to myself—as I would say to my clients—"you are more than you think you are."

In the first session with the Wilsons, the youngest daughter, Jocelyn, described a situation prior to the divorce in which her father had told her that he wished he were married to a different person. Jocelyn was visibly distressed, and the more she talked, the more I felt the need to do something to help. I had entered the session with the goal of keeping enough distance from the family that I would be able to watch their interactions with one another, but when Jocelyn's anxiety surfaced it was as if the "child rescuer" within my body slammed the "neutral observer" and took over:

Jocelyn:	The worst part was when my dad told me about a dream he had that mom was gone forever, and he had a different wife.	*I had observed Lori's apparent powerlessness in the face of her daughter's intense emotions, and I felt compelled to rescue Jocelyn. Even though I knew that my role as a family therapist was not to take care of Jocelyn, I responded as I would to any child in distress: I reached out to comfort her.*
Therapist:	That's what your dad said to you?	
Jocelyn:	Yes!	
Therapist:	Jocelyn, I think that in situations like this it can be very difficult when someone so important has hurt you, because sometimes what you're left with is a whole set of feelings. You might be scared and angry and mad and confused and hateful, but at the same time you might also have feelings of love and missing the person and caring for them, and it can be very hard to have all those different things going on at the same time.	*This not only served to immobilize Lori, it also prevented me from paying attention to how the family system was operating. Jocelyn resumed her stream of memories as if I had not spoken.*
Jocelyn:	I've been writing letters to him. You see, I remember my dad always yelled at my mom that just because of her he'd lost all his money, all his fortune. . . .	

I realized immediately that I had acted impulsively based on my desire to soothe Jocelyn, which was not necessarily a useful therapeutic goal at that moment. Looking back on the session, I thought about the idea that for a therapist to be able to enter a family system and retain maneuverability, she must be capable of shape-shifting. At times, it may be more useful to be a cheerleader and at other times a cynic. When Dr. Minuchin gave his own ideas about how we might respond to our clients, I observed the many different ways that he had of creating an effect. I had been learning to listen, empathize, and be curious, but now I saw that a therapist might also need to startle, irritate, cajole, ignore, excite, confuse, unnerve, and amuse his clients.

During the exchange with Jocelyn, I could feel Dr. Minuchin's homunculus frowning over my shoulder and reminding me that I am more than a child rescuer. For the rest of the session, I resisted the urge to step in as Jocelyn's protector. I resumed my tactic of asking Lori and the girls to talk to one another, allowing me to remain in the role of a participant observer. Without feeling the pressure to *do something*, I found that it was easier to think more clearly. The experience was akin to staring at a Magic Eye picture: by stepping back from the conversation, my focus shifted, and from the jumble of content, patterns of relationship were suddenly revealed.

Lori and Jocelyn seemed to have reversed the traditional mother-daughter role in which the parent protects the child. Jocelyn spoke with fire, describing how she had put her father in time outs, thrown things at him, argued with him, and stood up to him in defense of Lori. In contrast, Lori presented herself as somewhat helpless in the face of her daughter's intense emotions. She spoke words of sympathy and encouragement, but the sound of her voice was hollow.

For the first half of the session, I had felt myself pulled by the family's painful story in which they were victims of Ken's pathology. Now that I could see Jocelyn and Lori's relationship as a contributing factor to Jocelyn's symptoms, I was willing to cause uneasiness, because I believed it would help to generate novel behavior. In retrospect, I can see that the importance of looking at the family in this way was not about whether it was "true," but whether it was useful. For the first time in talking to a client, I asked a question with the intention of creating discomfort. By taking a risk and doing something different, I turned myself from a crutch into a lever:

Therapist:	Jocelyn, it sounds like—and tell me if I'm wrong—but did you protect your mother from your father?	*I saw a child whose mother had made her responsible for keeping her safe. My goal was to begin to unbalance this relationship so that Lori could become competent and powerful, and Jocelyn could be freed of the responsibility of protecting her.*
Jocelyn:	Yes.	
Therapist:	How long have you been doing that?	
Jocelyn:	Since I was 5 years old.	

I suggested to Jocelyn that she was behaving like her mother's "knight in shining armor," and that as long as she "carried a sword" and "slept with it under her pillow at night," she would have nightmares. Then I turned to Lori and asked her how she could "take the sword" from her daughter. This was the beginning of a conversation that, over the course of several sessions, led to Lori and Jocelyn discovering alternative ways of relating to one another. I would never have been able to engage in this conversation if I hadn't been willing to step back from a role that was familiar to me. By increasing the complexity of my voice, I was making myself richer and creating the possibility for my clients to become richer too.

LESSON TWO: INTERVENE AT THE LEVEL OF RELATIONSHIP

When I presented my first session with the Wilsons to Dr. Minuchin, he proclaimed that I was an individual therapist. I was stunned. After a year of studying systems theory and several months attending his consultation group, I believed that I was beginning to conceptualize systemically and that I was operating relationally. What was the gulf that separated my intention from my practice? What specific qualities of the session determined that I was conducting parallel individual therapy versus relational therapy?

Hoping to find inspiration from Dr. Minuchin's work, I reread the first case in *Assessing Families and Couples* (Minuchin, Nichols, & Lee, 2007). However, rather than reading the session in its entirety, I skipped through the transcript, reading only Dr. Minuchin's questions and ignoring the context in which they were being asked. Almost immediately I realized what, in retrospect, was blindingly obvious: All of Dr. Minuchin's questions requested information about a relationship. When I compared the session to my own, the difference was clear. Dr. Minuchin's first ten questions were relational and over half of them indicated complementarity, whereas my first ten questions were almost exclusively requests for information about an individual.

Dr. Minuchin's questions from *The Parentified Child*

Question	People included in the question	Complementarity
1. But why did **the family** come, as well?	*Sarah + family*	
2. Are **you** the only problem in **the family**?	*Sarah + family*	
3. What do **you** think is happening to **Sarah**?	*Sister + Sarah*	
4. Could it be that **something or someone in the family** makes **her** sad?	*Sister + family + Sarah*	*The family makes Sarah sad*
5. **She's your** lieutenant? **Your wife** works for **everybody**?	*Mother + husband + family*	*The wife is conscripted by the husband/hired by the family*
6. Why did **you** take this job? Are **you** protecting **your father, your mother, or your brothers**?	*Sarah + family*	*The daughter was hired to protect the family*

Question	People included in the question	Complementarity
7. Are **you** the only one that can help **mother?**	*Sarah + mother + family*	*The failure of the husband pushes the daughter into her role*
8. Why don't **you** let **your mother** be the mother?	*Sarah + mother*	*The daughter prevents her mother from mothering*
9. No. **You** have become the mother of **your brothers.** Could you ask **your mother** when **you** began to work as her helper?	*Sarah + brothers + mother*	*The mother made the daughter into her helper. The daughter prevents the mother from mothering the boys, etc.*
10. What are the arguments at home?	*Mother + family*	

My questions from the first session

1. So, what would you like me to know from the get-go?	*Natalie*	
2. Who's that a problem for?	*Natalie + unspecified others*	
3. You used the word obsessive-compulsive. Is that something somebody's described to you? Where did you get that idea?	*Natalie + unspecified others*	
4. He used those words? So, I don't know, that means different things to different people. Could you tell me what that means to you?	*Natalie*	
5. How did you do that?	*Natalie*	
6. Oh, so double-checking has actually been working out?	*Natalie*	
7. What would be useful to you, coming here?	*Jocelyn*	
8. What flavor?	*Jocelyn*	
9. How long have your parents been divorced?	*Jocelyn + parents*	
10. And you've been having nightmares ever since?	*Jocelyn*	

Once I had made this realization, I returned to the family with a "wide-angle lens," and tried to keep myself from zooming in on each individual out of context. In the following conversation, Lori was describing her pain, and rather than engage in a detailed interview with her about her feelings, I expanded the conversation to explore how she was influencing Natalie and Jocelyn:

Mom:	I feel like a loser. I was trying so hard to do things right, but I got it wrong anyway.
Therapist:	You're nodding, Natalie?
Natalie:	No, I wasn't nodding to her. I was nodding to myself.
Therapist:	[To Lori] When Natalie hears you say those things, I wonder what she feels. When you call yourself a loser....

My intention was to explore the effect that Lori's words have on Natalie, but I was not seeing with the eyes of the sculptor. Lori and Natalie called themselves losers, and I accepted their label. To challenge the "loser" identity at the same time as finding out more about their relationship, I could have said, "It sounds like Natalie becomes your twin. How do you think that happens?"

Natalie:	I feel that, too.
Mom:	We do feel the same way. Unfortunately, I grew up that way and then I transmitted it to her without even knowing that I did.
Therapist:	So, if there is a connection between the two of you, when Natalie hears you feel like a loser, then perhaps she feels like a loser?
Mom:	But I grew up that way. Then it was the same with my husband. Anyway, that's in the past. I feel like a loser for 1 hour, but I feel a winner for ...
Natalie:	The rest of the day.
Mom:	The rest of the day.
Natalie:	That's how I feel.

This metaphor took Natalie and Jocelyn's symptoms and explained them in terms of a destructive relationship. I was changing the language of "depression," "anger," and "OCD" to language about interaction.

Therapist:	If you think about how things were before, when you were a family of four, it's almost like there were four people in your marriage. There was you and your husband, and because Jocelyn and Natalie were caught between you, it's almost like four people were married. And when you feel, "I am a loser," Natalie feels, "I am a loser," because she was caught up in your marriage.

[Later in the conversation the same theme came up with Jocelyn.]

Mom:	[To Jocelyn] You're not abandoning me. You can love your dad and me. He's always going to be your dad.	
Jocelyn:	No, he's not. And I'll return to normal as soon as we get the divorce.	*Having already laid the groundwork, I only needed to highlight Jocelyn's words. Lori immediately responded, and her firmness helped Jocelyn to step down from her habitual role of protector.*
Therapist:	Did you hear what she said? "As soon as **we** get the divorce."	
Mom:	You're not getting divorced. I'm getting divorced.	

At the end of this session, Lori said that it had been productive, and that she was now able to see how the children had become so emotionally attached to her. I was learning how to conduct relational sessions, but this was a lesson I would have to learn many times over. I still feel myself "zooming in" to respond to clients as if we were alone in the room, particularly when children are involved. However, from analyzing my sessions, I can see that I do so at the expense of maintaining a systemic perspective on the problem. The way I view a symptom completely changes the questions I ask and the interventions I make, and when I take on the task of trying to heal a client, I prevent the family from becoming the healing agent both now and in the future.

LESSON THREE: CARRY MESSAGES THAT ARE SOMETIMES UNCOMFORTABLE

Dr. Minuchin's startling assertion during our training that "all families that come to therapy are wrong" helped me to grasp a fundamental principle of family therapy. The reading for my classes had confirmed that systemic therapists of every orientation operate based on the belief that their clients' views of their problems are limited, and that every family has access to a greater range of interpersonal and intrapersonal resources than they are currently utilizing. Up to this point in my training, I had attempted to expand my client's sense of what was possible by eliciting ideas from them. Dr. Minuchin encouraged us to challenge our clients in ways that made them feel uneasy. As soon as I attempted to approach therapy with this goal, I became acutely aware of my clumsiness, and the Wilsons were forced to suffer through the growing pains that resulted from me trying to do something new.

I equate the experience of a beginning family therapist to that of a novice juggler attempting to practice with too many balls. It is extremely difficult to keep all the balls in the air at the same time, and quite often when you drop one, the whole act falls apart. The problem for the trainee therapist is that competence in one aspect of therapy may be rendered ineffective when other aspects of therapy are lacking. The following excerpt demonstrates my failure to remain connected with the family as I tried to incorporate a challenging voice into my style. Jocelyn had described a series of nightmares, and I asked Lori to help Jocelyn talk about them:

Mom:	She has those dreams because she's worried about what's happening. [To Jocelyn] You are strong and the dreams are going to go away, because you are going to find yourself more at peace. You will discover for yourself who you are deep down. You are a really special girl. You mean so much to me. I don't want you to worry about those dreams. Sometimes we don't even know why we dream something. But don't worry about those dreams. They're only dreams, they're not real.	*As I listened, I sensed incongruity between Lori's words and her body language. She sounded as though she were reading from a script that she didn't believe.*
Therapist:	What are your words doing to Jocelyn?	*I assumed that implicit in this question was a challenge to Lori that she could support Jocelyn more effectively. I wanted to explore how Lori's lack of authority might be preventing Jocelyn from letting go of responsibility but my question served to bolster rather than perturb the relationship.*
Mom:	About her dad coming round . . .	
Therapist:	No, I mean . . . what is happening to her?	

Mom:	What do you think, Jocelyn?	*A lot happened in the short exchange that followed: Lori turns to Jocelyn for answers and direction, Jocelyn responds with extreme aggression toward her father, Natalie tries to intervene and silence Jocelyn, and Lori implies that dad is "bad."*
		This is very rich information, but because I was fixed on my challenge of the family, I ignored what was happening.
Jocelyn:	It doesn't calm me down.	
Mom:	Okay. What would you like to hear? What do you want me to say?	
Jocelyn:	That my dad is dead.	
Natalie:	Jocelyn, that's not . . .	
Mom:	You can't say that, Jocelyn. No matter how bad people are, they can still change. He's the dad that God gave you and we're going to pray for him, but right now we're just going to worry about you being happy and feeling safe.	
Therapist:	Lori, I'm . . . I don't know. I'm confused. Tell me again what your words . . .	
Mom:	You're confused about what?	
Therapist:	Well, I'm trying to understand something and I'm missing it. Tell me again what your words are doing to Jocelyn?	*The abrasive repetition of my question was intentional. I believed that the family was stuck in a habitual pattern regarding Jocelyn's feelings about her father. I had read about "creating intensity," and by keeping the pressure on Lori I hoped to challenge her to try something new. Unfortunately, my unskillful use of this technique simply forced Lori into a defensive position.*

Mom:	Because she's worried about her dad. But she doesn't need to . . .
Therapist:	While you speak to her like that, what's happening to her?
Mom:	Well, I don't see how else I should be talking.
Natalie:	It's simply just Jocelyn pushing away help. I mean it's no different. . . .

This was a good example of Natalie in her role as rescuer, but again I missed it. I was hampered by having positioned myself at the center of the conversation, which prevented me from observing the family and prevented them from dealing with one another.

Therapist:	So it's Jocelyn's fault?
Natalie:	It's not all her fault.
Mom:	It's not her fault, but she needs to be positive.

Rather than helping the Wilsons to envision themselves with new eyes, I had succeeded only in reinforcing their positions. When I presented this session to Dr. Minuchin, he pointed out that joining is not an activity that happens in the first 20 minutes of the first session; it is a continuous process throughout every session that makes challenges to the family possible and effective. During this session, I had failed to connect with Lori, and instead of walking side by side with her to a different vantage point from which she might have seen things differently, I had backed her into a corner.

In addition to neglecting an essential element of the therapeutic relationship, I had based my challenge on an assumption. Dr. Minuchin pointed out that it was easy for clients to dismiss suggestions that could not be substantiated. Instead, he invited us to activate our clients "to dance," so that their relationships came to life in the room. By using the information we gained from enactments, it was possible to reflect back to our clients the specific things that we had observed. In the following conversation, I borrowed a question from Dr. Minuchin that I hoped would be startling to Lori, without pushing her into a defensive position.

| Mom: | Now they are free to express themselves, because they know I'm not going to yell at them. I even told them we should be best friends. I said, "I'm your mother and you should respect me, but at the same time I can be your friend too." Now they are know that if they make |

I was alert to the image of Mom and the kids as equals. Jocelyn seemed to be suffering partly as a result of taking on the a mistake they can tell me the truth, even if it's hard. So, sometimes I'm their mother, sometimes I'm not. Sometimes I'm Natalie's friend. Whatever questions she has, she can come to me.

responsibility of protecting her mom. I wondered if the fluid parent-child boundary that Lori was describing was benefiting her more than Jocelyn.

Therapist:	How old are you Natalie?
Natalie:	Fifteen.
Therapist:	So Natalie is becoming a young woman. Sometimes she needs a mother, and sometimes she needs a friend. But Jocelyn is 10. How is it different with Jocelyn?

Remembering Dr. Minuchin's session with the Menotti family (see Chapter 2), I decided to enter softly. I was saying the reverse of, "A good mother of younger children sometimes becomes a difficult mother for older children." I hoped that Lori would be more able to accept the upcoming challenge if she felt that I was not attacking her as a parent. It was my intention to communicate to Lori that I was challenging a specific behavior rather than challenging her as a person.

Mom:	With Jocelyn, I think I play the same role. Sometimes she likes to hide things from me, and I say, "Jocelyn, you're not telling me the truth, I need you to be honest."
Therapist:	So that's when you're being a mom?

I had heard Dr. Minuchin ask a similar question.

Mom:	Exactly. I say, "Come on, we're going to talk seriously. Don't do this again, because I want to be able to trust you."
Therapist:	[To Jocelyn] So, I'm hearing what Mom's saying. Is she always Mom? Is she sometimes a friend?

[Mom and Jocelyn both nod]

Therapist:	So, who is Jocelyn's mom when she's being your friend? Is she her own mom?
Mom:	Yes, she becomes my mom.

Therapist:	She becomes your mom?	
Mom:	[Laughing] Sometimes, she's my mom. Yeah, she pampers me and does my nails and. . . .	*These questions were embedded in a conversation in which Lori felt more respected. I hoped that they would create enough of a "kick" to make Lori take notice, but not so much that she had to defend herself against them.*
Therapist:	So who is her mom when she's your mom?	
Mom:	I don't know. We didn't talk about that.	

In the next session, Lori reported that she had been thinking about this conversation: "When you said, 'where were you?' I felt it. When she tried to be me, when she took my part." At first I was concerned that I had hurt Lori's feelings and my response was to assure her of my respect for her as a parent. It was Lori herself who helped me to understand that she had felt unsettled but not disrespected by my question.

My initial attempts to challenge the family could have placed our relationship in jeopardy, and I am lucky that Lori was both a strong, resilient woman and a devoted mother. She weathered my incompetence and stuck around long enough for me to adjust and reconnect with the family. I had learned the importance of being attuned to the quality of our connection, and I was beginning to understand how to work within that connection to create imbalance.

LESSON FOUR: BE COMFORTABLE THAT YOU ARE AN UNCERTAIN EXPERT

One of the main themes that repeatedly surfaced in our consultation sessions was the dilemma surrounding the therapist's authority. As new therapists, we were painfully aware of our lack of experience and were very afraid of making mistakes. Because of this timidity, we were uncomfortable saying things to our clients that were provocative and challenging. What if we were wrong? Dr. Minuchin's response to this doubt was to remind us that we were *always* wrong, because reality is always made up of multiple perspectives. The point was not to be right, but to be useful.

I had learned that in order to challenge my clients' certainty, it was necessary to balance a critical voice with a voice of empathy and respect. Ironically, as I continued my effort to introduce doubt I began to speak with my own sense of certainty. From a position of "not-knowing," I moved to a position of "know-it-all." The following conversation took place as I was trying to explore Lori's relationship with Natalie, who had been asked to a school dance:

| Natalie: | It gave me a certain kind of confidence. Just to know that I have a place in this world. My mom tells me a thousand times a day. . . . | *This information from Natalie was a wonderful opportunity to explore the relationship, but instead of taking the time to find* |

		out more about the interaction and perhaps to initiate an enactment, I immediately intervened to try to fix the interaction. This distracted me from a very revealing interaction.
Therapist:	Do you need her to tell you that a thousand times a day?	
Natalie:	No.	
Mom:	I don't say it a thousand times.	*When Lori became defensive, Natalie immediately back-peddled. She accused herself of exaggeration and retreated to a position of protection. Because I was in the mode of a "fixer," I missed the transaction that was unfolding between Lori and Natalie.*
Natalie:	No.	
Therapist:	Tell your mom what you need.	
Natalie:	It's just an exaggeration. You tell me "you can make it" once a day.	
Mom:	Yes, that's what I say. I push you up. I want you to know that you're able to do it.	
Natalie:	Lately, I've been happier. I mean. . . .	
Therapist:	Do you need your mom to push you up?	*I intended to support Natalie in asserting herself, but I actually pushed her further into defense of her mother.*
Natalie:	I mean, every so often, yes.	
Therapist:	Well, tell your mom what you do need and what you don't need.	*It might have been much more useful to wonder aloud how interesting it was that Natalie had learned to be a chameleon so that she would not upset her mother.*
Mom:	What do you need?	
Natalie:	When I get into that depressed state, I need you to push me up . . . Shake me up.	

Dr. Minuchin once told us that the family tells the therapist a story and the therapist tells the family a parallel story that is slightly different. Looking back at this session I saw that I was not so much telling as trying to convince the Wilsons of a story. It was as if I was running one step ahead, trying to drag them along to see things from my perspective. Understandably, Lori and Natalie dug in their heels and tried even harder to convince me of the way they saw things.

I needed to become a better observer of the family so that I could help them to become self-observers. This was essential to the task that Dr. Minuchin set us week after week: to make what is familiar unfamiliar. He asked us, "How do you help people realize that they're doing something repetitive, that they're prisoners? How can you make them look at themselves anew?" I knew that my goal was to introduce ideas that were currently unavailable to the family. The problem was that I had not developed the skills with which to operationalize my objective.

Dr. Minuchin suggested that we think of the therapist as an "uncertain expert" whose function is to make observations about the absurdity of life with a sense of curiosity and amusement. He explained that a therapist can introduce strange and outlandish ideas to the family with the freedom of knowing that if the family disagrees, the therapist can apologize and say, "I'm sorry. I must have been quite wrong. Please explain it to me."

Dr. Minuchin provided the following examples as suggestions for how we could have responded to our clients:

- *To the mother of a young girl who told her mother that she had accidentally cut her hair:* I am fascinated that you are so dismissive. She did a perfectly good job of cutting her hair and you focused on the lie. Are you like that always? Do you have a tendency to zero in on what is negative?
- *To the husband of a woman who is very outspoken about her husband's faults:* Does she always talk that much? She is very poetic. Does she always talk that long?
- *To the father of a teenage girl who is failing at school:* You are keeping her at 6 years old. I'm sure you don't want to do that. What makes you do that?

I knew that I could not and should not try to precisely emulate Dr. Minuchin's style, and that I needed to create my own version of this bemused, curious way of reacting to clients with a twinkle in my eye. If I could go back to the conversation with Natalie and Lori and take the position of the uncertain expert, I might make the observation that Natalie seemed to have the ability of changing her responses when she thought her mother's feeling were hurt, and then ask if she was always such a talented chameleon.

LESSON FIVE: THE BEGINNING OF WISDOM IN FAMILY THERAPY IS COMPLEMENTARITY

Even though I was learning to maintain a relational perspective, I was still caught up in the family's version of reality when it came to Natalie: she was depressed, she was overwhelmed with obsessive thoughts, she had been damaged by years of living with her parents' hostile marriage. The "child rescuer" within me repeatedly took over when I was speaking to her, which centralized my role and prevented me from observing Natalie in relationship to the other members of her family. When Dr. Minuchin suggested that Lori had recruited Natalie to protect her, I found it difficult to imagine how Natalie's behavior functioned as a shield.

After wrestling with the question for a few days, I was still puzzled. I knew that I needed to experience uncertainty where the family experienced certainty, but it was like trying to remove a pair of glasses that had been Superglued to my face. Fortunately, later that week, I happened to read a case described by Jay Haley (1982) in which a family is struggling with a young man's addiction. In the first session, the therapist observed that the parents had ceased to deal with one another directly and were communicating largely through their son. They were not responsible for their son's addiction but it provided stability to their relationship. Thus, while their son's recovery was something they desired, it was also very threatening to them.

I finally understood what Dr. Minuchin had meant when he produced the statue and told us that a hammer could be both a hammer and a horse's head. Of course Lori wanted the absolute best for her children, but she and her husband had placed them in a position that was damaging. She had done her best to protect her children from harm, but she had also used them as a shield. By regressing into a childlike state, Natalie was binding herself to Lori, and as long as she remained helpless, she would not be able to leave home and abandon her.

Dr. Minuchin had told us, "The therapist is not the fixer; the therapist is the arranger of the context in which the family members change each other." Bearing this in mind, I thought about how to use my own relationship with the family to unbalance the habitual family roles, and I decided to speak to Lori alone at the beginning of the session. My intention was to create an alliance with her that might help to strengthen her role and weaken the girls' position of responsibility. By letting the children know that Mom and I had something private to talk about, I was setting the stage to disrupt the dynamic in which Lori was supported and protected by her children.

Lori has been describing Natalie's recent history of calling to be picked up early from school.

Mom: It was 8:30, and she called me and said, "Mom, you need to pick me up. I can't be here anymore. Please pick me up." It really upset me. I didn't know what to do.

Lori believed that Natalie was mentally unwell. I wanted to introduce the idea that Natalie's behavior was a response to Lori. The image of Natalie as a little child was the beginning of a relational metaphor. Rather than accepting Lori's story that Natalie was sick, I described her behavior in relationship to Lori: a little girl dependent on her mother.

Therapist: Well, I want to ask you what you think about this. In the last year, your family has gone through some major changes, and of course, that's been really hard on Natalie and Jocelyn. Sometimes in situations like this, children try to protect their parents. Like we talked about with Jocelyn. It seems that when you and your husband argued, she came in and said, "Look at me!" and she distracted everybody. It's possible that Natalie—in a different way—is trying to protect you right now. When you describe her meltdowns, and calling you from school, she sounds like a little girl, like a little kid.

Mom: She said she couldn't even read! She couldn't understand the teacher!

Lori seemed to accept my redefinition of Natalie's behavior.

Therapist: Right! It's almost like she's regressing back to an infant!

Natalie had gone from being a depressed teenager to a little girl, to her mother's keeper.

Mom: To a child.

Therapist: Now, I don't know what might be driving her to do it. It might be that she's protecting you—because then you get to be her mom and take care of her. She might feel like that's a safe place for you. Because she knows if she grows up, that she's going to leave you.

Lori changed the subject shortly after this exchange, and then went back to the image of Natalie as depressed.

Mom: I've learned that she can't be alone anymore. Not until she gets help.

Therapist: It's almost like . . . you know when people have a little kid and they put them in a harness? It's like she's saying, "I'm a baby! Here, hold this. You need to keep me close to you." You know . . . reins, or a harness?

I reframed Lori's description of her feeling that she cannot leave Natalie alone. The image of the harness suggested that not only was Natalie in control of her symptoms, but that she and Lori were co-constructing one another's behavior.

Mom: Yeah, there is a belt.

Therapist: Yeah, it's like you're tied together.

Having introduced the possibility that Natalie's behavior was an unconscious attempt to protect Lori, I said, "I would like to help you give her permission to grow up." We discussed how this might help Natalie, and Lori agreed. Thus, when Natalie and Jocelyn were invited back into the room, Lori and I operated as co-therapists. Lori began by telling Natalie that they were both ready for Natalie to become more independent:

Natalie:	It's good to know that I can leave you, and not have to worry so much about everybody.	
Mom:	I'm glad to hear that. I want you to feel free. You're ready to go and I'm ready to be alone.	
Natalie:	I know.	
Therapist:	What do you hear your Mom telling you?	*I wanted to support Lori, but to push her and Natalie to explore further.*
Natalie:	She's saying that she's there to support me, but not to worry about her. It's kind of an interesting thought, because, we're there to help each other but we shouldn't worry about each other.	
Therapist:	So that's confusing?	
Natalie:	Not if you think about it deeply enough. Mom was basically saying not to worry about her. Just to worry about myself. But if somebody's in danger to help them . . .	*I wondered if Natalie had heard a contradiction.*
Mom:	In that case, we all protect each other.	*At the end of her statement Natalie added "small print" to the verbal contract that she and Lori had made. It was still Natalie's responsibility to protect her mother.*
Natalie:	Yes, we'll protect each other.	*Lori leapt in to agree.*

At the time, I failed to see what had occurred and so I missed out on the opportunity to challenge the underlying nature of the relationship. In the following conversation I do a much better job of noticing the relationship transactions behind what Natalie and Jocelyn are saying:

Therapist:	What do you think about leaving Mom alone?	*I was curious about how Natalie and Lori would manage a conversation about separation.*
Natalie:	Am I willing to move on and not worry about my mom and sister? I guess it's a new step for me.	
Therapist:	Can you have a conversation about how it's going to work? [To Lori] How is Natalie going to get ready to leave you? How are you going to get ready to let go of her hand and then kick her out the front door? [I mime kicking. Everybody laughs]	*By asking Lori how she would get ready to let go of Natalie's hand, I implied that she was to some extent holding her daughter back. My intention was to challenge Lori to do something different that would help Natalie to thrive.*
Natalie:	You have to kick me out.	
Mom:	Kick you out.	
Natalie:	But you're not going to hold my hand.	
Jocelyn:	But Mom and I will still be there for you.	*In retrospect, I can see that Jocelyn was protecting Lori. If I had seen this at the time I could have asked Lori to intervene.*
Mom:	Yes, but. . . .	
Therapist:	Maybe Jocelyn's not ready to let you go. Maybe she's going to hold your hand and keep you in the house.	*Instead, I highlighted Jocelyn's actions to Natalie.*
Jocelyn:	Of course.	
Natalie:	No, Jocelyn, don't. Don't hold my hand.	*I continued to support Natalie, now a warrior, in her attempt to cut the ties that bind her.*
Jocelyn:	It's my job.	
Therapist:	So you might have to put up a fight to get rid of Jocelyn, so you can run.	*I have a tendency to overstate my confidence in my client's abilities. It might have been more energizing to the session for me to have taken a position of pessimism.*
Natalie:	I never wanted to hold onto Jocelyn's hand.	

Therapist:	Okay, so Jocelyn's maybe going to try and hold you back. She might try and make you stay, but you're not going to let her.
Jocelyn:	Because I want to protect my family.
Natalie:	Jocelyn, don't worry about me. Mom was willing to do it. You should be willing to do it to.

For the first time since meeting the Wilsons, I had entered the session with a clear sense of how each person's behavior was tied to that of the other family members. Our conversation had shifted from an examination of individual suffering to a relational exploration of the family organization that maintained that suffering.

LESSON SIX: BECOMING MARY POPPINS

Dr. Minuchin provided a consultation with the family for their seventh session (see Chapter 12). During that meeting, he had a connection to each family member that was simultaneously intimate and detached. After the session, I was struggling to articulate this quality when Dr. Minuchin jokingly compared himself to Yoda—an analogy that perfectly captured his ability to relate to clients from a position of detachment, authority, and playfulness. It suddenly became clear to me that much of the craft that Dr. Minuchin had been teaching us required that we find our own version of this therapeutic stance. I knew that I was generally too proximal to my clients, but I had struggled to envision what the alternative might look like. Having observed Dr. Minuchin I knew I had to develop a way of relating to my clients that was qualitatively different from the way I relate to everyone else in my life, and I began to search for a female character with the qualities of Yoda that also fit my personality. Luckily, an astute colleague provided me with the perfect person: Mary Poppins!

Mary Poppins transforms the lives of the Banks family precisely because she enters their family system without accepting their rules. It is her intention from the first moment to stay only "until the winds change," and her brisk, self-assured, enigmatic way of relating to the family communicates that she is essentially separate from them. I knew that modeling myself after her would give me the maneuverability and authority that I currently lacked. The next time I met the Wilsons, I carried Dr. Minuchin on one shoulder and Mary Poppins on the other. The following three segments illustrate subtle differences in how I conducted the session:

| Therapist: | Natalie, you're not a little kid anymore. | *Jocelyn and Natalie related as if Jocelyn was the big sister, which supported the family organization: Lori depended on Natalie to be weak and on Jocelyn to be strong.* |
| Natalie: | Yes, and at my age.... | |

Therapist:	Why do you need your mom to keep reminding you of all these things?
Natalie:	I really can't explain it. It's hard to say.
Jocelyn:	Natalie, say it!
Natalie:	And I know. Because from what I see. . . .

I abruptly shifted gears to comment on the sibling subsystem. Jocelyn was trapped in a role of responsibility, and I wanted to help Lori, free her from this position.

Therapist:	Stop! [To Lori] Can you help Jocelyn to stop treating Natalie like her little sister?

I asked Lori about parenting the two girls differently and she described her difficulty getting the girls to complete their chores. The conversation was off track from what I had intended to talk about: how Lori and Natalie's relationship had become a "prison."

I had observed how Dr. Minuchin remained free of the demands of the family. He ignored or interrupted what was not useful, what was repetitive, and what pulled the conversation away from a relational understanding of the problem. Now that I felt free of the need to respond to everything the Wilsons said, it was easier to work in the medium of relationship. In a small way, I felt like a theatre director arranging actors on a stage. My goal was not to tell the family how to behave, but to highlight the implicit rules of their current system and explore alternatives.

Therapist:	[To Lori] Natalie watches Jocelyn, Natalie and Jocelyn watch you, and you watch them. I have this image of all of you in your house, paying so much attention to each other. Natalie, you're not going to be able to grow up living like that.	*I intended this statement to rouse emotion in both Natalie and Lori. During the consultation, Dr. Minuchin had introduced the idea that Lori was growing back the umbilical cord between herself and Natalie, as well as the idea that Natalie was restricted by Lori's observation of her. Lori wanted desperately to help her children, but she also seemed stuck in a position that entraps them. Natalie seemed to have grasped Dr. Minuchin's message, so I enlisted her as the spokesperson for an alternative family life.*
Natalie:	Yes. It's more like dependence. Being loved and treated respectfully and being given what I need.	

	It's good for me and I appreciate it, but sometimes it just goes too far.	
Mom:	Mmm?	
Natalie:	It's just that sometimes it goes so far that we start taking it for granted.	*Natalie frequently softened criticism of Lori, and here she began to blame herself for being ungrateful.*
Therapist:	How can she open the cage?	*I rejected this notion and sent the message that Lori had the power to free Natalie from her anxiety.*

My enhanced sense of being a foreigner in the family system gave me a different perspective in the room. It was like having a bird's-eye view that enabled me to continually engage with the entire family. When I asked Natalie how Lori could "open the cage," it was a way of indirectly communicating to Lori what I felt I could not say to her directly. I wanted her to hear the challenge without feeling the need to respond and potentially become defensive.

Therapist:	[To Lori] I think that they need to know that you have someone else to go to, because if they think that you don't have anyone else to turn to, they will feel responsible.	*I wanted to kick the children out of the spousal subsystem and I chose to be very directive at this point.*
Mom:	When I talk to them it's not because I don't have support. I tell them so they'll know why I was upset. That's the only reason.	
Therapist:	I think they need to know that you have somebody else.	*Lori had challenged my assertion but I was momentarily positioning myself between her and the children, and I held my ground a little longer.*
Mom:	I mean, actually I do. They know I have Amelia and Katherine. . . .	
Therapist:	Can you talk to them about that and help them to understand?	*I shifted from an oppositional position to one in which I was supporting Lori. I had pushed just enough to ask her for a different response, but I didn't want her to become defensive.*
Mom:	Amelia, Katherine . . . even Joanie, they support me a lot.	

Natalie:	So you just don't want me to react to your feelings? I think that would be awkward, because then it would be like I don't care for you.	*Natalie did not find it easy to step out of the role of her mother's confidante.*
Mom:	No. Just focus on your own life. On all the things you have to do every day.	*Natalie's previous statement suggested that she recognized her role as mom's protector. By asking her to describe to Lori how long she had been in this role, I hoped to set the stage for Lori to give Natalie permission to step down.*
Therapist:	[To Lori] Can you find out from her when she took this job?	
Mom:	When did that happen, Natalie?	
Natalie:	I think it started when I was 6 or 7. I thought, who shall I side with—Mom or Dad? Because there is no such thing as neutral. Because sooner or later, you're going to side with somebody. I used to think about the difference between you and Dad. And then, many times you would share your feelings about how much pain you've been in from Dad. And then I felt like I had to be on your side and just to be around you, because it made me feel like I was doing a good deed.	*Natalie's description of her childhood experience was very touching and I am sure that for Lori these words were far more potent than anything I could have said. I had used the conversation to challenge the family organization around Lori's pain, which had created space for a new interaction to occur.*

This final lesson had allowed me to choose what distance to take from the family at each moment in the session. With this added flexibility, it was much easier to create enactments, to shift between a supportive and a challenging role, to sit back and observe the functioning of family rules, and to relinquish the desire to fix everybody.

The process of learning from Dr. Minuchin was in some ways isomorphic to the experience of being his client. He knew just how hard to push me, and when to pat me on the back. His challenges confused and flustered me, but that was ultimately what I reacted to when I pushed through my own limits and dared myself to try something new. It will take years for me to master the skills he introduced me to, but thanks to his supervision, I have begun to see through the multiple lenses of a family therapist. I am deeply grateful to Dr. Minuchin for challenging the certainty with which I saw myself as a therapist and a human being.

12

MINUCHIN AND THE WILSONS

Shortly after the session presented in the previous chapter, Minuchin conducted a consultation with the Wilsons in what was their seventh session of family therapy. Mother, Natalie, and Jocelyn were all present, as was Helen. As Helen's supervisor, Minuchin came into the consultation with a lot of information and was able to join from a strategic point of view. He had already discussed with Helen and the Friday group the presenting problem and how to externalize it, aspects of identity in the family, and the way in which family organization was making demands on the therapist. Entering the therapy room, Minuchin had two clients: the Wilson family and Helen. His goal was to enhance each of these systems so that they would leave the consultation richer than when they entered.

Mother:	Hello, good afternoon. Good to meet you. You are Helen's teacher? I don't remember your name.
Minuchin:	Minuchin. I was a professor of Family Therapy at Penn University. And now I am a retired old person living in Boca. And I want to help Helen to help you. So we will have one hour and a half together, and I will see what I can do. I have seen some sessions that Helen had with you because she showed it to me in the class. And so let's start by asking you why do you come to see her?
Mother:	You want to start, Natalie, or do you want me to start?
Natalie:	You can start.

Mother: Okay. We're here because we need help to go through the hardest times of our lives. My family, my husband, my kids, and I, what we've been through,.... but not realizing what we have been through until the end with the last straw. It's too hard to see what we didn't see before—what I didn't see.

Minuchin: Help me to understand your thinking, because you are too generic. Put some details in what you are saying.

Mother: Abuse, strong words, touch....

Minuchin: What is the nature of the abuse? Are you talking about your husband and you?

Within the first minutes of the consultation, Minuchin has brought forth a very serious topic, domestic violence. This fact from the family's past acts as a significant organizing principle in how they currently function. Minuchin attempts to uncover details about the abuse and how it affects the different family members, because he knows that the family has most likely remained organized around dealing with the abuse, which they are no longer facing.

Mother: My husband and I. Yes.

Minuchin: What was the nature of the abuse?

Mother: General abuse. Strong words. Very strong words. Very ugly words.

Minuchin: There was physicality at times?

Mother: He was physical some times. He tried to choke me once or twice.

Minuchin: Okay. Now, when that happened, were the children present?

Mother: Natalie was present.

Minuchin: [To Natalie] You were present. So tell me what was your experience about that? What happened?

Natalie: When I personally saw it, it was scary because my dad, he ... it was scary because my dad is....

Minuchin:	Let me tell you what I see. I saw you responding to me. And I saw your mother helping you and me by saying to you "sit forward" and "talk louder." Is that something that your mother does frequently?	*Minuchin begins the session by allowing the family to present their story of the presenting problem. While this conversation is occurring he is paying attention to the nonverbal communication among the family members. This is the beginning of his interventions at the level of relationship. He interrupts the narrative with a surprising focus on the pattern of control (and support) between Natalie and her mother. Issues of proximity and enmeshment among the family members will continue to be important in the session . . .*
Natalie:	Yes. I won't deny that.	
Minuchin:	And why does she do that?	
Natalie:	She wants the best for me.	
Minuchin:	Ah ha. And she thinks that you cannot do it yourself?	
Natalie:	I don't know about that. . . .	
Minuchin:	I mean, she's your crutch? Or your cane? See, I have a cane. Don't use your mother. Take it. [Minuchin gives his cane to Natalie] Don't use her. Tell her you don't need a cane.	*Minuchin joins the family as an "old person" who uses a cane, but continues his focus on the relationship between Natalie and the mother. He uses his cane as a metaphor for the mother-oldest daughter relationship.*
Mother [To Natalie]:	Tell me.	
Natalie:	I don't need assistance or a cane.	
Minuchin:	You see? Natalie, I am 90 years old. I need that cane. If I don't have that I fall down. But you . . . how old are you?	
Natalie:	Sixteen.	
Minuchin:	So you certainly don't need it. So that's a first impression. It's an interesting thing that you are so helpful. [To the youngest daughter] And your name is?	
Jocelyn:	Jocelyn.	

Minuchin:	Jocelyn, does your mother also feel that you need her help?	*Minuchin has made contact with each family member and begun to explore the idiosyncratic organization of a divorced family in which there was abuse. As a consultant, Minuchin continues Helen's exploration from previous sessions; it is not a new area.*
Jocelyn:	Sometimes, my mom does need my help. And I'm always there to help her.	
Minuchin:	How old are you?	
Jocelyn:	I'm only 11.	
Minuchin:	You're 11. So maybe you still need more help than Natalie does. Do you think so?	
Jocelyn:	I guess so.	
Minuchin:	There is a time when children don't need the mother and the mother still needs the children. [To Lori] So you still need Natalie. Is that more since your separation than before? Have things changed since you separated? See, now you are a family of three. You were a family of four. Were you a family of four or were you two families? I am asking you, Natalie, because I hope you understand what I am saying. When your father was at home, was your family organized in terms of two groups? Your father was separate and your mother and two children together?	
Natalie:	Yeah. My father tried to avoid my Mom most of the time and so . . . either I was talking to my Mom primarily at one moment or to my Dad another moment, but I never talked to Dad and Mom together.	
Minuchin:	Okay. So that was the way in which the family was organized before all this in which you and the two children were a unit.	*This exploration of the past is a prelude to talk about the present. By highlighting how the family was previously organized Minuchin is setting the stage to discuss how that familial configuration is no longer necessary.*

Mother:	Mmm-hmmm.
Minuchin:	And your husband was separate. And then he and you were in conflict, and what happened to the children when you were in conflict? Were they trying to enter in between both of you?
Mother:	No. Because most of the time they were not supposed to be there when I had issues with him. I tried not to fight in front of them. I tried to be quiet, to not start a fight. If he said the carpet is black but I knew it's white I tried to say "okay."
Minuchin:	You were holding back. It's very difficult to sit in silence.
Mother:	It is. But I learned to be silent a lot of times. To avoid fights.
Minuchin:	But do you think that they didn't know?
Mother:	Sadly, I thought that they didn't know, but they saw. I didn't know until now. I didn't know until 10 years later that Natalie saw her dad doing that. I didn't know that until now.
Minuchin:	She told you?
Mother:	Natalie told me just two or three months ago that she had seen Dad trying to choke me. I didn't know. I didn't know many things. I thought I was avoiding a lot of things for them not to see, not to hear, and when I tried to talk to Dad, I tried to talk to him when they were not present. But I did not accomplish anything.
Minuchin:	Can I talk with the children a little bit to find out what is their experience?
Mother:	Of course.

This casual question has a very important function. Minuchin entered the session as an expert, but asking Mother for permission to talk more with the children, he is placing her in the position of competent adult figure.

Minuchin:	Okay. Jocelyn, what's the difference in the family from the time in which your father was at home to now? Are there any differences?
Jocelyn:	Well, there were some differences after my father left. After my dad left, there were no more arguments in the house.
Natalie:	Or less. More specifically, there were no arguments for pointless topics.
Minuchin:	Explain that because I don't understand.
Natalie:	My father would make great arguments whenever we tried to push up his self-esteem. He would get mad for little things. If he was suffering for something little, many times my mom and my sister primarily would try to come and try to comfort him, but my dad for some reason took it as a severe annoyance, so yeah he got really mad. I guess he has a fear of success, really. Or he's just lazy.
Minuchin:	When did you become a psychiatrist?

Minuchin joins through humor, but is shifting the Identified Patient from having an individual disorder to developing symptoms because of her observations of others, especially her mother, and her desire to help and protect her. He is expanding the family members' views of each other, starting with the IP and shifting her into a position at the same level as he is.

Natalie:	I mean I observe a lot of things.
Minuchin:	I am asking you, because I am impressed with you. You are a good observer, but I am interested in when you began to become an observer of people?

Minuchin joins with Natalie, focusing on her competence. He explores areas of difficulty which other therapists might describe as pathology, but he reframes as competence. Natalie, described as a "people watcher," is connected to others through this observing habit.

Natalie:	It started really when I was young, because I notice people's emotions. I talk and socialize but I am not as social as most people. So when I see people, I observe their characteristics, I try to figure out things, why they are the way they are.
Minuchin:	So you are a people watcher.
Natalie:	Many times, yes. And then I try to ask questions, like why is the human mind that way, why is it that we learn skills and we don't have to check every single piece of the skill we need to know. For example, speaking, we don't solve the definitions of every little word which is. . . .
Minuchin:	You're losing me and it's not useful.
Natalie:	I know it's not useful.
Minuchin:	Because I am here for you, and at this point you are entering into a monologue that doesn't include me. Do you understand what I am saying?
Natalie:	Yes, you're saying that I am not relating the information to you.
Minuchin:	That's correct. You are entering into monologue. And you are entering into monologue as if it's a dialogue with me and it isn't. So I am telling you, I disappeared for you. You are not engaging me. You are ruminating inside of yourself. And I am wondering if that is a common experience to you.
Natalie:	Yes, it is.
Minuchin:	So you must be lonely, dear.
Natalie:	I mean I have friends and I talk to people but I just. . . .
Minuchin:	You do?
Natalie:	I just . . . yes. And it's really my fault.
Minuchin:	No, it is not your fault. Absolutely not. [To Lori] I am very interested

Minuchin engages Natalie in a conversation about the characteristics of her thinking. It is part of the exploration of an individual as a subsystem. Later, he will use this information as part of exploring a dyad, a triad, or the whole family.

Here, Minuchin moves from the exploration of an individual to the in this young woman. I am wondering if the voice that she hears in her brain is her voice or your voice. Are you entering into her brain? You know what I am saying?

idea that she is controlled by her mother. This line of discourse challenges the enmeshment between mother and daughter.

Mother: I don't know. I understand the question but I don't know.

Minuchin: I have a feeling sometimes she talks with her voice and then sometimes with your voice, at times without realizing. You become a puppeteer. [To Natalie] Do you know what I am saying?

This metaphor of a ventriloquist and her puppet contains within it many of the ideas inherent in Minuchin's work. He has presented new identities to the family members that they have not thought about before. This focus on complementarity, externalizes the problem of Natalie having ideational overload to the connection with her mother.

Natalie: Yes. We follow what we are taught . . . in this case, my Mom. And so I learn her morals.

Minuchin: She pulls the strings and you talk, and you think you are talking but she's a ventriloquist. You know, a ventriloquist is usually in the theater. He is sitting, he has a doll in his lap and the doll talks, but actually it is his voice. But when you look at him, you think that the puppet is talking because the ventriloquist has the skill of projecting his voice in such a way that you think it is a puppet. And I have a feeling you've got that skill.

Minuchin is increasing the intensity of the message that had begun during the sessions with Helen. This visual representation of an enmeshed mother-daughter dyad moves beyond the verbal explanation of the dynamic to a mental representation intense enough to push them toward new patterns of relating.

Mother: I don't think so, because I don't talk too much. I don't say, "You put this and you've got to put that. . . ." I don't think so. Because I don't interfere too much in their decisions and opinions.

There is now a polemic between Minuchin and the mother. He will increase the intensity of his intervention through an enactment.

Minuchin: Are you sure of that?
Mother: Maybe I'm not aware, but I don't. . . .
Natalie: I don't know if it's significant enough, but I will say it anyways.

	For example, you ask me, "Do you want to go to this place?" And I say yes. Then you say, "Are you sure?" And it makes me think "no" because "hey I am not going to please my mom."
Minuchin:	[Indicating another chair closer to her mother] Sit here. That's interesting what she said. Can you talk with your mom about that?
Natalie:	Because I feel . . . because . . . when you ask, whether it's clothes or . . . these are just miniscule things but . . . when you ask me what places do you want to go, or if we have to go to a place . . . let me think of a few things. . . .
Minuchin:	Help her, Lori. Help her to explain that to me because she's quite an interesting young woman.
Natalie:	My problem is that . . .
Minuchin:	No, no, no, no, no. You're talking with your Mom. And you are one of the people who watches. So she measures her experience by your face. It's successful if you smile. It's unsuccessful if you frown.
Mother:	I smile most of the time.
Natalie:	Yes, many times.
Mother:	I very seldom. . . .
Minuchin:	Isn't that interesting?
Mother:	I smile most of the time. Even if I'm sad or mad.
Minuchin:	So, even if you are silent, she listens to what you are saying. That's a fantastic thing!
Mother:	Yeah, I do smile because I choose to be positive regardless.
Minuchin:	Is Jocelyn as attuned to your moods as Natalie is?
Mother:	She's cheerful, outgoing, she is like a teacher trying to teach me ways to do things better. She's very soft-spoken.

Minuchin:	But you know Natalie has a problem in that she's a people watcher. And she's tremendously alert to your moods. She needed that distance to have freedom from your moods probably during the time in which you were married to your husband. She was alert to your conflict, wasn't she?
Mother:	Well, we didn't have conflicts at the beginning.
Minuchin:	When did it start?
Mother:	After he lost all his money. (Jocelyn murmurs something)
Minuchin:	What did you say, Jocelyn?
Jocelyn:	That he made a bad business move.
Minuchin:	You were helping your mom just now. That's nice. This helpfulness seems to be a family affair. What did your father do for business?

Minuchin describes the intrusion of Jocelyn into the dialogue as a helpful act. The challenge that follows below is implicit; he is trying to get family members not to intrude in the process in other subsystems.

Mother:	He bought and flipped properties.
Minuchin:	Jocelyn was talking.
Mother:	I'm sorry. I thought you were asking me.
Minuchin:	No, I was asking her. I am just alerting you to how sensitive you are to the needs of the children. That's lovely for Jocelyn, and it's too much for Natalie. Because Natalie is living your emotional feelings. So if you're depressed, she will be depressed. Or she will ruminate. She goes into those kinds of questions that are questions about where am I in life.

Minuchin is creating distress in the mother-older daughter subsystem. Because they are engaged in an enmeshed relationship, he is pointing out this destructive dynamic, hoping to challenge them to find a new way to relate.

Natalie:	Yes.
Minuchin:	But instead of saying where am I in life, she says why is two plus two four, and not six? It's a strange way of asking fundamental questions.

Natalie:	It is. . . . Yes.
Minuchin:	No. I am talking with Mom.
Natalie:	Sorry.
Minuchin:	I'm talking to you, Mother, but I am talking to Natalie, as well. When Natalie was born the doctor cut the umbilical cord, but you made it grow again.

This metaphor contains a stroke and a kick. It was challenging to Lori but the image was bound up with a mother's love, which helped her to hear it. Visual image increases the intensity of a relational message.

Mother:	I love her so much.
Minuchin:	Of course, no question of that.
Mother:	Of course. She was the happiness of my life.
Minuchin:	Do you know what happened to your children?
Mother:	I know they've been damaged. I know they need a lot of help. That's what I know.
Minuchin:	No, no, no, no, no.
Mother:	To figure out what I did wrong. Even though I thought I was doing right.
Minuchin:	I am not talking about wrongs and rights. I am talking about something that is quite natural. And it is how difficult it is for mothers to see the children growing up. You know, you probably were a perfect mother of young children, because you have a lovely sense of protection and you are loving with your children, and they are very loving children. But they look at you continuously. Lori, you have very bright children. That's very nice. And you have children that are a hybrid. They are too adult and too childish. It's quite an interesting combination. [To Jocelyn] What do you think? Sometimes when you talk with me I think you are 15. How old are you?
Jocelyn:	Eleven.

Minuchin:	Wow. And sometimes you talk like you are 15. And at other times you talk like 9. How did that happen?
Mother:	I don't know.
Minuchin:	It's like an accordion. This is a fantastic accordion because she goes like that. She's very, very adult.

Minuchin uses another metaphor as a bridge between some of the abstract thinking occurring in the family and a more concrete representation that might be more useful.

Mother:	Yeah, she is. That I know.
Minuchin:	And then she's very childish. [To Natalie] And how did you also become this strange animal that stretches and shrinks?
Natalie:	I like to question things. And the thing is I just go overboard, but I mean in my mind, if I don't answer it, it will stop me from doing everything and I have to . . . must answer.
Minuchin:	My dear, you talk about your brain as if it is separated from you.
Natalie:	Yes, that's what it feels like. I know it's not true.
Minuchin:	It's not true.
Natalie:	I know it's in my subconscious. I know.
Minuchin:	But you know people are more than one person. People have many aspects of them and so at some point you tend to be a very adult, life-observing person. I think you will need to change, Lori, for Natalie to grow up, because you are also a child observer. She's a mom observer and you are a child observer. [To Natalie] Your mom is always like that. A magnifying glass. And you see yourself under a magnifying glass. She's saying, "What does my mom feel when I do that?" And when she does that, her brain is saying, "Look at yourself doing that." It's a fantastic painful experience. Natalie then becomes tongue-tied, a stammerer.

Minuchin [to the therapist]:	So, Helen, you have a very interesting group of people here. Loving and prisoners in a cage of love. Love can be a golden cage, but it is a cage. Natalie, that has such a wonderful mind, is restricted by her mother's observation of her mind.	*Minuchin supports Lori's competence by framing her as an observer of her daughter, but he also states that "love can be a golden cage." This phrase challenges enmeshment while at the same time undercutting resistance.*
Mother:	But how did I do that when I was gone most of the time? I was gone because I was forced to work two jobs.	
Minuchin:	Just by love. Just by protection. My dear, do you know what happened with Natalie? She felt very much that you needed her. That is a lovely feeling, because you probably needed that. I don't think you need that now. Both of your children are lovely, like you. I think that you are very nice people. How do you think you can cut the umbilical cord? And continue being a mom? Loving them as you do, letting yourself be loved as they are. But I don't know how that can happen. You are a very nice family. How can I help you, because, you see, I am concerned about all of you.	*Here we can see a therapist move back-and-forth in proximity to make interventions. Minuchin's use of "my dear" and his explanation to the family that he is concerned about them shows his tenderness. This is an intimate position, one of close proximity. However, he is also challenging a destructive "pattern of love", which is a more distant position.*
Natalie:	Yes it's been killing me. Normally I am making A's here and there but I got a C+ on my science test that I could have gotten an A, because, I don't know what my issue is, because I study and I am not confident enough to even trust my own knowledge. That's basically what's happening.	*Natalie is saying, "I am damaged." Minuchin challenges this individual symptom. He explores the power of mother "coloring" Natalie's brain. This image, that Natalie's mother is in her head providing direction and preventing her from growing, will be expanded throughout the rest of the session.*
Minuchin:	No, that's not it.	
Natalie:	It got to a point I couldn't speak English . . . I couldn't speak anything. I would talk like I never knew how.	
Minuchin:	But that is because you have inside of you a homunculus. A homunculus is an imaginary small person inside of you and the homunculus is looking at you doing whatever you do. And that is a handicap to	

	growth. And your homunculus looks very much like your mother. And the question is, how can you kick the homunculus without kicking your mom?
Natalie:	I really don't know how to do that.
Minuchin:	Of course.
Natalie:	For every solution that I have been receiving, I am trying to work it out like there's mechanics in all little things. Because in the mind there is no mechanics.
Minuchin:	And I am saying whenever you do anything you are saying to yourself, "How am I being observed?" And that is a prison. And you said it's in your brain and I am saying it's outside of your brain. How that happened, I don't know.
Mother:	I was thinking because I don't give them enough time, I should, and now I see that I give them too much.
Minuchin:	But you see I don't blame you.
Mother:	But I can see how I give them love but I wasn't there all the time hugging them . . . I wasn't doing that. I didn't do enough as a mother.
Minuchin:	It happened because they were watching you and your husband. They were watching their mother and their father. And they were caught in between. So this is a traumatic experience for children, because they took sides and this young woman took your side and at the same time she felt—I think—guilty for taking only your side and not seeing her father's side. That I am not certain, but I hypothesize that this happened to her. So she is very uncertain.
Natalie:	Yes. For many of years of my life I was going between my mom and dad—sometimes neither—and I didn't know what to do. I just see the truth now. So that's why I am siding with my mom now.

Minuchin connects the individual symptomatology to the family history. He is saying that symptoms are not due to an inherent characterological deficit; they are a product of traumatic family organization.

Minuchin:	[To Lori] It's something you didn't want. It's something your husband didn't want either. But it happens to children of conflicting parents. They don't know what side to take and then they are absolutely befuddled. It's easier to know how it happened than to help in the process of growth. Because she's stuck, I know that she is conflicted and confused. I think that Jocelyn is still free. [Jocelyn shakes her head] You don't think so, Jocelyn?
Jocelyn:	Well, only one thing. It's not about my family. It's not about my mom. It's because, you see, ever since I made a promise when I was 8 years old I've been trying to protect the family from my dad. I had a dream that I had a sword and needed to kill my father to save my family.
Minuchin:	And you told me that you're 11?
Jocelyn:	Mmmm-hmmmm.
Minuchin:	So, you will fail. If you take that job, you will fail.
Jocelyn:	For me, it's like I can't. If I fail it's breaking a promise.
Minuchin:	You cannot win that job. Who gave her that job? Isn't that an absurd job?
Jocelyn:	I need to help them.
Minuchin:	[To Lori] Look at the job that Jocelyn is taking. That is an absurd job for an 11-year-old girl. And she needs to know that it's absurd. Because the idea that she will protect you is absurd. Can you tell her in ways that she can hear that you don't need her protection?

Jocelyn claims a voice as the carrier of the symptom. In this family, each member insists on claiming the identity of victim at times as well as savior. Neither position is beneficial or useful.

The daughter, youngest in the family, had it in her mind that she needed to protect the family from the abusive father/husband. Minuchin's question is another challenge to viewing symptoms individually. Jocelyn cannot take on the role of family savior without someone else allowing her to have that job.

Mother:	I tell you at home and I will tell you again. You don't need to protect me. I can do it by myself. You need to be a child.
Minuchin:	Beautiful.
Mother:	You need to be an 11-year-old and have friends and do your homework and do your best for yourself. Spend time with the dog. With your friends. Read.
Jocelyn:	I am not going to give up until Dad is gone forever.
Mother:	Well, don't worry about me. I'm safe. I am doing things that I am supposed to do as a mother and an adult. That is my job to do. Okay? And your job is to go to school and do your best and make more friends.
Natalie:	And you should study a lot more.
Minuchin:	Whenever you talk with Jocelyn at home, does Natalie stay quietly out or does she enter?
Mother:	Sometimes she's quiet and sometimes she enters.
Minuchin:	And when she enters, do you tell her, "No."
Mother:	I say, "Stop it."
Minuchin:	You need to do that much more. This is very important, because she is taking a parental job. And that robs you. And you will need to help Natalie to be out so that Jocelyn can be in. Jocelyn suffers because Natalie is so protective of her. So, you need to find a way to say lovingly, "Natalie, stay out. I can handle this." [To Natalie] Can you do that? Can you let your sister be with your mother and let your mother do the job of helping her to grow up?
Natalie:	It sounds simple, because most of the time I am not really around

A family's organization needs to change over the course of its life cycle.. This family was organized around a very abusive situation, with the children moving into the parental subsystem and trying to protect the mother. That function, if previously necessary, is not required in their current situation. Minuchin works with the mother in an effort to help her delineate the boundaries so that Natalie is not a parentified child. He then shifts his attention to Natalie in order to help her move out of the mother-Jocelyn subsystem.

them and when I am around them, for some reason, I don't know why, I just find it annoying to hear my sister's voice. It's been like that for me.

Minuchin: That would be nice if you then don't listen. Your sister needs to not hear your voice, so that your mother's voice will be amplified. She needs your mother's voice. But when you enter, she feels ganged up on. So tell your brain that that's not your job. You have a wonderful brain. Tell your brain that Jocelyn has your mother's voice to help her and to guide her and not yours. Is that possible?

Helen: I think that might be difficult.

Minuchin: You think that might be difficult? Yeah. Because Natalie is such a protector. She's continuously watching. [To Natalie] I was like you. I had 10 uncles, 10 aunts, 100 cousins, and I lived in a very small town, and I was always watching them and they were always watching me. I was a member of a large tribe and that creates people watching. Your situation is different. You became a people watcher out of protection for your mom. And so that's different because my situation was easier, because I just watched without the feeling of threats.

Natalie: Yes.

Minuchin: That's dangerous. That makes for an increase of sensitivity. And you will probably always have that talent. I think it's a talent. It made me a very famous psychiatrist, because I have your talent. So keep it. It can be very useful. But now, you are my student. When you will be a psychologist, which will be many years from now, I will not be here anymore. So I will talk to you now as a teacher, okay? One of the problems of people that have your kind

Minuchin challenges Natalie by joining with her. He then explains that the competence Natalie has as a people watcher is the same talent that he has as a famous psychiatrist. He then recruits her to be a learner from him, saying "You are my student."

of brain is how to observe without intruding. Because you intrude as much as your mom colonized your brain. I think without knowing that she colonized your brain, you intrude in Jocelyn's and mother's dialogue. And for a people watcher, it's important to know when not to intrude. So it's important to know to let your mom be the mother of Jocelyn without you wanting to be a parent of Jocelyn. Because that's wrong. And that is damaging.

We are coming to the end of our time together. It's very nice to have met you. Any questions?

Mother: I wonder how this happened because, as you said, I captured them too much, but I feel the opposite.

Minuchin: I will tell you what happened. You were busy in a conflict, with your husband. All your energies were involved in this conflict. They became observers of this conflict, and in some strange way they decided that you needed them as a shield and poor little Jocelyn dreams of killing her father. That's a terrible thing.

Jocelyn: It wasn't Mom's fault.

Minuchin: [Interrupting Jocelyn] And she needs to know you don't need that. You need to protect her from these kinds of dreams. You see, you are in a different situation now. You are a family of three. There is no danger. You are going to continue seeing Helen?

Mother: Maybe a few more sessions.

Minuchin: Can you see her sometimes with Jocelyn alone? Without Natalie? So that you can work together without her? I think it will be very helpful to Jocelyn to have that possibility, because she is a very bright kid. They are both tremendously bright kids. It's a pleasure to talk with them. You did a good job with them.

WHAT CAN WE LEARN?

This family was seen by two very different therapists. One was a novice therapist who was unaware, at first, of how she was getting caught up in the demands of the family. Her penchant as a child rescuer overwhelmed her systemic training, so she tried to make a distressed child feel better, rather than helping the family learn how to heal themselves. The other therapist was more experienced and effective. He explored new alternatives for the family to view what was happening. Although it may have been difficult for them to hear how they were all maintaining their difficulties, the Wilsons were challenged to view themselves and their possibilities in a new way.

Externalizing the Problem

Although this family had gone through a divorce involving a marriage with domestic violence, they still came to therapy offering up the oldest daughter, Natalie, as the Identified Patient. Their main concern was that Natalie ruminated on ideas, demonstrated aspects of depression, and had trouble socializing. Minuchin did not accept this as the true story of the family. Instead of focusing on Natalie's problems, his interventions deal with metaphors (mother as a puppeteer and Natalie as hearing her mother's voice) and with Natalie's constant observation of her mother's moods and behavior. In this position, Natalie remains young. This is not seen as an individual dynamic but as a situation in which mother is maintaining an umbilical cord between herself and her 16-year-old child, Minuchin tells the mother that she will need to change in order for Natalie to grow up.

Layers of Identity

Throughout Helen's narrative, we saw her struggle with trying to expand not only her own voice but that of her clients. In this consultation, Minuchin works to expand the identities of the family members, describing himself in multiple forms to prepare the way.

Mother's identity goes through a variety of descriptions, including a crutch (for Natalie), a very helpful parent, a puppeteer, a ventriloquist, a perfect mother for younger children, and a child observer.

Natalie, the IP, shifts from incompetent to competent. Minuchin frames her as being a psychiatrist, a people watcher, lonely, a puppet, an observer of her mother, a stammerer, a parentified child, and a protector.

Jocelyn's identities shift from a helpful child, cheerful and outgoing, to an 11-year-old who sometimes talks as a 15-year-old and sometimes as a 9-year-old.

Family Organization

The family presents itself as a three-person system, but, Minuchin helps to expand this narrative. He brings the idea of the father into the session, discussing how, during the marriage, there were two groups in play: the mother and children, and the isolated father. This is an essential understanding, as both children are dealing with loyalty issues—siding with mother against father.

Minuchin also sees various configurations within this three-person system. He tries to remove Natalie from the parental subsystem, as she has been acting at times as a parentified child. He also tries to shift the boundaries between mother and oldest daughter so that they are not engaging in a relationship between a mother and young child, rather a mother and emerging adult.

Minuchin provides three primary metaphors connection to one another. The first is that he sees Natalie using her mother as a cane for help, and tries to have Natalie walk upright on her own. He then tells mother that when Natalie was born the doctors cut the umbilical cord, but she is growing it back. The third metaphor is about mother being a ventriloquist and Natalie her puppet, where she can put her words into the puppet's (Natalie's) mouth. There are more instances of presenting the family's complementarity, demonstrating how each person is maintaining the current way of functioning in the family. It follows, as a basic message, that each person will have a role to play in healing one another and helping to change the family.

13

HONING ONE'S CRAFT IN A CHANGING FIELD

In the early 1960s, Don Jackson wrote that there were six centers in the United States doing family therapy. Some 50 years later, the authors of *Family Therapy Review* (Rambo, West, Schooley & Boyd, 2013) summarized the current situation by listing eight models of family therapy: (1) Psychoanalytic/Experiential, (2) Intergenerational, (3) Structural/Strategic, (4) Brief Therapy, (5) Narrative, (6) Collaborative, (7) Integrative, and 8) Psychoeducational. Each of these contains submodels and there are six other models for couples. The number of universities and institutes that teach family therapy in the United States is probably in the hundreds.

What has happened to the field? Is there a cacophony of voices? Can someone who is just learning, or even a seasoned veteran, orient him or herself within the plethora of models? It's a question worth considering. To address it, the authors invite you along on a short trek to a not-very-distant past.

Beginning in the 1950s, the field was invested in describing how families functioned, and exploring the ways in which they created idiosyncratic pathologies in their members. The study of the "double bind" (Bateson, Jackson, Haley, & Weakland, 1956) is one of the clearest examples of how such explorations brought new information—in this case, the theory that communication patterns in the family were responsible for "producing" schizophrenia. Minuchin's *Families of the Slums* (Minuchin, Montalvo, Rosman, & Schumer, 1967) explored the way in which family organization, particularly in troubled poor families, encouraged acting-out behavior in children. And *Psychosomatic Families* (Minuchin, Rosman, & Baker, 1978) demonstrated the connection between family relationships and the emergence of somatic responses in young family members. In these first decades, the primary focus was on the ways of being a family as an explanation for pathology in its members.

With time, as the field expanded, the focus changed, moving actively toward techniques for changing families. Any search through the literature of the 20th century would reveal a wide variety of different approaches, such as cognitive-behavioral, solution-focused and others, along with publications and training centers focused on their models.

In Minuchin's work, this expansion resulted in two books: *Families and Family Therapy* (Minuchin, 1974) *and Family Therapy Techniques.* (Minuchin & Fishman, 1981).

An important point about the beginning years of family therapy is that the early practitioners, probably still influenced by individual and psychodynamic approaches, emphasized not only the function of the therapist but also the use of self in the process. When Bowen(1971) directed a family therapist to focus first on working toward differentiation in his or her own family of origin, or Whitaker (1989) suggested that therapists should "nurture your confusion," it was clear that they were working from an asymmetrical position, were aware of the purpose of their interventions, and were in control of the therapy. That emphasis on the self and activity of the therapist was to change toward the end of the 20th century.

POSTMODERNISM AND SYSTEMIC FAMILY THERAPY

A major change in the position of the therapist occurred in the late 1980s. The postmodern movement in family therapy brought a paradigm change. Under the influence of the French radical philosopher Michel Foucault, who posited that language controls reality and language is controlled by the powerful, postmodern thinkers and practitioners challenged the hierarchical position of the early pioneers.

Postmodernist schools vary in their approach, but they all voiced their concern about two aspects of family therapy as it had generally been conducted: the imposition by therapists of viewpoints that ignore or violate family norms; and the use of therapeutic procedures they felt were subjugating the family. This postmodern ideology was strongly held and very influential, changing the conception of the appropriate role for practitioners from a self-aware therapist to a restrained therapist.

As must be obvious to readers of this book, we do not share this conception or train our students with this goal. To us, this view damages the possibilities for effective change in the family. It makes the new therapist dependent on techniques that maintain the family certainty about explanations and efforts that are not working

In this second decade of the 21st century, traditional systemic therapy and postmodern therapy co-exist, and these viewpoints are not completely opposed. It seems useful to clarify what positions they share and where they disagree. To do so, we have prepared a brief comparison between the thinking and techniques of a narrative approach and the concepts we have presented in this book, being careful to avoid the danger of distorting our colleagues' work since this is not a dialogue. We start with a listing of what is shared, then describe our understanding of the principal ways in which we differ.

What Systemic and Narrative Therapies Share
1. A rejection of the symptom localized on one family member.
2. A concern for social justice, working with disadvantaged populations, and involvement in communities.
3. An orientation toward diversity; a focus on growth and strength.
4. A rejection of focusing on pathology.
5. An emphasis on multiplying alternative ways of being.
6. An acknowledgement of multiple identities.
7. A focus on context and the significance of witnessing.

How Systemic and Narrative Therapies Differ

Although the two models share these similarities, they have different theoretical explanations concerning family functions and the process of change, and they have different therapeutic techniques for meeting their therapeutic goals.

We cannot describe those differences in detail here, but we can offer an example of a major difference by considering how the function of family members in therapy is seen. Narrative therapists encourage family members to join in challenging the pathology of the culture which, by restricting people to narrow ways of being, is implicated in the creation of their pain and problems. We have a different conception of the source of problems as well as the pathways through which they can be alleviated. We see family members as implicated in maintaining the localization of the symptom in the symptom bearer, albeit unwittingly, and we make them responsible for healing each other. For us, this is the basis of being systemic.

BEING SYSTEMIC

Throughout this book, we focused on challenging family certainty as a way to release the inherent potential for improvement in the family's organization. And when we said to family members, "You are richer than you think," we were exploring diversity, in the search for change, as an alternative to exploring pathology.

In Systemic Family Therapy, the therapist understands that family members are interactionally involved with one another, and that the therapist also comes in contact with those members. That realization entails a necessary exploration of the self and style of the therapist. Further, a systemic viewpoint requires an awareness of larger contexts, such as gender, class, race, culture, nationality, and language.

We do not think that we are presenting a new therapeutic model. Rather, we are encouraging you to view *the craft of family therapy* in a unique way. Almost any model of family therapy can encompass concepts and techniques we have presented within its structure and in its own way The family therapist's pouch will be available for you, as a therapist, regardless of the model from which you operate.

REFERENCES

Anderson, H. (2012). Collaborative practice: A way of being "with". *Psychotherapy and Politics International, 10,* 130–145.

Bateson, G., Jackson, D. D., Haley, J., & Weakland, J. (1956). Toward a theory of schizophrenia. *Behavioral Science, 1,* 251–264.

Bowen, M. (1972). *Family therapy in clinical practice.* New Jersey: Aronson.

Haley, J. (1982). *Problem-solving therapy.* California: Jossey-Bass.

Hare-Mustin, R. T. (1994). Discourses in the mirrored room: A postmodern analysis of therapy. *Family Process, 33,* 19–35.

Jackson, D. D. (1957). The question of family homeostasis. *The Psychiatric Quarterly Supplement, 31,* 79–90.

Minuchin, S. (1974). *Families and family therapy.* Massachusetts: Harvard University Press.

Minuchin, S., & Fishman, H. C. (1981). *Family therapy techniques.* Massachusetts: Harvard University Press.

Minuchin, S., Montalvo, B., Guerney, Jr., B. G., Rosman, B. L., & Schumer, F. (1967). *Families of the slums.* New York: Basic Books.

Minuchin, S., Nichols, M. P., & Lee, W-Y. (2007). *Assessing families and couples: From symptom to system.* Massachusetts: Pearson.

Minuchin, S., Rosman, B. L., & Baker, L. (1978). *Psychosomatic families.* Boston, MA: Harvard University Press.

Nichols, M. P., & Fellenberg, S. (2000). The effective use of enactments in family therapy: A discovery-oriented process study. *Journal of Marital and Family Therapy, 26,* 143–152.

Parsons, T., & Bales, F. F. (1955). *Family, socialization, and interaction process.* New York: Free Press.

Rambo, A., West, C., Schooley, A., & Boyd, T. V. (2013). *Family therapy review.* New York: Routledge.

Sullivan, H. S. (1947). *Conceptions of modern psychiatry.* Washington DC. The William Alanson White Psychiatric Foundation.

Whitaker, C. (1989). *Midnight musings of a family therapist.* New York: W. W. Norton & Company.

White, M. (2007). *Maps of narrative practice.* New York: W. W. Norton & Company.

INDEX

abuse, physical 147–8, 204–6
accordion metaphor 214
addiction 195
affect, blocking of 58
age 133, 138
Anderson, H. 8
anger: of IP 75, 139, 143, 145, 147–8; of mothers 83, 104, 141, 143, 145–6, 186
anorexia nervosa 12–15; challenge and 18–20; as control 18, 21–2, 23–6, 27; decision-making with 24; transactions around 19–20
anxiety 8; control from 171, 176, 182, 201; performance 131–3, 138, 154–5
appetite 14
apprehension 147–8
archetypes 166
Argentina 66
armed camp metaphor 71–2
assertiveness 159, 172–3
Assessing Families and Couples (Minuchin) 184
Association of Child and Adolescent Psychiatry 67
authority: of fathers 17; of mothers 188; of therapist 71, 105, 120, 140, 141, 160, 166, 167, 177, 178, 188, 199
autonomy 23, 26, 35; control and 27; therapist's support for 18, 20, 24, 27

Baker, L. 223
Bateson, G. 68, 223
bias: of client 122; of parents 39; in questions 114; of therapist 109, 112, 113, 115
blackmail 21
blame: in couples 164; -self 201
Borges, Jorge Luis 29, 65–6
"Borges and I" (Borges) 29

Bowen, Murray 9, 224
boxing metaphor 72

cane metaphor 172, 178, 205, 222
certainty: challenging 4–5, 15–17, 30, 48, 53, 56–7, 63, 134, 161, 168, 192; as enemy of change 4, 56, 71; of families 4–5, 6, 10, 13, 17, 29, 30, 48, 49, 53, 56, 57, 71, 72, 73, 79, 127; joining in 124; as prison 109, 125; respect for 130, 132; about therapist 122; of therapist 192; uncertainty 3, 168, 172; of unique identity 29
challenge: ability to hear 59; abstract 171; anorexia nervosa and 18–20; by being 82; of certainty 4–5, 15–17, 30, 48, 53, 56–7, 63, 134, 161, 168, 192; confidence for 192; of control 157; dismissal of 190; enactment of 35; of enmeshment 205; hidden 34, 53; of IP 80; joining and 27, 28, 113, 129, 148, 192, 219; nonconfrontational 191; of parents 36–8, 43, 48, 52, 61, 74, 75; by supervisor 202; support of 20; by therapist 4–5, 15–17, 30, 34, 35, 37, 62–3, 65, 71, 72, 75, 105, 107, 109, 111, 112, 115, 119, 120–1, 140, 155, 161, 163, 167–8, 188, 192
chameleons, children as 193, 194
change: acknowledgment of 36–8; certainty as enemy of 4, 56, 71; through complementarity 23, 210, 222
chaos 132
chicken coop metaphor 72
children: as chameleons 193, 194; complementarity of, with mothers 170, 184–5, 194, 210; as damaged 180, 194, 196, 213, 215; after divorce 180, 182, 221; in family therapy 67; as helpers 134, 148–50, 185; homunculus of 215–16; as manipulative 146, 155; mothers and, as

140–1, 157, 177–8, 224; silent monologue of 15; style of 56, 65–6, 110, 111, 112–13, 124, 127, 130, 120, 121, 179, 181, 199; subsystems with 61–2; as Supernanny 130, 132, 134; techniques of 4–8, 56–7, 127, 192–3; topics by 6–7; *see also* co-therapist; questions
therapist pouch 3; basic principles 4; metaphor in 71; techniques 4–8; therapist's self 8–9; utilization of 70–106
therapy: comfort zone in 124–5; intimacy in 124; narrative therapy 224–5; play therapy 131, 133; systemic therapy 134, 169–70, 181, 224–5; *see also* couples therapy; family therapy
three-stage session 65
time 69, 171
transactions: around anorexia nervosa 19–20; in families 19–20, 113, 184–5

translation 87, 88
trust 54; of children 147–8; control and 171–3; repair of 59

umbilical cord metaphor 210–1, 221, 222
uncertainty, acceptance of 168, 173

venting 116
ventriloquist metaphor 208–9, 222
victim: claiming identity as 217; IP as 37, 73, 163, 164; parents as 36

Whitaker, Carl 10, 224
White, Michael 10, 19
Wiltwyck School for Boys 65
witnessing 224
worry 197